The Book of John Mandeville

Medieval and Renaissance Texts and Studies

Volume 231

The Book of John Mandeville

An Edition of the Pynson Text
with Commentary on the
Defective Version

by

Tamarah Kohanski

Arizona Center for Medieval and Renaissance Studies
Tempe, Arizona
2001

The image on the dust jacket,
British Library Manuscript Harley 3954,
is reproduced with the kind permission of The British Library.

® Copyright 2001
Arizona Board of Regents for Arizona State University

Library of Congress Cataloging-in-Publication Data

Mandeville, John, Sir.
  [Itinerarium. English]
  The book of John Mandeville : an edition of the Pynson text / with commentary on the defective version by Tamarah Kohanski.
    p. cm. — (Medieval and Renaissance Texts and Studies ; v. 231)
  Includes bibliographical references.
  ISBN 0-86698-273-6 (alk. paper)
  1. Mandeville, John, Sir. Itinerarium. 2. Mandeville, John, Sir—Journeys. 3. Palestine—Description and travel. 4. Orient—Description and travel. 5. Geography, Medieval. 6. Travel, Medieval. I. Kohanski, Tamarah. II. Title. III. Medieval & Renaissance Texts & Studies (Series) ; v. 231.

G370.M2 M3613 2001
915.69404'3—dc21

00-045355

This book is made to last.
It is set in Goudy, smyth-sewn,
and printed on acid-free paper
to library specifications.

Printed in the United States of America

CONTENTS

Introduction
    Overview   vii

    Beyond Original Author and Original Text:
    The Case for Reception- and Variance-Based Study   xx

    Investigating the Defective Texts   xxix

    Textual Variation and Some "Truths" about the *Book*   xli

Notes to the Transcription   liv

The Pynson Edition of *The Book of John Mandeville*   1

Appendix I   95

Appendix II   99

Glossary of Proper Names   104

Bibliography   127

INTRODUCTION

Overview

The Book of John Mandeville was a popular work in its own day, perhaps one of the most popular in Europe. The *Book* was known in a variety of forms across the continent and achieved fame as a traveler's tale, a kind of eyewitness encyclopedia, a source of geographical information, and much more. Appealing to a powerful imaginative yearning Eastward in late medieval Europe, energized not least by the Crusades and later by a growing commerce with the East that necessitated a greater effort on the part of the average European to locate himself in an expanding real and ideological world, the book mapped the religious, cultural, political, and economic territory of the unknown: the sites of remote Christian miracle and martyrdom, the struggle of Latin Christendom with Islam, the perceived threat of Judaism, as well as the riches of the Far East, the natural wonders and monstrous races to be encountered there, and the societies and power structures that held sway in the non-Latin world. It is a book balanced amidst geography, history, romance, propaganda, satire, and a multitude of other generic patterns, offering a complex and multifaceted view of the world it describes, and seeking not only to represent and interpret that world but also to make it available to a broad base of readers.

The vernacular production of the *Book* was one important factor in the achievement of that goal. The issue of the *Book*'s original language of composition—Continental or Norman French—remains in some dispute, but there can be no dispute about its vernacular origins, or its popular success. Even though the surviving manuscripts somewhat occlude the issue of the original language of composition, variously claiming it as Latin, French, or English, the *Book*'s emphasis on the importance of vernacular transmission is universal. The standard claim in the French manuscripts is that the author has chosen to render his work not in Latin but in French "so that everyone can understand." The English Cotton version alters this to suggest that the book, while originally written in Latin, has been translated by its author into French and finally into English "that euery man of my nacoun may vnderstonde it" (M. C. Seymour, *Mandeville's Travels* [Oxford: Clarendon Press, 1967], 4). The English Egerton and Defective versions remain silent on the language issue, thus tacitly suggesting their own English as the original form, but express a similar commitment to rendering the book in a form accessible to a popular audience.[1]

That impulse toward vernacular production was highly successful. The *Book* survives today in over two hundred fifty manuscripts, in ten languages: French, English, Latin, German, Italian, Spanish, Dutch, Czech, Irish and Danish.[2] The survival of early paper manuscripts, as well as the pricier vellum, suggests a readership not confined to the upper class. Josephine Bennett's research on the early manuscripts (*Rediscovery*), and C. W. Moseley's on the availability of the *Book* ("The Availability of *Mandeville's Travels* in England," *The Library* 5th ser. 30 [1975]: 125–33), suggest that it was well-represented in medieval European libraries. Moseley goes so far as to assert that "few literate men in the fourteenth and fifteenth centuries could have avoided coming across the *Travels* at some time" ("Availability," 126).[3] The manuscript survival includes carefully produced texts by professional scribes, known to have been commissioned for

---

[1] For discussion on this point cf. David Ruddy, "Scribes, Printers, and Vernacular Authority" (Ph.D. Diss., University of Michigan, 1995), 92–93, and George Warner, "Sir John Mandeville," *Dictionary of National Biography* 12: 909.

[2] Most estimates of the number of manuscripts range between two hundred fifty and three hundred, but seldom do they agree completely. M. C. Seymour's *Sir John Mandeville* (Aldershot: Variorum, 1993), 38–49, the most widely accepted source for such information, lists two hundred sixty-three. That number is somewhat open to interpretation, however, as Seymour often includes abstracts, poetic derivations from the *Book*, and other such texts in his count. Also, Klaus Ridder's monograph *Jean de Mandeville's "Reisen"* (Munich: Artemis, 1991), a study of the von Diemeringen version of the *Book*, lists fifteen German manuscripts not counted by Seymour. Christiane Deluz's table of 251 manuscripts (*Le Livre de Jehan de Mandeville* [Louvain: Institut d'Études Médiévales, 1988], 370–82), drawn largely from Josephine Bennett's catalog in *The Rediscovery of John Mandeville* (New York: Modern Language Association, 1954), is noticeably incomplete.

The number of languages is more certain, the ten listed here being generally accepted. George Warner listed eleven languages however, giving Walloon and Bohemian in the place of Czech ("Sir John Mandeville," *Dictionary of National Biography from the Earliest Times to the Present* [1922–23], 913). Iain Higgins, listing the usual ten, suggests an eleventh, Catalan, of which "only a bibliographical reference remains" (*Writing East: The "Travels" of Sir John Mandeville* [Philadelphia: University of Pennsylvania Press, 1997], 23).

[3] M. C. Seymour concurs with regard to the English texts specifically: "There can scarcely have been anyone in the realm who had not heard of the wonderful adventures of the English knight, and most who had the means and opportunity would have read or heard his story" ("The English Manuscripts of *Mandeville's Travels*," *Edinburgh Bibliographic Society Transactions* 4 [1996]: 175).

the libraries of rich clerics and aristocrats, as well as tidy, cheap texts more suitable for the common market, and a number of hastier productions in nearly unreadable mixed hands. The swift multiplication of early editions also suggests a strong public demand: the fifteenth century alone saw thirty-one separate editions in French, German, Italian, Latin, Dutch, and English.[4] The *Book* first saw print in English with Pynson's 1496 edition of a Defective text, which spawned three more editions in the following fifteen years and remained in print for almost three centuries.

If one thinks of the *Book* as an encyclopedia or geography, with which genres it often seems to have more in common than with the itineraries and travelers' diaries the modern title *Mandeville's Travels* calls to mind, one can understand why attention is called, in most versions of the book, to the decision to render it in the vernacular. Whereas an authoritative encyclopedia or geography might be expected to be in Latin, the *Book* is a more popular geography and one that draws its authority from the apparent experience of the well-travelled narrator, rather than from the accepted legitimacy of its numerous but unacknowledged sources. It appeals to the more general, non-scholarly audience: both real travelers and those who seek from their armchairs a vicarious experience of a world they will never see at first hand. The suggestion that the book would normally be in Latin, or was originally, offers some scholarly legitimation, while the decision to write in the vernacular emphasizes the work's non-scholarly objectives and ostensibly non-scholarly origins. While the prologue suggests a special effort to assist "theym that woll and are in purpos for to vysite the holy cyte of Ierusalem and the holy places that ar theraboute" (Pynson sig. a3^r)[5], the book is also for those who merely draw "solace/ and comforthe" (Pynson sig. a3^r) from talk of the Holy Land, for those who would know of the world's marvels, and for those with commercial interests at stake in the East (cf. especially von Diemeringen's version, which clearly states that it has been translated into German to provide useful knowledge for a primarily mercantile audience). Thus, while the *Book* asserts its right to be in Latin, it offers itself in a variety of vernacular languages so that those who want or need this information can more easily have access to it.[6] The encyclopedia, the geographical treatise, the history, and all the

---

[4] Cf. Seymour, *Sir John Mandeville*, 50–56, for a complete listing of European editions. Czech and Spanish editions were first printed ca. 1510 and 1515, respectively. The Irish and Danish versions did not apparently circulate widely, and never gave rise to early printed editions.

[5] The Pynson edition is bound in signatures a–g^8, h–i^6, k^4. Cf. p. liv.

[6] I am deeply indebted here to David Ruddy's discussion of the *Book*'s claims of Latinity and vernacularity in "Scribes, Printers, and Vernacular Authority," 84–98. Ruddy argues persuasively that the *Book* is presented to early audiences as an informational work, worthy of

other classically authoritative, Latinate genres upon which the *Book* draws have become real-world tools for people living in a period of growth for travel, discovery and commerce.

The *Book of John Mandeville* was, without doubt, a fixture in the late medieval and early Renaissance world-imagination, inextricably linked to Europe's developing interests in Eastern exploration, trade, and empire-building. C. W. R. D. Moseley, in his "Availability of *Mandeville's Travels*," suggests a strong correspondence between those interests and the publication of editions. The brief Spanish interest in the *Book*, for example, "exactly corresponds with Magellan's circumnavigation and Ponce de Leon's discovery of Florida" ("Availability," 132). The search for the Terrestrial Paradise and the Fountain of Youth were engaging subjects for the Spanish in this period, on which the *Book* could offer insights. In England, events such as Cabot's voyage, Drake's circumnavigation, and the granting of a charter to the East India Company all ushered in periods of intensified publication. The sixteenth and seventeenth centuries, when England had begun to build an empire, brought a particularly heavy influx of new editions. "The *Travels* certainly influenced the early voyagers; their exploits seem to have influenced the public appetite for the *Travels*" ("Availability," 133).

While the book has in modern times been regarded as everything from an abominable fraud (owing to the wealth of unacknowledged sources that scholars began to identify and catalogue in the nineteenth century) to an unsung piece of "literature" with no clear responsibility to fact or truth, the *Book* in its own day was almost certainly regarded as a source of information, both interesting and useful. The Cotton version's suggestion that it was originally in Latin, as well as the French texts' explanation for why it wasn't, lend credence to the idea that readers saw it as a learned work. The known facts about the *Book*'s early uses and cultural currency support this view as well. Columbus, Frobisher, Mercator, and many others used the *Book* as a source. Generations of Europeans placed far more confidence in it than in the *Travels* of Marco Polo, "Il Milione," whose extravagant claims about the Orient were not to be credited.

The *Book* offered its readers a view of an expanding world: generally up-to-date, at least by the standards of a culture used to appealing to classical authorities for this sort of information, and verified by the eyewitness experience of the narrator, whose persona helped lend form and shape to the audience's response to that world. Ironically enough, the *Book* has become, in modern Western studies, less a source of information about the

---

academic status, but interested in the more democratic project of making the knowledge of the world it contains accessible to all.

distant other than about the self: the European world now reads itself in the *Book*, analyzing its own centuries-old construction of the Oriental. The "otherness" modern Westerners seek to understand in reading the *Book* has become more temporal than geographical. What exactly did the early readers, hearers, scribes, and redactors see in the *Book*, and how did they interpret it? What did the Holy Land and the Far East mean for them? To what degree did they imbibe the much-proclaimed "tolerance" of the narrator for other cultures and religious communities? To what degree did they internalize the satirical aspects of the *Book*'s comparisons of Christian practice with Saracen or even idolatrous religious devotion? How much did they believe of the stories of dog-headed men, of people without faces, or even of men with fingernails so long that they could not feed themselves? How such matters influenced Europeans' view of the world and of their place in it is a matter of no small interest, and many studies of the *Book* have grappled with exactly these problems.

What most studies have not grappled with, however, is the diversity of the subject material itself: the multiple nature of the *Book of John Mandeville*, as a work that exists in some twenty-one attested versions,[7] with a high degree of substantive as well as incidental variation. It has been usual until quite recently for scholars to use a "best text" of the *Book* as a stand-in for the original, and to dismiss textual variance as textual corruption—a practice that has left the majority of extant texts of the *Book* undervalued and insufficiently studied because of being perceived as in some way "corrupt." A number of scholars have recently begun to challenge that approach, however, looking at "best texts" in terms of their relationships to other extant texts of the *Book*, and devoting in-depth study to versions that have historically received little attention. Christiane Deluz, in her *Livre de Jehan de Mandeville*, and Klaus Ridder, in his *Jean de Mandeville's "Reisen"*, both work exclusively with specific versions, but still maintain a constant awareness of and sensitivity to the claims of other texts. Deluz studies a single Continental text as authorial, but also works hard to situate that text in the context of others, rather than treating it in isolation. Ridder's subject, the German von Diemeringen version, stemming from a 1398 German translation of the Latin Vulgate version, can make no claims on originality, and Ridder approaches it as a study in variance, outlining the ways in which that version creates its own sense of audience, its own organization of the material, and thereby a unique reading dynamic. The most groundbreaking study in recent years, Iain Higgins's *Writing East* (1997), fully integrates the *Book*'s multitextual nature into its methodology, juxtaposing several different texts of the *Book*, studying their variation,

---

[7] Based on Seymour's classification of the manuscripts in *Sir John Mandeville*, 38–49.

and attempting to understand it in the context of the world and the people that produced it. Higgins systematically investigates textual variation and its implications in ten separate versions, in four languages: Continental and Insular [French]; Bodley, Cotton, Defective, Egerton, and Metrical [English]; Velser and von Diemeringen [German]; and the Vulgate Latin.[8]

Higgins suggests that there are many ways of usefully investigating the *Book*. The traditional method of choosing a "best text" and treating it as authorial, can, he says, be instructive, as the work of critics like Josephine Bennett, Donald R. Howard, Emile Montegut, Mary Campbell, and Christiane Deluz amply demonstrates. Similarly, it can be illuminating to compare a specific translation or redaction against a more original version, as Ridder does, in order to understand rather than discredit the altered version. But while this is to do well, it is possible to do better, Higgins suggests, if we "read two or more related versions of *The Book*, with reference to their immediate sources ... treating each as a specific response to a particular received text. The result would be a kind of diachronic reading, tracing the text's transformations through time, space, and languages." A further refinement of this approach would be to undertake, as Higgins does, a "palimpsestic or topological reading" (*Writing East*, 19–20) of many versions simultaneously, paying heed to transmission history but without according the primacy to the original text that usually leaves variant texts on the critical fringe.

A philological model based on the printed text suggests that a book has a single "correct" form that is the property of a single author; but for works produced in a manuscript culture, such assumptions do not necessarily hold. While there are certainly medieval texts that were not considered open to alteration, especially those of great scriptural or theological authority, popular manuscripts such as the *Book* were by nature in a constant state of flux: scribes, translators, and redactors all treated alterations to such texts as potential enhancements. Medieval popular texts, in the words of Gerald Bruns, "are never fully present" ("The Originality of Texts in a Manuscript Culture," *Comparative Literature* 32 [1980]: 126): new potentialities are constantly being realized in the course of transmission. Because medieval texts are variant by nature, variations produced through error are also more accepted. The opening of the "Egypt Gap," for example—the omission of a long section on Egypt that has come to define the Defective version—was not a conscious choice, but the fact that the version had been "corrupted" did not prevent its gaining stature, in

---

[8] I have chosen not to treat the "Metrical version" as a version of the *Book*, for reasons outlined on pp. xiii–xiv. That the Metrical text may be something new and not another version of the *Book* does not, however, interfere materially with Higgins's conclusions.

manuscript and in the Pynson and following editions, as the most widely-read version in England. Insofar as the medieval world perceived the alteration of texts as an integral part of the process of transmission and embraced the variant texts that process produced, it behooves medieval scholars to emulate that attitude and embrace those variant texts as well.

Higgins's groundbreaking effort in that direction has been an important catalyst for the present edition. Studies of the English variants have been hampered up to now by a prevailing attitude that these texts are unworthy of study and, correspondingly, unworthy of editing. The unavailability of any Defective editions to work from thus resonates with both cause and effect in the prevailing scholarly disinterest in the Defective version as a whole. One effect of Higgins's work has been to help legitimize the Defective version by making the Pynson text—based on a Defective manuscript—one of the central "isotopes" in his discussion of textual variance. Reading Pynson in concert with the more accepted versions such as Cotton, Egerton, Continental, and Insular affirms the importance of such "Defective" texts for reception- and variance-based studies and will, it is to be hoped, generate an interest in the Defective version that an available edition of Pynson's text of that version may help along.

A more general understanding of the status of the English versions will be useful here in demonstrating the Defective version's very real claims to scholarly attention. In the English tradition, M. C. Seymour has classified five distinct versions of the *Book*, all derived ultimately from the Insular version, in French: Cotton (1 exemplum), Egerton (1), Defective (35),[9] Bodley (2), and Metrical (1). The Metrical version is, it may be argued, not a "version" of the *Book* at all, acknowledging itself as a "little treatise *drawn from* that book" (cf. Seymour, *The Metrical Version of Mandeville's Travels* [London: Oxford University Press, 1973], 43-44; emphasis mine). While it clearly uses *The Book of John Mandeville* as its main source, it does

---

[9] The number of texts classified as "Defective" has been recently in flux. M. C. Seymour's 1966 classification ("English Manuscripts"), long the standard for scholars of the *Book*, lists only thirty-two Defective texts, and notes that the Epitome (London, British Library MS Additional 370459), Extracts (Oxford, Bodleian Library MS Ashmole 751) and Ripon Fragment (Ripon, Library of Ripon Cathedral), though listed separately, are affiliated with Defective. The catalogue to his 1993 monograph, *Sir John Mandeville* (43-45), however, lists thirty-six Defective manuscripts plus two which are listed among them but not numbered, apparently because they are so short: the Ripon Fragment and a previously unlisted set of extracts (Oxford, Bodleian Library MS Digby 88, fol. 28).

The changes to the classification remain unexplained. In addition to the four newly listed manuscripts, one has also been silently reclassified under a new name: MS. Penrose, a Defective E-manuscript in the 1966 classification, appears now as Princeton MS. Taylor 10, a Defective D-manuscript. The Defective A-manuscript subgroupings have been altered as well. See Appendix I for a complete listing of manuscripts in English.

not claim to be the *Book*, but only a derivation from it.¹⁰ The Bodley version is an abridgement of an English translation of the Royal version, itself a Latin translation of an Insular text, in French. The Defective version is generally considered to be a direct English translation of the Insular version, while Cotton and Egerton are both conflations, apparently based in part upon the Defective version.¹¹ Even from this brief account, it can be seen that the Defective version is, among the extant versions in English, apparently the most directly connected to the acknowledged Insular archetype.¹² Add to this the version's overwhelming numerical superiority in terms of manuscript survival, and the fact that the first English edition, Pynson, was based on a Defective manuscript, and Defective begins to emerge as a version well worth looking at. Remarkably, however, it has scarcely been looked at at all. To date, every manuscript exemplum of the four other versions in English has been printed in a modern edition;¹³ of the Defective manuscripts, however, only one abbreviated exemplum (The Epitome; British Library MS. Additional 37049) and one even shorter related text (The Extracts; Bodleian Library MS Ashmole 751) have been edited.¹⁴ The full-length Defective manuscripts have been left in com-

---

¹⁰ David Ruddy, "Scribes, Printers, and Vernacular Authority," 34, argues this point at greater length.

¹¹ The Stanzaic Fragment is sometimes treated as a separate "version" as well, but has even less claim to be so than the Metrical. Bodleian MS e Musaeo 160, the only surviving Stanzaic manuscript, conflates material based apparently on chapters 15 and 23 of the Cotton version with material from Marco Polo's *Travels*. The objective here is not to revise *The Book of John Mandeville*, creating a new version of that text, but to write something new, using the *Book* as a source-text.

¹² While most scholars agree that Defective is the earliest English version and the basis for Cotton and Egerton, some doubt does remain. The issue is discussed more thoroughly at the beginning of the next section, p. xxii.

¹³ Cotton has been edited by A. W. Pollard (*The Travels of Sir John Mandeville* [London: MacMillan, 1900. Repr. 1905, 1909, 1915, 1923; New York: Dover, 1964]), Paul Hamelius (*Mandeville's Travels, Translated from the French of Jean d'Outremeuse*, 2 vols., Early English Text Society os 153–54 [London: Kegan Paul, 1919]), and M. C. Seymour (*Mandeville's Travels*) among others. Egerton has been edited by George Warner (*The Buke of John Maundeuill* [London: Roxburghe Club, 1889]), Malcolm Letts (*Mandeville's Travels: Texts and Translations*, Vol. 1, Hakluyt Society 2nd ser. 101 [London: Hakluyt Society, 1953]), and C. W. R. D. Moseley (*The Travels of Sir John Mandeville* [New York: Penguin, 1983], with additions from Cotton). Both extant texts of the Bodley version have been edited, Bodleian Library MS Rawlinson D 99 by Letts (*Mandeville's Travels: Texts and Translations*, Vol. 2, Hakluyt Society 2nd ser. 102 [London: Hakluyt Society, 1953]), and Bodleian Library MS e Musaeo 116 by Seymour (*The Bodley Version of Mandeville's Travels*, Early English Text Society os 253 [London: Oxford University Press, 1963]). The Metrical version has been edited by Seymour (*Metrical Version*).

¹⁴ Both by Seymour ("The English Epitome of Mandeville's Travels," *Anglia* 84 [1966]: 27–58; and "Secundum Johannem Maundvyle," *English Studies in Africa* 6 [1961]: 148–58). Cf. Appendix I for their placements within the Defective schema.

plete editorial obscurity, as has the Pynson edition that stemmed from them. Scholars who wish to work with the Defective version have had available, up to now, only a cheaply produced facsimile of the Pynson text, unreadable in places and without any points of reference that might encourage comparison with other versions.[15]

The central reason for this lack of critical attention to the Defective version has been an overriding concern in scholarly circles with the ideal of the authorial work, and the perceived distance at which the Defective texts stand from the lost original version. This may seem initially surprising, as Defective, out of all the extant English versions, seems to derive most immediately from the Insular source. But the Defective texts have long been outcast for essentially two reasons: a) the existence of the "Egypt Gap," the defining attribute of the Defective version, and b) the plethora of extant Defective manuscripts, with all their attendant textual variance. Pejoratively named for a sizable lacuna in its descriptions of Egypt (believed to stem from the lack of a second quire in the Insular copy-text), and perceived by many scholars as progressively debased by its flourishing transmission history, the Defective version has fallen into the category of scribal effluvia—a falling off from the purity of the original text. The version with the most convincing claim to a clear line of descent from the archetype is seen as least authorial because of the "Egypt Gap," while its ongoing manuscript transmission, compared with the almost total dearth of evidence of transmission for the other English texts, comes to count against it—as if to be reproduced, circulated, and read were somehow a bad thing, and texts that went uncopied and unread are in some way more important for study because they appear unadulterated.

Editors and critics alike have demonstrated this bias in favor of the original text and its original author. Proponents of critical and best-text editing encourage us to think of scribes' contributions to and alterations of their texts not as revisions of the work they transmit, but as debasements of it. The author writes the book, but then scribes and redactors progressively deface it—adding, deleting, and corrupting where instead they ought simply to have copied the authorial work. This view allows scribal alteration no legitimacy whatsoever. Because the book is perceived as a finished work when it leaves its author, it can only be marred by any change: scribal effort, which never produces an exact replica of its copytext, is therefore perceived as essentially destructive rather than productive, even though it is solely through that effort that the book is ever trans-

---

[15] *The Travels of Sir John Mandeville. Facsimile of Pynson's Edition of 1496.* Exeter Medieval English Texts and Studies (Exeter: Exeter University Press, 1980), with a short introduction by M. C. Seymour.

mitted at all. Embracing this view of authorial ownership of books, scholarship has for most of this century been content to pass over variant texts of medieval works as unoriginal and therefore unimportant, rather than studying them as artifacts, as cultural and historical exempla, or as important phases in an ongoing system of production from which books in a manuscript culture never emerge completed.[16]

Lachmannian or critical editing, with its objective of reconstructing the lost original, has traditionally been considered the ideal approach to editing the *Book*. Once texts are placed in a stemma, they can be assessed in terms of what came from their antecedents and what must be interpolation or alteration, thus allowing the editor to work backward to a clear sense of what comes from the original. The major problems with this approach are simply those of having too little information with which to create meaningful stemmata, or of being unable to interpret conclusively the information one has. In the case of the *Book* these obstacles have proven difficult to overcome. While scholars have been promising critical editions for over a hundred years, no critical edition of the book, or even of any of its three major European versions, has so far been produced.[17] Long is the list of those who have taken up the challenge only to lay it down again, seemingly in despair. While some broad areas of consensus have been reached about the integrity of versions and the general relationships among texts, the obstacles in the way of bringing the *Book of John Mandeville* back to its roots have so far proven insurmountable. Critics and editors continue to speak hopefully of a critical edition, but the tremendous complexity of the *Book*'s textual tradition renders it unlikely that any definitive edition will be produced soon.

Because efforts toward a critical edition have been so fraught with practical difficulties, editors have been thrown instead upon a Bedieran approach—the effort to identify and transmit a single "best text" of the work, with minimal editorial intervention—simply because there has been no recognized alternative. Thus the Cotton and Egerton texts, British

---

[16] Perhaps the best modern corrective to this view is Bernard Cerquiglini, *In Praise of the Variant: A Critical History of Philology*, trans. Betsy Wing (Baltimore: Johns Hopkins University Press, 1999), from which Higgins takes a line as the foundation for his isotopic reading: "... medieval writing does not produce variants; it is variance" (77–78; *Writing East*, viii).

[17] The three major paths of development of the *Book*, Continental, Insular, and Liège, will be discussed at greater length later. Among others, Johann Vogels was reported to be finishing a critical edition of "the French texts" when Warner published his Egerton edition in 1889 (Warner, *Buke*, viii), Guy de Poerck announced his work on a critical edition of the Liège version in 1955 (G. de Poerck, "La tradition manuscrite des *Voyages* de Jean de Mandeville," *Romanica Gandensia* 4 [1955], 125, n. 5), and Luc Schepens suggested in 1962 that he would have an edition of the Continental version forthcoming (L. Schepens, "Au sujet de deux manuscrits de Jean de Mandeville," *Scriptorium* 16 [1962]: 377). None has ever appeared.

Library MS Cotton Titus C. xvi and British Library MS Egerton 1982, have become the standard "best texts" in English by virtue of their real or imagined closer connections to the original text of the *Book* than the other English texts. What this means, in fact, is that they have been accorded primacy as the most original texts in English because they do not have an "Egypt Gap."

There are compelling reasons to question the primacy of the Cotton and Egerton versions. Even if one accepts the credo "original text is best text" out of hand, these two texts remain problematic. While both do provide full coverage of the Egypt material, that full coverage is acknowledged to be the product of conflation: as noted above, both Cotton and Egerton are believed to have been partially based on some form of the Defective version, with the Egypt material added in from another source. M. C. Seymour, the ranking genealogist of the *Book* manuscripts, describes Cotton as "a conflation in English based on the Defective Version, subgroup A and expanded by reference to the Insular Version, subgroup A [in French]," and Egerton as "a conflation in English based on the Defective Version, subgroup A, and a lost English translation of the Royal Version [in Latin], with reference to an Insular manuscript [in French]" (*Sir John Mandeville*, 45).[18] Both versions' claims to originality, in the sense of being closer to the original text of the *Book* than the Defective version, are thus complicated by their own derivations from the Defective version. Are they in fact more original for having been conflated with other texts? Or are they in some ways even further removed?

Intimately connected with this quandary is the fundamental paradox of Bedieran editing itself: if the original text is the goal, and scribal alteration equals debasement, how does one justify putting the process of scribal conflation and alteration that led up to one specific text in a privileged position, as integral to the book, while that same process, as it applies to all other texts of the book, continues to be viewed as destructive of it? This problem is especially obtrusive in the case of Cotton and Egerton in that both show signs of pervasive scribal intervention. Cotton was initially chosen as the best text of the *Book* in English based on the belief that it derived from the conflation of two French texts, thus connecting it more closely than Egerton with the original French text. Malcolm Letts complained of Egerton that it "at times gives the impression of being a paraphrase rather than a translation" (*Sir John Mandeville* [London: Batchworth Press, 1949], 132–33), not connecting at all firmly with its presumed French antecedent. But Cotton, while preserving closer ties to the French (albeit now considered to stem more directly from the Defective), is not

---

[18] The subgroups are set out on pp. xxxiv–xxxv.

without its problems. Paul Hamelius, an early editor of the Cotton text, was so offended by it that he attacked its writer as "one who distinguishes himself by his ignorance and stupidity" (*Mandeville's Travels*, 2: 17) and went on to call him both "careless" and "slovenly" (2: 18). While all students of the text have not been as hotly condemnatory as Hamelius, Cotton does contain a number of egregious errors. Cotton's early selection as the best text authorized a problematic translation on genealogical grounds, while the later selection of Egerton authorized a more graceful text, but one believed to be less original genealogically.

That the Cotton and Egerton versions are represented each by a single manuscript is also cause for concern in that, while the manuscripts of the Defective version show evidence of a strong and continuous transmission history, there is no evidence that either Cotton or Egerton was known outside the walls of the library in which it was kept, except for the possible association of Cotton with the Stanzaic Fragment (cf. note 11).[19] In a large corpus of texts and references from the Middle Ages and early Renaissance, there is no indication that either was ever copied, nor widely read. It was from the Defective version that Chaucer, the *Cleanness*-poet, and a host of other writers gleaned source material for their own literary works.[20] It was to the Defective version that British explorers turned for geographical information, and the Englishman-on-the-street turned for stories of the sanctities of the Holy Land and the mysteries of the Far East. A simple lacuna in the Egypt material is no good reason to ignore such a mine of potential information. If one is interested in the contemporary influence of the *Book*, the Defective version has marked advantages over Cotton and Egerton, but these two texts' questionable claims to originality have for the past century been allowed to overshadow the very real interest of the Defective version.

Twentieth-century scholarship on the book is still laboring to break free of a nineteenth-century focus on the original author and the original text that elevates the original text to a position of supreme authority, as

---

[19] Seymour associates the Egerton manuscript with Thomas More in his "English Manuscripts," but without convincing proof.

[20] Chaucer borrowed from the *Book* most notably in the *Squire's Tale*. On Chaucer's debt to the *Book*, see J. W. Bennett, "Chaucer and *Mandeville's Travels*," *Modern Language Notes* 68 (1953): 531–34; C. W. R. D. Moseley, "Chaucer, Sir John Mandeville, and the Alliterative Revival," *Modern Philology* 72 (1974): 182–84; and D. May, "*Mandeville's Travels*, Chaucer, and the House of Fame," *Notes and Queries* ns 34 (1987): 178–82. On *Cleanness*, see L. Purdon, "Sodom and Gomorrah: The Use of *Mandeville's Travels* in *Cleanness*," *Journal of the Rocky Mountain Medieval and Renaissance Association* 9 (1988): 63–69; and C. Brown, "Note on the Dependence of *Cleanness* on *The Book of Mandeville*," *Publications of the Modern Language Association* 19 (1904): 149–53.

the unsullied vehicle of its author's intentions, and thereby elevates two of the most apparently obscure versions of the book to the status of "best texts" because their complete Egyptian information is believed to render them the most original English survivals. This pervasive focus on originality does a continuing disservice to the *Book* by directing critical attention away from study of the book in its contemporary context, as a dynamic, constantly adapting part of a manuscript culture. This fixation on the original author and his original text has played a major part in the decrease in scholarly interest in the *Book* in the twentieth century, a decline that has only begun to reverse itself very recently with the growth of interest in colonial literature, travel literature, and the literature of the outsider. Faced with the *Book*'s continued intractability to an original-focused methodology, many critics simply abandoned it: hence the remarkable lack of any extended study of the *Book* in English from Bennett's 1954 *Rediscovery of John Mandeville* (itself in part a response to prevailing scholarly neglect, though Bennett's authorial focus remains marked) until Higgins's 1997 study. Criticism has perhaps reached a point at which it is necessary to change the rules, as Higgins does, in order to go forward.

Those new rules require that, rather than attempting to study the *Book* as the product of a single author, with a single goal or meaning instilled by him, we instead study the *Book* as an organic work, continuously metamorphosing over the course of its transmission from manuscript to manuscript, and coming over time to mean many different things to many different audiences. In short, the focus of criticism must be adapted to the *Book* as it is, rather than as scholars would like it to be. A New Philological model would define "authorship" more loosely than twentieth-century sensibilities generally allow, taking into account that in a manuscript culture a book is in a continuous state of production, not fixed and immutable when it leaves its author's hands but constantly being written and rewritten. The first version, like the first author, becomes only one part of a system that allows for constant reshaping of the narrative.

The future of scholarship on the *Book of John Mandeville* lies in the systematic study of the variation found in the surviving manuscripts and early editions, and of what it means in terms of the people who read the book, copied it, added to it, deleted from it, and wrote their notes in its margins. The Defective version is at the very heart of that variation. With its active transmission history and often striking difference from the more accepted versions, as well as a broad spectrum of internal variation, this version provides an invaluable record not only of how books spread to their readership in the Middle Ages, but also of how people understood the larger world around them.

If one seeks to understand the *Book* as a product of its culture, and also as a producer of that culture, it is necessary to work with the facts of manuscript transmission, rather than against them. The *Book* was much altered in the course of its dissemination, and those alterations were passed on, often with new ones made on top of them. Some of the changes (like the opening of the "Egypt Gap") were almost certainly errors. Others just as certainly were not. What is important is that early audiences read the book as transmitted: revisions, additions, deletions, warts and all. In order to understand that reading experience and discover what the *Book* was to the Middle Ages, scholarship must reclaim the great body of evidence that the Defective version represents. The Pynson edition clearly merits our attention as an authorizing agent for the Defective version and as the progenitor of the English editions, while the variations among Defective manuscripts offer a compelling and unusual opportunity to study how different writers, illustrators, and audiences perceived or wanted to perceive the *Book* and the world it describes. It is my hope, with the publication of this edition, both to press the case for a more variance- and reception-oriented approach and to encourage study of the Defective version by making one exemplum, at least, available in a convenient form, keyed to the chapter breaks of Cotton and Egerton for easy cross-referencing, thus inviting comparison among texts.[21] The variance among the texts called "Defective" (a classification which may itself have outlived its usefulness, as I shall suggest below) has much to teach us, if we will pay attention. The combination of recent refinements in approach to the *Book* and the publication of the Pynson text will, it is to be hoped, mark the first steps toward the reclamation of all the texts of the Defective version, for both our profit and our delight.

BEYOND ORIGINAL AUTHOR AND ORIGINAL TEXT: THE CASE FOR RECEPTION- AND VARIANCE-BASED STUDY

While we are mainly concerned here with the English *Book*, it will be useful to look briefly at the larger European textual situation in order to understand the magnitude of the stemmatic problems that have defeated every attempt to fix the form of the original text. The strong early demand for manuscripts of the *Book*, with the resultant frequency of copying, translation, and conflation, gave rise over the course of the book's manuscript

---

[21] As the Egerton text is not chaptered, editors of Egerton generally import the thirty-four chapter divisions of Cotton, as Warner does in his 1889 edition, Letts in 1953, and Moseley in 1983 (qq. v.). It is perhaps worth noting, for the sake of clarity, that Paul Hamelius (*Mandeville's Travels*) separates the standard Cotton chapter 8 into chapters 8 and 9, thus giving his Cotton edition an anomalous thirty-five chapters.

transmission to widely divergent versions across Europe, including poetical versions, a picture-book, a series of extracts dealing almost solely with the Holy Land, a series of texts focusing on Liège and the Danish hero Ogier, von Diemeringen's "encyclopedic" version, and many others. The complexities surrounding the *Book*'s Continental transmission complicate the issues of its Insular transmission and of its earliest origins as well.

Until the nineteenth century, the idea of John Mandeville, the English knight personally responsible for the English versions of the book, was more or less accepted in the English-speaking world. Most English texts, including the Defective texts and Egerton, tacitly claim English as the original language. In the Cotton version, "Mandeville" tells us that he has personally "put this boke out of Latyn into Frensch and translated it ayen out of Frensch into Englyssch" (Seymour, *Mandeville's Travels*, 3–4). After decades of work disentangling the lines of transmission of the extant texts, however, scholars were able to firmly establish that the earliest texts were in neither English nor Latin, but French—either Continental or Anglo-Norman.[22] What this means in terms of the original author's nationality and the *Book*'s country of origin remains a subject of some debate.

Dissension over whether the Continental or Anglo-Norman (Insular) texts are most original runs high. Guy de Poerck attempted to codify the textual tradition of the book in 1955 by delineating three separate French versions, each independently derived from the lost original, which he considered to have been a Continental French text. De Poerk's three French versions—Continental, Liège, and Insular—have been adopted by many modern students of the *Book*, as has his idea that the original would have been a Continental work. His argument is bolstered by the facts that the texts of his Continental version are in the main the most complete, and that Paris 1371, the earliest dated text we possess, is of Continental origin. J. W. Bennett, however, had delineated the French manuscripts a year earlier along the same lines, as the Paris [Continental], Ogier [Liège], and Norman French [Insular], and was a vocal champion of a Norman original. Paris and Ogier she calls "redactions," arguing that Paris 1371, often called the "best and oldest" manuscript,[23] is in fact "a poor copy of a redaction, and the manuscripts written in England in Norman French represent most faithfully the work of the author. The Ogier version is a redaction of a redaction, the least authentic of the three versions" (*Rediscovery*,

---

[22] The first critic to suggest that the original text was in French rather than English was M. D'Avezac in his introduction to the *Historia Mongolorum* of John of Plano Carpini (noted in Warner, *Buke*, vi).

[23] The Wells *Manual* cited it as such. Also cf. Bennett, *Rediscovery*, 135 n. 1.

146).²⁴ She makes a strong case, using detailed analysis of variants among different texts of each version, and her view has more recently been bolstered by Moseley, who suggests in "Chaucer, Sir John Mandeville, and the Alliterative Revival" that "Mandeville" could have been a dependent of the Bohuns, writing in the north of England (182-84). This would explain why so many of the texts in English that show direct borrowing from the *Book* are Alliterative Revival works, mainly northern. Most recently, Deluz too has approved Bennett's conclusion, although without arguing the case.

M. C. Seymour, in his *Sir John Mandeville*, attempts to prove once and for all that the *Book* was written in Continental French, calling Bennett's assessment of the textual situation "very cursory" (4) and throwing his not inconsiderable critical weight behind de Poerck. Seymour's main arguments are that the internal evidence for the author's Englishness is not conclusive and that the source materials would have been more available in a Continental library. Still, while Seymour marshals his evidence well, it is scant and often conjectural. Seymour may be in a better position to conjecture than most, having studied the texts for some forty years, but the arguments he advances cannot be said to decide the issue. Higgins follows de Poerck in suggesting, with his schematic of the versions' relationships (*Writing East*, 21), that the extant Continental and Insular manuscripts arose independently from an earlier archetype to which Continental is most closely related.

Of the English texts, it is generally agreed that all stem at least in part from an Insular archetype that already contained the "Egypt Gap." Most critics will also allow that Defective is the earliest of the English versions and the basis for both Cotton and Egerton, but pockets of dissent remain here as well. While George Warner and more recently M. C. Seymour have held that Cotton was based on Defective, Johann Vogels, the great nineteenth-century genealogist of the *Book*, postulated that the Defective version was based on Cotton. Vogels also suggested that Egerton might be based on Cotton rather than on Defective, an idea rejected by Nicholson and Yule ("Mandeville, Jehan de," *Encyclopaedia Britannica* 11th ed., 1911. xvii: 563 n. 5) as well as by Seymour ("The Origin of the Egerton Version of *Mandeville's Travels*," *Medium Aevum* 30 [1961]: 159-69). While Defective's claim to being the earliest English version and the root of the two other major versions in English is, I think, convincing, Vogels's

---

²⁴ Even so, as Bennett goes on to note, Johann Vogels, Paul Hamelius, and even Malcolm Letts, all longtime students of the *Book*'s textual tradition, had selected Ogier texts as good texts of the *Book*.

arguments to the contrary have never been decisively disproved. Higgins, while he does not subscribe to Vogels's view, does indicate uncertainty on the derivation of Cotton, representing it as derived from Insular but not clearly from Defective (*Writing East*, 21–23).[25] Seymour has subdivided and schematized the Defective version in an effort to decide this issue, but the manuscripts mightily resist such efforts. Several texts simply do not fit into the stemma as constructed, and the precise relationships of Cotton and Egerton to the Defective stemma remain unclear.[26]

What cannot but be clear, given all these textual convolutions, is the very unsettled nature of our understanding of the *Book* as an artifact. Although scholars have generally accepted certain broad hypotheses—that Continental predates Insular, and that Defective predates the other English versions—the evidence is not so conclusive as one might wish, and, when one attempts to engage more particular questions, such as the specific derivation of the Cotton manuscript, the facts become even more slippery. It is therefore notoriously difficult to acquire anything like a full sense of the book as a unity or even to find a convenient place from which to start.

Efforts to unify the *Book* in one way or another have traditionally been at the heart of its scholarship. Criticism's historical impulse to determine the facts about the original author and his original text reveals on its most basic level the desire to reduce these issues to manageable proportions, to find something to cling to amid the welter of variant texts and conflicting hypotheses about how they relate to one another, where they come from, and what they are supposed to mean. Inquiry focused on "the man and his book" has been important, not only as a means of managing the sheer bulk of the *Book* in all its myriad forms, but also as an essential underpinning for a criticism based on the idea of authorial control over meaning. The desire for an author, a "Sir John Mandeville" whose experience and vision would give shape to this maddeningly formless and multitudinous book, has energized a long and largely fruitless effort to find or reconstruct him based on the available evidence.

Almost all versions of the *Book* include some information about the

---

[25] Higgins's table lists Cotton's source as "Insular," while Egerton's are listed as "Defective, Insular, Lost" (*Writing East*, 22). But the schematic (21) shows Cotton's derivation from Insular through Defective, with a question mark suggesting the uncertainty of the derivation.

[26] Seymour says in *Sir John Mandeville* that ". . . it is now possible to construct a stemma which comprehends the affiliations of all versions and their subgroups, with the important qualification that the relationship of the two primary French versions has still to be resolved exactly" (3). That stemma has not yet been unveiled, however, and it seems improbable that it will be conclusive, as significant dissent on essential textual issues persists.

narrator, which was long accepted as authorial biography. It is thin at best, however, usually coming in two short passages: one at the beginning, one at the end. The Pynson edition gives as fair a representation as any. At the outset:

> [I] John Maundevyle knyght. Thoughe it so be that I be nat worthy that was borne in englonde in the towne of saynt Albone and passed the see in the yere of the Incarnacion of oure lorde iesu crist M.CCCxxxii on the day of saynt Myghell and hyderwarde hathe be longe tyme over the se and have sene and gone thorowe many landes and many provynces/ and kyngdomes and Iles and have passed thorough Turky/ thorough/ Ermony the lytell and the greate thorough Tartary Thoroughe Percy/ thorough Syry/ thoroughe/ araby/ thorough Egypt the hygh and the lowe. thorough lyby thoroughe Caldee/ and a great party of Ethyope/ thorowe Amozome. thoroughe Inde the lesse and the more. a greate party. and thorough many other Iles whych are aboute Inde Where many dyvers maners of folke dwell in dyvers lawes and shappes/ of whyche londes and Iles I shall speke more playnly/ and I shall devyse a party of thynges what they are whan tyme shall be/ after it may come to mynde/ and specyally for theym that woll and are in purpos for to vysite the holy cyte of Ierusalem and the holy places that ar theraboute/ and I shall tell the Wey that they shall holde thyder for I have many tymes passyd and ryden it wyth good company/ and of many lordes. (a3^{r-v})

At the end:

> And I Iohn Maundvyle that went oute of my countre and passed the se the yere of oure lorde a M ccc. xxxii. and I have passed thorowe many londes and Iles and countrees/ and nowe am come to rest I have compyled this boke and do wryte it the yere of oure lorde M. ccc. lxvi. at xxxiii. yere after my departynge fro my countre. and for as moch as many men trowe nat but that they se with theyr iyen or that they may conceyve in their kyndly wytte therfore I made my way to rome in my comynge homwarde to shewe my boke to the holy fader the pope and tell hym of the marveylis that I had sene in dyvers countrees so that he with his wise counsell wold examyne it wyth dyverse folke that ar at rome for there dwell men of al nacions of the worlde. and a lytell tyme after whan he/ and hys counseyle had examyned it all thorowe he sayde to me for certeyne that all was sothe. for he sayde he had a boke of laten that conteyned all that and moche more of the whych the Mapa mundi is made/ the whych boke I sawe. and therfor the holy fader the

pope hath ratyfyed and confermed my boke in all poyntes. (k3ᵛ)[27]

The facts, of course, differ in different manuscripts. In many of the Insular French texts, "Mandeville" claims to have begun his travels in 1322 and to have written the book in 1356. Most Continental texts say it was written in 1357. The Defective texts vary widely on these dates, from Bodleian MS Douce 109, which says that "Mandeville" left England in 1300 and returned home after thirty-three years (fol. 73ʳ), to British Library MS Arundel 140, no. 1, which says he left in 1332, then crosses it out and substitutes 1366, making the date of composition, after thirty-four years of travel, 1400.[28] Likewise, the author/narrator's visit to the Pope is mentioned only in the English versions and in the Latin Durham University MS Cosin V. iii. 7.[29] Thus in over two hundred fifty extant texts, many of which vary widely in the biographical data they supply, one is faced with quite an array of "Mandevilles," and, given the climate of dissent surrounding which texts and readings to view as most authorial, critics in search of the real John Mandeville have seldom agreed fully on where and when he might be found.

Certain constants, however, are apparent: "Mandeville" consistently claims to be an Englishman, a knight of Saint Albans who has traveled the world since leaving England in the mid-1300s. For centuries this, at least, was taken as fact. But even this thin core of information about the

---

[27] This last is the famed "papal interpolation," a section apparently added into the *Book* sometime after it was first translated into English. Efforts to use the interpolation to help date the English versions of the *Book* have met with limited success.

Higgins gives a detailed account of the interpolation in its various forms (*Writing East*, 254–60), noting that it is especially elaborate in one of the Latin translations, Durham University Cosin MS V. iii. 7 (fol. 83ᵛ), which names "authoritative" sources to which the Pope has had recourse in endorsing the *Book*: Higden's *Polychronicon* and a globe, possibly the Nuremberg Sphere of 1492 which, ironically, cites John Mandeville as a source. See also D. May, "Dating the English Translations of *Mandeville's Travels*," Notes and Queries ns 34 (1987): 178–82; C. W. Moseley, "Sir John Mandeville's Visit to the Pope," *Neophilologus* 54 (1970): 77–80; J. D. Thomas, "The Date of *Mandeville's Travels*," Modern Language Notes 72 (1957): 165–69; and K. Sisam, *Fourteenth Century Verse and Prose* (Oxford: Clarendon Press, 1975), 94–106.

[28] Due to ambiguous sentence construction, there is some confusion over whether 1366 is meant to be the date of his original departure from his home or the date of his trip to Rome thirty-four years later (which would make the original date of departure 1332, as in the overstrike). Viz.: "And I *Johan Maundevyle*. that wente oute of my contre and passede the see the yeer of our lorde a. m¹ ccc ~~xxxii~~ lxvi. at xxxiiii yeer aftre my departynge fro my contre// And for als moch als many men trowe noght/ bot that thei see with their eighen/ or that thei may conseyve in their kyndely wyt therfor I made my way to Rom in my comyng/ hamwarde to schewe my boke to oure holy fader the pope. . . ." Other Defective texts list varying dates of departure throughout the early fourteenth century.

[29] The papal interpolation is a feature of all the English texts, with the exception of the two texts of the Bodley version (Bodleian Library MSS Rawlinson D 99 and e Musaeo 116).

author's life was thrown open to question, and scholarship on the *Book* subsequently thrown into some disarray, by Stanislas Bormans's discovery in 1866 of this modernized extract from the lost fourth book of the *Myreur des Hystors* of John d'Outremeuse, a fourteenth-century Liège notary:

> In the year 1372 there died in Liège on the 12th November a man greatly distinguished by his birth who was content to be known by the name of Jean de Bourgogne, called "with the beard." He opened his heart however on his death-bed to Jean d'Outremeuse, his friend, whom he appointed his testamentary executor. In truth he called himself in the precis of his last will Master Jean de Mandeville, Knight, Count of Montfort in England, lord of the isle of Campdi and of Chateau Perouse. Having had the misfortune to kill, in his country, a count whom he did not name, he obliged himself to traverse the three parts of the world. Came to Liège in 1343.[30] (quoted in Letts, *Sir John Mandeville*, 15)

The very association of Mandeville's name with a French one seems to have solidified the growing general sense that the book was originally French, in the late 1800s, into a conviction that it and its author were definitely so. E. B. Nicholson and Henry Yule's decision to title their 1883 entry on Mandeville for the *Encyclopedia Britannica* "Mandeville, Jehan de," emphasizing the French connection, materially changed the way "Mandeville" and the *Book* would be viewed for decades to come.[31] But even this reversal of the general opinion was not to be unclouded by doubt. To complicate matters, in the Latin vulgate version of the *Book* the narrator tells us he has a Liégois friend, a doctor called John ad barbam (i.e., "with the beard") whom he had met in Cairo and met again in his old age in Liège, who encouraged him to write his book. This would make John Mandeville and John de Bourgogne two separate people, a possibility swiftly taken up as an alternative.

The "Liège controversy" has been a central theme of scholarship on the *Book* ever since, and efforts to integrate all the pieces of conflicting testimony have resulted in a wide array of hypotheses. Warner, Nicholson and Yule agreed that the Liégois writer John de Bourgogne used "John Mandeville" as an assumed name under which to write the *Book*.[32] Paul

---

[30] The original language of the passage is a difficult French-Flemish dialect. Early notices and translations appear in Warner, *Buke*, xxxiv and in Hamelius, *Mandeville's Travels*, 2: 8.

[31] Nicholson, E. B. and Henry Yule, "Mandeville, Jehan de," *Encyclopedia Britannica* 9th ed. (1883), xv: c. 473.

[32] Warner, "Sir John Mandeville"; Nicholson and Yule, "Mandeville, Jehan de." Nicholson backed up his position a year later with "John of Burgundy, alias 'Sir John Mandeville'," *Academy* 25 (12 April 1884): 261.

Hamelius, in 1917, countered with the argument that it was really John d'Outremeuse, a Liégois writer of greater note, who was "in all probability the real author of the *Travels*," having been given permission by the real Sir John Mandeville, an English doctor and traveler, to use his name (*Mandeville's Travels*, 2: 3-8).

Most critics of the early part of the century lined up behind one viewpoint or the other,[33] and throughout the early 1900s it was fairly well accepted that "John Mandeville" was merely a pen name for a Liégois author. The only question was, for whom? But Malcolm Letts, in 1949, turned the tables somewhat with his assertion that the opposite was true: John Mandeville had assumed the name John de Bourgogne because, as Outremeuse had said, he was a fugitive from England (*Sir John Mandeville*, 13-22). This at least would seem to fit the evidence better and was upheld by Rita Lejeune in her 1964 study of the Liège association.[34] Josephine Bennett in 1954 took the common-sense approach still further, asserting that John Mandeville had no assumed name and was connected with Liège only in the fevered imagination of John d'Outremeuse, who "spent his whole literary life in the glorification of Liège and its cathedral. ... It would be entirely in character for him to attempt to connect the author of the *Travels*, a work which he extravagantly admired, with Liège in some way" (*Rediscovery*, 103). C. W. Moseley, some thirty years later, emphatically agreed with Bennett that "John Mandeville" was not a pen name for John de Bourgogne and said that "the case for an English author is quite good" (*Mandeville's Travels*, 10). Oddly enough, Ralph Hanna a year later stated categorically that no one still believed Mandeville to be English ("Mandeville," *Middle English Prose: A Critical Guide to Major Authors and Genres*, ed. A. S. G. Edwards [New Brunswick, N.J.: Rutgers University Press, 1984], 122). In fact, opinion is still very much divided on both the author's name and nationality, and looks as if it will remain so for some time to come.

---

[33] C. Brown, "Note"; D. W. Singer "Note," *The Library* 3rd. ser. 9 (1918): 275-76; and J. J. Jusserand, *English Wayfaring Life in the Middle Ages* (New York: Putnam, 1930), for example, all throw in with Warner. A. P. Newton, ed., *Travel and Travellers in the Middle Ages* (London: Kegan Paul, 1926); A. Steiner, "The Date of Composition of *Mandeville's Travels*," *Speculum* 9 (1934): 144-47; and G. Kimble, *Geography in the Middle Ages* (London: Methuen, 1938) follow Hamelius. Hamelius's theory was attacked with particular vehemence by Bennett (*Rediscovery*).

[34] R. Lejeune, "Jean de Mandeville et les Liégeois," *Mélanges de linguistique romane et de philologie médiévale offerts à Maurice Delbouille*, Vol. 2 (Gembloux: J. Duculot, 1964), 409-37. Lejeune's discussion of the topic is both exhaustive and clear, attributes with much to recommend them in the presentation of such a complex and difficult critical problem. Her article deals in depth with the positions of Warner et al., Letts, and Bennett (below).

There is no way to determine which, if any, of the theories about the author's name, nationality, and life story is to be believed, and, despite the disproportionate amount of attention the search for the "real" John Mandeville has received, criticism can go on without him. One can sympathize with the sentiments of Malcolm Letts, who mourned, "Although I have plunged into the controversy myself, I feel that far too much paper and ink have been expended on the problem. After all these centuries it is the man as disclosed in his book that is important, not the man himself. The man himself can now never be anything but a ghost" (*Sir John Mandeville*, 21). Indeed, the man has become many ghosts. The "Sir John Mandeville" who was once accepted so uncomplicatedly as both author and narrator of the *Book* has become two separate personae, author and narrator, and a multitude of variations on each, as scribes and redactors have left traces of their authorship in the texts, and the narrating Mandevilles they created are seen to vary from text to text. It is the multiple Mandeville and the multiple *Book* that are truly "real."

While the pursuit of the *Book*'s original author occupied criticism for decades, it has done little to advance our knowledge about or understanding of the book itself. That author-focused criticism is perhaps not the most desirable approach is emphasized by the success of recent work by scholars like Deluz, Ridder, Higgins, and Ruddy, which emphasizes the book rather than its author, and the multiplicity of the book rather than its original form. Deluz's study of manuscript associations, Ridder's in-depth analysis of a specific non-original version, Higgins's exploration of variant "isotopes," and Ruddy's analysis of the *Book*'s early reception suggest that there is much to be learned from non-traditional approaches that work with rather than against the forces of change. By investigating the *Book*'s variance we may come to a greater understanding of its meaning, insofar as that meaning is constituted over time in a dialogic system of authors, texts, and readers, rather than by a single author in a single act of writing.

This is not to suggest that knowledge about the origins of the *Book* would not be useful. Not only would it enable scholars to identify and understand later variations in a more informed way, but it would also help us to quantify the generic contract the book originally attempted to make with its readers. Even if we accept the *Book* as multigeneric by nature, we must also acknowledge that its generic markers have been much altered by transmission—some texts focussing more strongly on the martial element, others on the religious, some on the romantic aspects, others on the encyclopedic, and so on. Certainly it would be helpful to have a baseline from which to measure such change. What is important is that we use that baseline as a starting point for study of the book in all its forms, rather than as a tool for reducing the variance of the *Book* as it exists over time to a single "best," most original version.

INVESTIGATING THE DEFECTIVE TEXTS

Almost all classic criticism of the *Book* works from some "best text": in English usually the Cotton manuscript, but often Egerton as well. This selection of a "best text" satisfies the traditional desire to be as true as possible to the original, and also makes the task of talking about the *Book* manageable, but only by casting the work in an unreal light, as something far more unified and cohesive than it actually is. Certainly it is tempting to reduce the *Book* to a unity. A commitment to the variance of medieval texts necessitates opening the closet door on something of a mess. But one cannot ignore the possibility that that mess, the hodgepodge of variant manuscripts of the *Book*, is really more the *Book* than any neat construct, written or unwritten, and more the *Book* than any single "best text." Both critical and "best text" approaches rely on a sense of the primacy of an original that is both irrecoverable and unreflective of all that the *Book*, in its long career, came to be. The *Book*, as a work whose original text is lost and whose widespread transmission over several centuries led to a profusion of different versions, cannot be characterized by a single text: scholarship would be better served, and would better serve the *Book*, by an increased emphasis on the texts' variation, rather than essentially reductive efforts at critical or best-text editing.

As a broader range of variant texts of the *Book* becomes available, scholars will have a greater opportunity to understand the *Book* as a unity in diversity, incorporating varying degrees of difference without the loss of a common bond. Small moves in this direction have been made over the years, with regard to the texts in English: Malcolm Letts' edition of Bodleian Library MS Rawlinson D. 99 of the Bodley version, A. C. Cawley's publication of the Ripon Fragment (two discontinuous leaves of a Defective text), and M. C. Seymour's editions of Bodleian Library MS e Musaeo of the Bodley version, the Epitome (an abridged Defective text), the Stanzaic Fragment, the Metrical version, and the Extracts (taken from a Defective text).[35] It is no coincidence, however, that these are universally the most fragmentary texts or those with the most striking variations. The Bodley version—an embedded genealogical curiosity, the closest extant manuscript to one of the texts upon which Egerton was probably based—is arguably the only one among them that might really be called a text of the *Book*, the rest being abstracts, extracts, and poetic texts that draw

---

[35] Letts, *Mandeville's Travels*; A. C. Cawley, "A Ripon Fragment of *Mandeville's Travels*," *English Studies* 38 (1947): 262–65; Seymour, *Bodley Version*; idem, "English Epitome"; idem, "Mandeville and Marco Polo: A Stanzaic Fragment," *Australian University Modern Language Association* 21 (1964): 39–52; idem, *Metrical Version*; and idem, "Secundum Iohannem Maundvyle."

on the *Book* for material but are so loosely connected to it as to be separate works. Not coincidentally, none of these texts bears a particularly close resemblance to Cotton or Egerton, and it is more than happenstance that the Defective texts that do resemble Cotton and Egerton have never been edited.

The more irregular texts are interesting to read precisely because they are so far removed from what critics see as the "real" English texts of the *Book*. Most critics still think of the full-length Defective texts, however, simply as bad versions of the "real" texts, too different to be important and not different enough to be interesting. Lacking both the authority of the more "original" texts and the élan of the wildly irregular, these manuscripts have been left in editorial obscurity. Jules Bramont in 1928 published one edition of the *Book* that might be construed as a Defective text, based on Thomas East's 1568 edition, which stems from Pynson, but it is printed "with certain passages restored, which the Elizabethan printers omitted in error."[36] The most notable of those passages is, of course, the material from the "Egypt Gap," which the editor fills in from the 1725 Cotton edition. Thus Bramont's effort is directed not toward preserving a Defective rendering of the *Book*, but toward making this early published version accord with what later critics consider the best English manuscript version.

While the irregular texts that have been printed in modern editions have failed to excite sustained critical response, largely because they have not traditionally been seen as important texts in and of themselves, they have at least the advantage of visibility. Scholarship makes far more mention of the Metrical version and the Stanzaic Fragment than of all the Defective texts put together. The bulk of the Defective survival of the *Book* remains all but invisible: unedited, and rarely even mentioned. While most scholars using "best texts" make some kind of apologia for their choice of Cotton over Egerton or vice versa, few so much as note any of the Defective texts as a possibility. These texts are, however, valid parts of the *Book*'s tradition, with much to offer scholarship. They do not differ from Cotton and Egerton solely by what they lack, nor can every difference in the Defective manuscripts be written off as an omission or an error. There are other, more subtle differences, more difficult to quantify, which have been largely ignored by a critical tradition reluctant to look beyond the "Egypt Gap." Higgins's recent work comparing Pynson (his exemplar for the Defective version) against other versions of the *Book* has begun to suggest some of the new kinds of questions and answers study of the Defective version may have to offer scholars; but because Higgins uses,

---

[36] J. Bramont, ed., *The Travels of Sir John Mandeville and the Journal of Friar Odoric* (London: J. M. Dent, 1928), xii.

The Defective Texts xxxi

as he must in a work of that scope, only the one text to represent all of the Defective version, variation within that version remains obscured. The Pynson edition is without question an important exemplum of the Defective version, and emerging efforts to take it into account are long overdue: but it must be stressed that no single Defective text can reasonably be called upon to exemplify the whole. The study of Pynson is both interesting and illuminating, but it must proceed as the study of Pynson, a single text, not a stand-in for its entire family of texts. The Pynson text no more exemplifies the entire Defective version than Cotton or Egerton exemplifies all of the *Book of John Mandeville*.[37]

To illustrate, let us compare these parallel descriptions of burning the dead on an Ile in India, found in Egerton, Trinity College MS R. 4. 20 (Defective), and Pynson. While they are substantially the same, each puts a subtly different twist on the question of whether the spouses of the deceased shall be burnt along with them or not. Egerton has:

> when any man dies in that land, thai brynne his body, for that he suld suffer na payne, when he es in his graue, thurgh etyng of wormes. And, if he hafe na childer, thai brynne his wyf with him. For thai say that it is resoun that scho bere him cumpany in the tother werld as scho did here in this werld. And, if scho hafe childer, thai late hir liffe for to bring tham vp, if scho will. And, if it be swa that scho chese rather to liffe with hir childer rather than to be brynned with hir housband, than sall scho be arettid vntrew and vnkynde, and scho sall neuer be praised, ne na man sall efter that tyme trist on hir. And, if the wyf dye before hir husband, he schall

---

[37] The Pynson edition, because it is the first in English, apparently widely known and certainly broadly influential over subsequent editions, is often taken as representative of the Defective version as a whole. Higgins remains commendably aware, throughout his study, that Pynson cannot fully exemplify the Defective texts, but the tendency to speak of Defective as a single unit, either reducible to Pynson or in general terms, as if a critical edition did exist, has been long entrenched. For example, M. C. Seymour, in his edition of the Cotton text, can say that he has filled in a lacuna in Cotton "from the Defective Version" (*Mandeville's Travels*, xxi). Even the Defective texts' most vocal champions have underplayed the diversity within the classification. Ralph Hanna in his "Mandeville" strongly urges the necessity of studying the Defective version, arguing that it alone has "any real claims to be the English Mandeville": it "provided source material for three of the five other English recensions (only the Bodley and metrical versions are completely independent). Further it alone, so far as one can tell, achieved any wide dissemination.... And this text alone exerted influence on Renaissance readers" (123). He caps his argument by saying that "no compelling reason, other than unavailability of the Pynson print, compels one to ignore this centerpiece of the Middle English Mandeville tradition" (124). Hanna's argument for the Defective version is at root an argument only for Pynson: a sensible argument to be sure, but still tending to hold up Pynson as the Defective text, rather than a Defective text.

noght be brynt with hir agayne his will; bot, if him list, he may take him another wyf. (*Buke*, 85)[38]

Cambridge, Trinity College MS. R.4.20 has:

¶And if ony man dye in that londe they brenne hym in tokenyng of penaunce. that he shal suffre no penaunce if he were leid in the erthe. of etyng of wormes. And if his wyf have no child thei brenne hir/ with hym. and seien it is good resoun that she make hym companye in that other world. as she dide in this/ and if she have childre. she may lyve with hem and she wol. and if the wyf dye bifore men brenne hir. and hir husbonde also if he wole. (fol. 51ʳ)

Pynson's edition has:

if any man dye in that countre they brenne hym in tokenynge of penaunce that he shulde suffre no penaunce if he were layde in the erthe of etynge of wormes and if his wife have no chyldren they bren hir with hym/ and they say it is gode reoson that she make hym company in the other world as she dyd in this/ and if she have children she may lyve with theym and she woll and if the wyfe dye before men brenne hir and hir housholde as if he woll. (sig. f3ʳ)

The similarities here are obvious, yet the three treatments stress entirely different points. Egerton stresses the primacy of the male, a man's free choice not to be burned as opposed to his wife's choice of death or ostracism. Similarly, a woman who chooses life is clearly depicted as having a perverse will, being untrustworthy and unwholesome, whereas a man's choice of survival is without moral overtones. Also, by placing the possibility of a man's choosing to be burnt in the negative ("he will not be burnt with her against his will"), Egerton stresses the survival potential of the husband as opposed to the wife far more strongly than does R.4.20 with its "men brenne hir. and hir husbonde also if he wole." While R.4.20 preserves the notion of man's free choice, it does so in terms far less strikingly favorable to the male. Pynson, by contrast, stresses the gender issue in quite a different way. It does not even suggest burning the husband, but focuses instead on the cultural practice of being burnt with one's chief possessions: for a man, his wife; for a woman, her household goods.

In a cursory reading, one might easily construe these three passages as functionally identical, yet the difference in stress is powerful. Egerton's

---

[38] Egerton references in this introduction are to Warner, *Buke*. Cotton references are to Seymour, *Mandeville's Travels*.

strong emphasis on masculine authority and the moral duty of women is far less marked in the other texts, which approach the same material in very different ways. If scholars never look at the Defective version at all, this kind of variance is not noted and its implications go unconsidered. If scholars look only at Pynson, they get a clear indication that variance on this point exists, but no fuller understanding of what forms that variation may take in the other Defective texts.

The Defective version shows marked internal differences in style, in tone, and in effect which may not always be revealed by examination of a single Defective exemplum. As a case in point, let us consider the concentration of set phrases, especially the *Book*'s trademark phrase "And ye shall understand," in Pynson, Egerton, and Cambridge University Library MS Gg. I. 34. iii (Defective). The phrase is a striking feature of even the earliest French texts, but in Gg. I. 34. iii its incidence is multiplied out of all proportion, rendering the narrator extremely present to the reader and insisting at every turn upon the manuscript's self-proclaimed ability to instruct and enlighten. In a short discussion of the wonders of Constantinople, the quality of Gg. I. 34. iii's insistence upon its own authority becomes clear. Pynson tells us that Christ was nailed to the cross lying down, "and therfore he suffred the more peyne. Also [those] in Grece and the crysten men that dwell over the see say that the tree of the crosse that we call Cypresse was of that tree that adam ete the appyl ... " (sig. a5^r). In this it agrees closely with Egerton (*Buke*, 6) and with texts of the Insular version. But Gg. I. 34. iii has instead "therefore he suffred the more pain as grekes and Xn men seye that dwell in that country. *And ye schal understand* that the tree of the cross ..." (fol. 7^r; emphasis mine), emphasizing the text's assertion of its own role as educator of the reader. Where Pynson, similarly to Egerton and their Insular ancestors, tells us that "A party of the crowne of oure lorde ihesu wherwithe he was crowned/ and of the nayles/ and the spere hede and many other relyques ar in fraunce in the chapell of the kynge of fraunce" (fol. a5^v; *Buke*, 6),[39] Gg. I. 34. iii begins, "*And ye schall understand* that a partie of the crown ..." (fol. 8^v; emphasis mine). Where Pynson and Egerton tell us, with Insular, that "at constantynople lyeth saynt anne" (sig. a6^v; *Buke*, 8), Gg. I. 34. iii announces, "*And shall understand* [sic] that at Constantinople lyes saint anne" (fol. 9^r; emphasis mine).

"Ye shall understonde," "Ye shall wete," "Ye shall wele wete," "Ye shall wele understonde": everywhere in Gg. I. 34. iii one encounters the

---

[39] Where Pynson and Egerton agree closely, quotations are taken from Pynson and the appropriate reference to Warner given for the reader's convenience.

multiplication of direct address from the narrator, made doubly noticeable in almost every case by being highlighted with a red paraph. These frequent, striking reminders of the narrator's presence and of his attempt to create an authoritative voice through assertion of his right to act as teacher render the reader's experience of the narrator quite different from what it is in Egerton or Pynson, where these assertions figure less largely. Indeed, Gg. I. 34. iii bolsters the sense of its own authority in a variety of small ways. There is, for example, contention between Paris and Constantinople over which of them possesses the head of the spear that pierced Christ's side. Pynson and Egerton side with Paris, but do so subtly: "the hede is at parys and many tymes sayth the emperoure of Constantynople that he hathe the spere hede. And I have often sene it but it is gretter than that of parys" (sig. a6ᵛ; *Buke*, 7). In this they agree with their Insular antecedents. Gg. I. 34. iii, however, repudiates Constantinople's claim far more bluntly: "I have oft seen it but *it is not that* for it is greater thanne it is a paris" (fol. 9ᵛ; emphasis mine). Throughout, Gg. I. 34. iii is a more insistent text, more interested in dictating and controlling audience response to its information. Study of the Pynson text alone would suggest that the Defective version as a whole follows its antecedents fairly closely on this point, and accords with Egerton in doing so—a conclusion that would simply be incorrect.[40] There is reason to believe that this more authoritarian approach to the *Book* was disseminated fairly widely in England, but in order to see it scholars must return to the individual Defective texts.

In order to study the variance of the Defective texts as it should be studied, it is necessary to question the classification that makes of them a single entity. Over thirty separate manuscripts, by far the majority of the extant texts in English, cannot so easily be dismissed as interchangeable and unimportant simply because they share the lack of a quire of copytext. As Seymour's division of the Defective version into subgroups suggests, all the manuscripts within that version are not alike:

> Each sub-group is distinguished by recognizable features. Thus, sub-group A (ch. xx) includes an account of the rotundity of the world, otherwise found only in the exceptional MS. Royal 17 C. xxxviii; sub-group B (ch. xxxii) gives a duplicate account of Alexander's discomfiture by the virtuous islanders; sub-group C (ch. xii) omits the Hebrew alphabet; sub-group D corrupts the phrase roys ils (which marks a major lacuna in ch. vi) to yles and valeyes; and sub-group

---

[40] Warner's edition of the Insular version in his *Buke* will serve for comparison on the points raised here. His text is based largely on British Library MSS Harley 4383, Sloane 1464, and Royal 20 B. x of the Insular version, which he had ready to hand.

D [sic] (ch. xxxii) interpolates a Latin translation of part of Dindimus' correspondence.[41] ("English Manuscripts," 169)

Seymour also tells us,

> Sub-groups A and B derive independently from the lost archetype, and sub-groups C, D, and E represent successive dependent stages in the transmission of the text of sub-group B. The tripartite division within subgroup A [manuscripts are classed as Ai, Aii, and Aiii] represents three independent lines of descent from the common ancestor; and the five manuscripts of sub-group B derive independently from their common ancestor. ("English Manuscripts," 169)

If, then, A and B are independently derived and never in the course of their transmission came to be conflated together, why must they be accounted the same version? Granted, they stem from the same archetype, but ultimately all manuscripts of the *Book* spring from the same archetype. Although the concept of the Defective texts as a single "version" of the *Book* has been in force since the nineteenth century, that does not make it a necessary construction: only a long-lived one. Certainly it is not the only way in which these texts could be classified. Where one chooses to place the boundaries of a "version" is very much a subjective matter, and one could as easily consider all the A-variations as one version and all the B-variations as another. Or one could consider each subgroup a separate version. There is much more leeway in these classificatory systems than one is normally encouraged to think about. Even for the manuscript genealogist, for whom, if for anyone, the classification of all these manuscripts as a single "version" should be a boon, it is instead something of a problem. If, for example, one were trying to produce a critical edition of the Defective version[42] should one include the rotundity of the world? The texts of the A and B subgroups, deriving independently from their shared archetype, are presumably of equal "value" as texts. Without the archetype before us, we cannot know if the rotundity of the world has been added into A or left out of B. The decision of what to include as the authoritative reading for all the Defective texts must then be a highly subjective one.

The classification of all these texts as a single genealogical unit, a "ver-

---

[41] Chapter numbers refer as usual to Cotton's chaptering. Cf. note 21.

[42] Seymour notes in several places, including *Mandeville's Travels*, that the Early English Text Society has ready for publication a critical edition (presumably his own) of the Defective version. To date it has not appeared. He may have had this text in mind when, as mentioned above, he referred to having filled the lacuna in Cotton "from the Defective Version" (cf. note 37).

sion," suggests that their similarities outweigh their differences, but in many cases that is demonstrably not the case. Consider the two manuscripts Bodleian Library MS Rawlinson D. 101 (Defective) and Cambridge University Library MS Dd. i. 17 (Defective), both classed by Seymour in 1966 as subgroup Aii. Their accounts of the roundness of the world are the feature that most securely binds them together, that makes them similar. And yet those two accounts are quite unlike. Both speak of the two pole stars, Transmontaigne and Autertyke; they tell of how the heavens spin around them like "wheels on an axletree." They tell of how one might travel all around the earth and return again to one's own country, and even recount a story of a Norwegian who did it by accident. They give the earth's circumference variously as 30,452 miles (D. 101) and 20,425 miles (Dd. i. 17), after the opinion of old wise men. But Dd. i. 17 continues:

> ¶Bote after my lytil wyt me thynkyth, save hare grace that it ys more a boute ¶And for to under stonde better that I welle say I ymagyne a fygure whare ys a grete Compaas and a boute the poynt of that Compaas that ys y cleped centre by a nother litel compaas departid by lynes in many parties ¶And that thes lynes mete to gedre on the Centre so that as many parties other lynes alle the grete compas hase be on the lytell compaas of alle the space by lasse. now by the grete compas sette forth the firmamente the which by astronomers ys departid in xii. signes ¶And eche signe ys departyd in thritty degrees This his thre hundreth and sexti degrees that is a boute. Now be the erth departid in as meny parties as the firmament and eaych of theese ansswere to a degree of the firmamente ¶This been alle vii. hundereth and twenti ¶Now be this in all multiplied thre hundred tymes and sexti and hit schal mounte in alle to one and thrity thousand myle and fyve Ilke myle of eyghte furlanges as mylles been in oure countree and so muche hase the erthe in compas and in Roundenesse alle aboute after myne opynyoun and myn undirstondyng ¶And ye schal undirstonde after the opynyoun of alle Wyse philosophres and astronomers that Englond Scoland Wales ne Irlond bote nought rekened in the heyghthe of the erthe as hit semees welle by alle bokes of astronomye. ¶ffor the hyth of the erthe ys departid in vii. planetes wich been y clepid Clymates. and thees Countrees that y spak of ben nought in thes Clymates for thay bee dounward so to ward the West. ¶And also thes Iles of ynde which been even a gens us byth nought rekened in the Clymates for they bee towarde the Est to lowe. ¶And clymates goth aboute alle the world. (fols. 45^{r-v})

This passage in Dd. i. 17 is comparable to Cotton's and Egerton's, and can be traced back to both the Continental and Insular versions. D. 101's conspicuous omission of this material is suggestive. While it may simply be accidental variance, introduced by an incomplete copy-text or a page-flip, it may also be the result of a desire on the D. 101 writer's part to adhere to the opinions of past authorities, rather than pitting his "lytil wyt" against them.[43]

Such variation may well be significant, especially insofar as D. 101 is generally a less complex text, and one apparently more concerned with the reporting of "fact" than with interpretation, speculation, or inference. Dd. i. 17, following the French models more closely, goes into significantly more detail than its subgroup-mate, interpreting the facts, delving into the emotional as well as the physical, and frequently placing events within a context of cause and effect rather than simply reporting them as occurrences. Of the pygmies, for example, D. 101 tells us only that they are three spans tall and fair, that they wed at half a year and are old if they live to be eight, and that they have tall men to work for them, omitting an interpretation of their relationship with those tall men that Dd. i. 17 preserves: "thay haue as gret scorne of thes men: as we wold haue of Geauntes a mang us" (fol. 46ᵛ).

Recounting the story of the bishop Athanasius, D. 101 tells us:

> in this citte Seynt Atanas that was bisshope of Alysaunder made the psalme Quicuncz vult ¶ this man was a grete doctor of divinite and he was accused to the pope of Rome that he was an eretike and the pope send after hym and put hym in prison and ther he made the psalme and send it to the pope and seid if he were heretike than was that heresy for that was ys beleve and whan the pope saw that therin was all oure feythe he lete delyver hym oute of prison And the pope commaunded that psalme to be seid every day at prime And held Athanas for a good man but Athanas wold never after goy to his bisshopryche ageyn. (fols. 49ʳ⁻ᵛ)

Here D. 101 again omits that which Dd. i. 17 retains: a marked pattern of speculation about the motivations of both Athanasius's accusers and Athanasius himself. In Dd. i. 17, "This man was a grete doctour of Divy/ nitee

---

[43] It should be noted that neither computation in Dd. i. 17 is in fact the result of the writer's "little wit." In reference to Egerton's numbers, which are identical with Dd. i. 17's, George Warner notes: "The first of these measurements of the earth is very nearly the same as in Brun. Latini, who makes it to be 20,427 miles. . . . What Mandeville then proceeds to give as his own computation is none other than that of Eratosthenes (ob. 196 B.C.); and he may have found it in Vinc. of Beauvais" (Buke, 200n). Within the text, however, the second calculation represents not one more authority, but the narrator's questioning of authority; its omission might easily have been purposeful.

& for he spake so depe in divinitee and of/ the godhede. he was accused to the Pope of Rome" (fol. 42ᵛ; emphasis mine). And later, "*athanas wolde never afterward go to his bischopriche/ agen. for that thay hadde accused hem of heresye*" (fol. 42ᵛ; emphasis mine). D. 101 continuously suggests a reductive tendency on the part of its writer or its antecedents that would bear closer investigation. And yet the classification of these two manuscripts encourages us to think of them as essentially the same.[44]

The subgroups and their overarching classification within the "Defective version" suggest that we pass over the differences between the Defective texts in favor of their similarities, as texts with a "rotundity of the world" passage, or as texts with two accounts of the Brahmins, or, most encompassingly, as texts with an "Egypt Gap." Perhaps one of the most striking examples of a text whose difference has been sacrificed to classification is that of British Library MS. Harley 2386. Classified by Seymour as a B-text of the Defective version ("English Manuscripts," 187), this text omits nearly two leaves of prologue, some form of which is present in all other English texts of the *Book* (excepting verse forms and fragments), to begin with the passage "John maundevylle knyht of alle I be nouht worthy that was borny in englonde in the town of seynt albon and passed the see in the yere of our lord jhu crist. a. m.   xxxii" (fol. 74ʳ),[45] a passage which in some form usually appears in the midst of the prologue (or chapter one as it is considered in some manuscripts). Perhaps not coincidentally, the section that is not here is the only sustained mention of crusading and the need to conquer the Holy Land in the book,[46] the section upon which generic readings of the *Book* as "crusade propaganda" are essentially based. The opening material, absent from 2386, is the linchpin of such arguments, the clear statement of crusading zeal to which later, more vague military references can be connected to imbue them with crusading spirit as well. Without that opening material, the crusading force of the book is all but lost.[47]

---

[44] Seymour has silently removed Rawlinson D. 101 from the Aii classification in his 1993 listing of the manuscripts (*Sir John Mandeville*, 38–49), along with Bodleian MS Douce 33. Whereas the previous classification ("English Manuscripts") listed all the A manuscripts as Ai, Aii, or Aiii, the new listing has these two manuscripts plus the Extracts (Bodleian MS Ashmole 751) as simply A-texts. One wonders why this is so, and what effect it has on Seymour's previous statement that the A texts reflect three separate lines of descent, but no explanation for the change is offered.

[45] Space is left in the date for the insertion of the hundreds.

[46] See the Pynson edition for a fairly representative text of the material that has been left out of Harley 2386. Although all manuscripts do not, of course, agree verbatim, most of the English manuscripts do open with passages similar to that in Pynson.

[47] Cf. A. Atiya, *The Crusade in the Later Middle Ages* (London: Methuen, 1938), for an analysis of the *Book* as crusade propaganda.

Seymour claims that the text "Begins imperfectly" ("English Manuscripts," 187), with two leaves missing before folio 74, on which he says the *Book* begins. The collation of the manuscript he lists as "unknown." But R. J. Lyall has since determined the collation of Harley 2386 based on watermarks and finds no leaves apparently missing before folio 74.[48] Rather there has been, Lyall says, "the apparent cancellation of a watermarked half-sheet corresponding to folios 74 and 87" ("Materials," 23). Since there is no text missing from the place where folio 87 would have been, it seems reasonable to assume that no text is missing from the beginning either: indeed, if the half sheet was cancelled rather than lost, as the textual continuity surrounding folio 87 would suggest, it may even indicate a purposeful desire on the part of the manuscript's writer to leave off the introduction.

In addition, Harley 2386 gives no internal evidence of beginning imperfectly: just the opposite, in fact. Throughout the text, chapters are marked by the spaces left for large decorative initials which were never filled in. The first line of the text, "John maundevylle knyht of all I be nouht worthy ..." has space for such an initial before it, marking it as a chapter, a division that is highly unusual in manuscripts of the *Book*. In most manuscripts this passage comes midway through the prologue or first chapter and is marked as special only by a paraph. In some manuscripts it is underlined. In some it is even noted in the margin with the rubric "who made this book." But this is the only extant manuscript that considers that passage to be the beginning of chapter one. Immediately after the short paragraph in which Sir John identifies himself and sketches out where he has been in the world, the text continues with "The secunde chapitre," beginning as usual with "In the nam of god al myhte he that wyl passe see he may go meny weyes ..." (for comparison cf. Pynson sig. a3^v).

The only basis for an assumption that two leaves must be missing from the front of the text is the expectation that they should have been there. The fact that a chapter has been begun at "John Mandeville, although I be not worthy" suggests that the text is meant to begin there, whether because the scribe felt for some reason that the opening leaves should be removed or because the copy-text had lost them. Whatever the cause of their absence, the effect is striking: the creation of a *Book of John Mandeville* with a significantly less distinct martial component than others of its kind.

---

[48] By a singular stroke of luck, R. J. Lyall, "Materials: The Paper Revolution," *Book Production and Publishing in Britain: 1375–1475*, ed. Derek Pearsall and Jeremy Griffiths (Cambridge: Cambridge University Press, 1989), 11–29, uses Harley 2386 as one of its chief examples of how analysis of paper can help with dating, collation, and reconstruction of medieval manuscripts. Lyall makes the collation of the text "[five leaves] a^{14}, b^{16}–d^{16}, e at least 12 (5–? missing)" (23).

While Harley 2386 is plainly a special case, and most texts do include the propagandizing prologue, the fact remains that some people were producing and reading texts that simply could not support a propagandistic interpretation. Even if Harley 2386 springs from a copy-text missing the first folios, and the variation came into being by accident, it was nonetheless passed down. One might speculate, then, that the martial message of the first folios was not so central to readers' understanding of the *Book* that it could not be left off. The manuscript dates from the late fifteenth/early sixteenth century, by which time the *Book* had been in wide circulation for over a century. The book was well known by then, and it is unlikely that if it were generally perceived as crusade propaganda, a copy-text missing its crusading prologue would have been used without comment. Perhaps the writer of 2386 objected to the martial tone in the prologue of a book he did not consider martial, and so deleted it. Perhaps by the late fifteenth century, one scribe at least came to see the idea of crusading as outdated and so sought to modernize the text. The possibilities are as interesting as they are manifold. Regardless of our interpretation of Harley 2386's difference, it is clear that such a manuscript should not simply be buried among the other Defective texts as if not significantly different from them or from other texts of the *Book*. While the filling of the "Egypt Gap" from another manuscript is considered to be of the most signal importance, producing the best available versions, Cotton and Egerton, the opening of a gap such as that in Harley 2386 has not so far been considered even worth critical mention.

The classification of all texts with an "Egypt Gap" as a single version passes rather lightly over the striking oddities of a manuscript like British Library MS Royal 17C. xxxviii (Defective), as well. Royal 17C is notable not for the bits that are missing but for those that are included, most notably both a roundness-of-the-world passage (the defining mark of a Defective A-text) and a double account of the Bragmans (the defining mark of a Defective B-text). It is in fact the only English manuscript besides Egerton in which the two meet. Also interesting is that the "Egypt Gap" in Royal 17C is unlike that of any other manuscript. The site of the gap in Pynson, which corresponds fairly well to the gap in most other Defective texts except those that alter "Roys Ile" to "iles and valleys," reads like this:

> And this arre they of Canopate that is Egypte the kyngdom of Ierusalem wherof David and Salon were kynges: the kyngdome of Surrey. of the whych the cyte of Damas was the chef/ kingdom of anaple in the lond of Dameth/ and the kyngdom of arab was to one of the thre kynges that made offerynge to oure lorde whan he was borne. and many other londes he holdethe in his hande/ and also

he holdethe Calaphes that is a greate thynge to the Soudan/ that is to say amonge theym Roys Ile [GAP] and this vale is full colde. and than men goo up on the mount of saynte Katheryn/ and that is moche hygher than the mounte Moyses. (sig. b5ʳ)

Royal 17C has instead, at the gap, "... and that was oon of the three kynges that bar offryng to our lord. And many other londes he holdeth in his hand. And the mount of seynt katherine is moch heyr than the mount moyses ..." (fol. 16ʳ). What is striking here is how much more smoothly Royal bridges the gap, erasing the actual clause in which the gap occurs to join the surrounding material quite seamlessly, as if it knows the gap is there. Most Defective texts leave it as Pynson does, an obvious non sequitur in the middle of a sentence. While Royal's version may seem a non sequitur as well, it is far less so, being really no more disjoint than many transitions in the *Book*, which are often effected simply by changing the subject abruptly. The site of the "Egypt Gap" in Royal is much more coherent than others, and suggests a possible familiarity with several texts, out of which its writer has attempted to produce continuity.

While Royal 17C may not fall completely outside the genealogical lines of the Defective texts, its inconsistencies with respect to the other texts called "Defective" suggest that it is connected with them in a more complex and ill-understood way than is generally supposed: that it may be a conflation, that it definitely requires further study. Manuscript genealogy is useful in determining the connections between texts, but it should not be used, as it has so often been for the *Book*, as a means of crediting some texts while discrediting others. An understanding of textual interrelationships is an invaluable tool for studying textual variance, but to use that understanding instead as a means of narrowing the field, weeding out texts we consider inferior or unoriginal, is to make a grave error.

Textual Variation and
Some "Truths" about the *Book*

Not only does neglect of the variants cause scholars to miss the nuances of specific texts and lose the opportunity to study how those texts present themselves and their material to their audiences, but it also fosters an acceptance of generalizations about the *Book* as a whole that are based on very limited textual evidence, and thus may not be supported by the bulk of the texts. Two such long-held patterns of generalization which have recently been challenged are the idea of the *Book* as an essentially bipartite work, and the concept of the best texts of the *Book* as essentially similar and even interchangeable.

For over a century the idea of the *Book* as structured around a fundamental antithesis of East versus West, in which the Far East is rhetorically balanced against the Holy Land in an essentially antagonistic pattern, held nearly unconditional sway. So entrenched was this belief in the early part of the twentieth century that Paul Hamelius printed his edition of the Cotton version (*Mandeville's Travels*) in 1919 in two distinct sections, labelled I and II, despite the Cotton manuscript's complete lack of any such distinction. Modern scholars have, however, begun reenvisioning that pattern. Higgins rightly suggests that the remarkable thing about the movement from Holy Land to Far East in the *Book* is the continuity, rather than the discontinuity, between the two: "it is handled no differently from any previous shift in the text, being presented as a natural progression that entails only a minor change in subject, from territory and routes to territory and diversity" (*Writing East*, 124). Edward Said's discussion of Orientalism has also provided a corrective to long-held views associating the Holy Land with Europe and Asia with "the East," stressing as it does the very Oriental character of the Holy Land itself, for medieval and Renaissance Europeans.[49] We thus find ourselves at a crossroads for criticism and understanding of the *Book*, as scholars begin to envision it more as a coherent whole. A more in-depth investigation of some of the variant texts may be instrumental in supporting that view, as I hope to show here.

The bipartite view of the *Book* was popularized by George Warner in his introduction to the 1889 Roxburghe Club Edition of the Egerton text, where he said:

> Although there is no direct statement to that effect, *Mandeville's Travels* are made up of two parts. . . . In the French and English texts there are merely a few introductory words to ch. xvi, but in the vulgate Latin in Harley 3589 (f. 102) there is the rubric "Explicit prima pars. Incipit secunda." The printed edition (Grenv. 6700) expands this into "Incipit sec. pars et ultima tractatus huius que tractat de diuersis insulis et de mirabilibus dispositionibus hominum in illis habitantium." (*Buke*, xv)[50]

---

[49] Said notes that "the Arabs and Islam . . . for almost a thousand years together stood for the Orient" (*Orientalism* [New York: Vintage, 1979], 16–17). His discussion of modern Near Eastern Orientalism outlines the same basic cultural prejudices that medieval Europeans brought to their reading of the Islamic world and the Arab peoples, and also suggests the very Orientalist nature of the anti-Semitism so prevalent in the *Book* (cf. Said, 26–28). Said's statement that "In the Christian West, Orientalism [i.e., the study of the Oriental] is considered to have commenced its formal existence with the decision of the Church Council of Vienne in 1312 to establish a series of chairs in Arabic, Greek, Hebrew, and Syriac" (49–50) in the major universities of the day emphasizes, as does much of his book, the degree to which the Near East was perceived as far more alien than familiar.

[50] Warner's chaptering refers as usual to that of the Cotton text, which he adopts for his

The evidence of Harley 3589 seems definitive to Warner, making overt what he sees as implicit in the other versions he has seen. But a more thorough study of the surviving texts of the Book suggests that it is not nearly so definitive as it sounds. A small number of manuscripts do make the split into two parts very consciously, setting the Far East material off from that on the Holy Land in the most incontrovertible terms: these, however, are invariably later manuscripts, and most of the extant French and English texts do not mark any separation at all. The *Book* as bipartite work does exist, or come to exist over the course of its transmission, but the two-part division does not emerge as defining for the book as a whole. Especially with regard to its earliest audiences, the *Book* does not appear to have presented itself in this light. Indeed, if one reads the Pynson text, which formed the basis for the wide dissemination of the *Book* in England after 1496, one finds oneself strongly compelled toward Higgins's view of the essential continuity of the movement from Holy Land to Far East. There is, in fact, much more continuity of style, tone, and subject matter than the model of a bipartite narrative implies.

This is the passage from Pynson at which the narrative would be said to break:

> And sythen I have devysed before of the holy londe and countrees theraboute and many wayes theder/ and to mounte Synay to Babilon. and other places of the whyche I have spoken.
>   ¶ Nowe I woll tell and speke of yles/ and of dyverse bestes and dyvers folke/ for in those countres is many divers folke. and countres that are departed by the fowre flodes that came oute of paradyse terrestre. (sig. e4^v–e5^r)[51]

This would seem a clear enough indication of a major break in the text, but only if taken out of context. By the time one reaches this "break" in Pynson one has already read through three others that are very much like it:

> Nowe syth I have tolde you of many maners of men that dwell in countrees before sayde. Nowe woll I turne ageyne to my way. (sig. d6^r)

Egerton. The chaptering of the French and English manuscripts is far from regular: Defective texts rarely agree with one another or with Cotton. Bodleian MS Douce 33, for example, has twenty-four chapters, whereas British Library MS Add. 33758 has only sixteen. While a number of Defective texts have twenty-one or twenty-two chapters, they rarely agree throughout in where the chapter breaks are placed. Bodleian MS Rawlinson D. 99 of the Bodley version has sixty-nine chapters, and the second part, as Warner defines it here, would begin at chapter 43. The attribution of the same chapter 16 to all French and English texts can thus be somewhat misleading.

[51] The passages in Cotton and Egerton are quite similar to this one.

> Nowe have I tolde you of weyes/ by the whyche men go ferthest and lengest as by Babylony/ and mounte Synay/ and other places many/ thoroughe the whiche londes men turne ageyne to the londe of promyssyon. ¶ Nowe wolle I tell you the wey to Ierusalem. (sig. d7ʳ)

> Nowe have I tolde you somme wayes by londe/ and by water. howe men may go to Ierusalem. If all it be so that there be many other wayes that men goo by after countrees that they come fro. Nevertheles they turne all to one ende. (sig. d8ʳ)

And after the "break," one encounters still more:

> Nowe have I devysed you the londes towarde the north to com fro the londes of chatay to the londes of Pruys/ and Rosy where crysten men dwelle. Nowe shall I devyse to you other londes and kyngdoms in comynge downe fro Chatay to the grekes see where cristen men dwell. (sig. g8ʳ⁻ᵛ)

> Nowe have I saide and spoken of many on this side of the great kingdom of Chatay of Whom many ar obeysaunt to the greate chane. Nowe shall I say of som londes and countres and Iles that ar beyonde the londe of chatay. (sig. h1ᵛ)

In reading the Pynson text, then, one is hardly struck by any kind of abrupt distinction being made at signature e4ᵛ. All these other examples of similar passages are set off from the rest of the text in just the same way the "break" is: with a space in the manuscript and a large capital letter. The form "Now have I shown you this. Let us move on to the next" emerges as the pattern for the beginning of chapters, rather than as any momentous, one-time event. The "break" at e4ᵛ is not physically unique in the text, nor is it stylistically unique. It is one statement among many. Indeed, if one is going looking for major textual divisions, why not designate a third at h1ᵛ, where the text states its aim to move from Cathay to the Iles of India? This is certainly a major change of venue and is in fact set off as a separate section in some divided texts, as will be shown below.

Cotton shares chapter breaks with Pynson in four of the places cited above: Pynson's chapter at e4ᵛ is Cotton's chapter 16, at d6ʳ Cotton's chapter 14, at g8ʳ Cotton's chapter 28, and at h1ᵛ Cotton's chapter 29. Because Cotton shows only four chapter breaks of this pattern in thirty-four chapters, as against Pynson's five in nineteen chapters, the pattern never emerges as markedly in Cotton. But in Pynson it makes itself strongly felt, especially as so many of the other chapter breaks that do not strictly follow this pattern lean toward it as well: chapters break most often in Pynson at moments when one is changing course, leaving one

Textual Variation   xlv

country for another, going from here to there. A single instance simply does not stand out in the sequence. Warner's "few introductory words to [Cotton's] ch. xvi," which are supposed to denote a major change in the book's movement, are perceived as being very much of a piece with the introductory words to the other chapters in Pynson. Indeed, the most distinct physical "break" in Pynson occurs in the form of an indented heading in the midst of the early chapters on alternative routes to Jerusalem:

> ¶Howe a man may go ferthest and lengest
> in those countrees as herafter ben rehersed (sig. d6ᵛ).

This is the only such heading in the text, and while it precedes a chapter break in Pynson, it would be in the middle of Cotton's chapter fourteen— far from the site such a heading would need to occupy in order to ratify the accepted bipartite theory.

Warner does not note that in addition to the one manuscript he cites as having two distinct parts, there are also manuscripts in more than two. Bodleian Library MS Rawlinson D. 99 of the Bodley version, for example, is a text in English, roughly contemporaneous with Harley 3589 above, and is explicitly broken into not just two, but five distinct sections, with these headings:[52]

> Hic incipit liber qui vocatur Maundevile, quem quidam miles composuit sub hac forma peregrynis. Incipit prima pars [chaps. 1–30]
>
> Hic incipit secunda pars, de peregrinacione Ierusalem et de eius consuetudinibus, et quomodo peregriny se habebunt cum intrent civitatem illam. [chaps. 31–42]
>
> Hic incipit tercia pars huius libry, et de castello Nysy et domina eius. [chaps. 43–53]
>
> Hic incipit quarta pars, de terra prisbiteri [sic] Iohannis ac de statu venerabili eius nobilitate. [chaps. 54–62]
>
> Hic incipit quinta pars, de statu et nobilitate regis de Tharce vel de Chatan. [chaps. 63–69]

In this view of the work, then, the way to Jerusalem, Jerusalem itself, the Near East, the Lands of Prester John, and the Empire of the Khan are each considered separate entities, a view that would no doubt lead to very different suppositions about the comparisons and contrasts to be made between areas of the world and about the themes to be gleaned from the juxtaposition of parts in the work.[53] Some texts are divided into more than

---

[52] M. Letts, *Mandeville's Travels*, Vol. 2 has been used as my source here.

[53] William Ryding, in his *Structure in Medieval Narrative* (The Hague: Mouton, 1971), dis-

two parts; others, like Pynson, are not divided at all, except by the kinds of loose "Nowe I shal telle" chapter divisions outlined above. Such evidence poses a very real challenge to the received notion that the *Book* is essentially definable as a bipartite work that builds its main themes through opposition.

From a modern vantage point, we may be able to justify perceiving two sections in the book, as we are more aware of the Mandeville-author's use of written sources than earlier audiences were. We know that the author used different core sources for his material on the Holy Land and the Far East. The major source for the *Book*'s accounts of the Holy Land and ways thither is the narrative of William of Boldensele, a German Dominican who had traveled there in 1332–1333. This account is supplemented by information from William of Tripoli, Hayton the Armenian, Jacques de Vitry, and others.[54] The central source for the Far East is the Franciscan Odoric of Pordenone's description of his travels in the Middle and Far East during the early 1300s. The Mandeville-author supplements this account as well, most notably with information culled from Vincent of Beauvais and, through him, John of Plano Carpini. Thus, in terms of source materials, the *Book* does follow two separate models. But there is also a good deal of overlap: material from Jacques de Vitry, Brunetto Latini, and

---

cusses the romances of Chrétien and the Chanson de Roland as bipartite narratives, but he also notes that the division of texts into parts for interpretation is very much a matter of individual goals for reading the works:

> Others have been inclined to see tripartite and quadripartite schemes, which should serve to remind us that analysis can be more or less refined, and that stories can be divided into parts in many ways to serve many different ends. Voretzsch, for example, argues that Chrétien's romances divide into five parts; Le Gentil sees a quadripartite division in the Chanson de Roland.... On the basis of the presumed conditions of oral presentation at court, Frances Titchener argues a division of Chrétien's works into twenty or so units averaging three hundred verses in length, each reasonably independent and suitable for an evening's entertainment. On the same principle, Wechssler proposes a tripartite division into units of about 2000 verses, and Witte two divisions of 3500 verses. (116–17)

There is as yet no close analysis of the textual divisions across the range of manuscripts of the *Book*, although such a study would certainly be useful. Higgins notes one such study on the Dutch version: W. G. Ganser, *Die niederländische Version der Reisebeschreibung Johanns von Mandeville: Untersuchungen zur handschriftlichen Überlieferung*, Amsterdamer Publikationen zur Sprache und Literatur 63 (Amsterdam: Rodopi, 1985).

[54] A. Bovenschen, "Untersuchungen über Johann von Mandeville und die Quellen seiner Reisebeschreibung," *Zeitschrift der Gesellschaft für Erdkunde zu Berlin* 23 (1888): 177–306 is the central source study for the *Book*. Warner (*Buke*, xv–xxx) provides a useful overview of the sources. Deluz tabulates the sources at length in Appendix VI of her *Livre*, 428–91.

It is generally accepted that the Mandeville-author used William of Boldensele and Odoric of Pordenone in Jean le Long's 1351 French translation rather than in the original Latin, although he may also have had recourse to the Latin texts.

Hayton the Armenian, for example, is incorporated into both "parts" of the book. And, most importantly, the book as presented generally does not attempt to highlight a distinction between two sections. Rather it seeks to offer a continuous journey, in many ways highlighting the unified nature of travel through the Holy Land and beyond. Where Donald Howard sees in "the customs of the East a distorted reflection of the West, forcing a comparison of the two" ("The World of *Mandeville's Travels*," *Yearbook of English Studies* 1 [1971]: 16), it is perhaps possible instead to see West and East more interconnectedly, as sites in a continuum. While readers of the *Book* must often find themselves comparing, that drive toward comparison need not be constructed by scholars as the foundation of the book as a whole.

The evidence we find in the surviving manuscripts and early editions suggests that the bipartite view of the *Book* emerged fairly late in the book's manuscript history, and never became fully incorporated into the medieval and early-Renaissance view of it. Modern readers may perceive a thematic division, based on a differentiation between types of sources— an emphasis on pilgrimage narratives and guides to the Holy Land in the first "part" and a stronger emphasis on natural history texts and encyclopediae in the second. But we must also acknowledge that access to source information about the *Book* was not general until the nineteenth century. While the manuscript evidence suggests that some early readers and transmitters of the *Book* saw the comparative aspects as defining for the work, the majority did not. Similarly, no early edition incorporates any kind of clear bipartite division. When we look at the broad spectrum of manuscripts and early editions, it becomes increasingly clear that this aspect of the *Book*'s structure has been overemphasized by modern scholarship.

As a second example of the value of comparative analysis, let us look briefly at the overall character of the Cotton and Egerton texts. It is, of course, usual for scholars who have chosen one or the other of the accepted texts as a basis for their work to refer to it as "The *Book*" rather than as "Cotton" or "Egerton." The chosen text is considered to stand for the whole. And so, having reduced the "authorial" corpus of the English texts to only two, scholarship almost unconsciously reduces the two to a loosely conflated one.[55] But, as Higgins's study of the *Book*'s "isotopes"

---

[55] A striking instance of this process of conflation is found in the Thule interpolation, a feature of the Egerton text which has been published only once, by Letts (*Mandeville's Travels*, I: 212–14). Both Warner (*Buke*) and Moseley (*Mandeville's Travels*) leave it out because it appears only in Egerton and, as Moseley says, "clearly has nothing to do with the author of the book" (*Mandeville's Travels*, 183n). The "good text," Egerton, is thus made to conform to the pattern of other "good texts."

has begun to suggest, there are important inconsistencies—factual, tonal, and stylistic—even between these two versions, which have both been used to stand for "The *Book*." Overall, Cotton adheres more closely to its Insular roots than does Egerton: the Egerton text tends toward abridgment in such matters as developing the narrator's voice, ascribing motivation, and speculating about cultural practices, but tends toward interpolation for the purpose of strengthening its own authority with learned references and pieces of learned lore.

The respective endings of the two texts provide an immediately striking contrast. Cotton here employs a highly developed narrative voice that emphasizes Sir John's misery at being forced by age and ill-health to stop traveling, before coming at last to a formal, rhetorical prayer for himself and his readers. In this it accords fairly closely with its Insular antecedents:

> And I Iohn Maundevylle knyght aboueseyd, alle though I be vnworthi, that departed from oure contrees and passed the see the yeer of grace a m. ccc. and xxii., that haue passed many londes and manye yles and contrees and cerched manye fulle strange places, and haue ben in many a fulle gode honourable companye and at many a faire dede of armes, alle be it that I dide none myself for myn vnable insuffisance. And now I am comen home *mawgree myself to reste for gowtes artetykes that me distreynen, that diffynen the ende of my labour ayenst my wille, God knoweth. And thus takynge solace in my wreched reste recordynge the tyme passed* I haue fulfilled theise thinges and putte hem wryten in this boke, as it wolde come into my mynde, the yeer of grace a m. ccc. and lvi. in the xxxiiii. yeer that I departede from oure contrees.
>
> Wherefore I preye to alle the rederes and hereres of this boke, yif it plese hem, that thei wolde preyen to God for me and I schalle preye for hem. And alle tho that seyn for me a *Pater Noster* with an *Aue Maria* that God foryeue me my synnes, I make hem parteneres and graunte hem part of alle the gode pilgrymages and of alle the gode dedes that I haue done, yif ony ben to His plesance; and nought only of tho but of alle that euere I schalle do vnto my lyfes ende. And I beseche almyghty God, fro whom alle godeness and grace cometh fro, *that He vouchesaf of His excellent mercy and habundant grace to fullefylle hire soules with inspiracoun of the Holy Gost in makynge defence of alle hire gostly enemyes here in erthe to hire saluacoun bothe of body and soule, to worschipe and thankynge of Him that is three and on, withouten begynnynge and withouten endyng, that is withouten qualitee good, withouten quantytee gret, that in alle places is present and alle thinges conteynynge, the whiche that no goodness may amende ne non euelle empeyre, that in perfyte Trynyte lyueth and reg-*

neth, God be alle worldes and be alle tymes. Amen. Amen. Amen. (Seymour, *Mandeville's Travels*, 229-30; emphasis mine)

Egerton, by comparison, is what one might call "succinct," offering the basic outline of Sir John's career as a traveler, then moving on to a prayer for his own salvation and that of his audience that is moving in its simple humility:

> And I, IOHN MAWNDEUILL, knyght, that went oute of my cuntree and passed the see the yere of oure Lord Ihesu Criste m⌈cccxxxii, and hase passed thurgh many landes, cuntreez and iles, and hase bene at many wirschipfull iourneez and dedez of armez with worthy men, if all I be unworthi, and now am commen to rest, as man discomfitt for age and trauaile and febilness of body that constraynez me tharto, and for other certayne causez, I hafe compiled this buke and writen it, as it coome to my mynde, in the yere of oure Lord Ihesu Crist m⌈ccclxvi, that es for to say in the foure and thrittyde yere efter that I departed oute of this land and tuke my way thiderward ...
>
> Qwh[erefore] I pray til all thase that redez this Buke or heres it redd, that thai will pray for me, and I schall p[ray] for thaim. And all thase that saise for me deuotely a *Pater Noster* and ane *Ave*, that Godd forgife me my synnez, he graunt tham parte of all my pilgrimage and all other gude dedis that I hafe done or may do in tyme commyng unto my lyfez end. And I, in that in me es, makez tham parceneres of tham, prayand to Godd, of wham all grace commez, that he fulfill with his grace all thase that this buke redez or heres, and saue tham and kepe tham in body and saule, and after this lyf bring tham to the cuntree whare ioy es and endles rest and peesse with outen end. Amen. (Warner, *Buke*, 155-56)[56]

Cotton is more complete than Egerton on many counts, frequently retaining observed details and speculative explanations its cousin omits. In the section on the death of a Khan, for example, Cotton preserves an intriguing sidelight about the burial of the dead emperor. Both texts relate the practice of richly bedecking the Khan's tent, providing food, horses, and wealth for the next world, and burying all together in an enormous pit, after which the Khan is never spoken of again. But Cotton goes on,

> And yit natheles somtyme falleth of manye that thei maken hem to ben entered preuylly be nyghte in wylde places and putten ayen the

---

[56] Egerton places the papal interpolation in the ellipsis here. Cotton places it directly before the "I John Mandeville" passage.

> grass ouer the pytt for to growe. Or elles men coueren the pytt with grauelle and sond, that no man schalle perceyue where ne knowe where the pytt is, to that entent that neuer after none of his frendes schulle han mynde ne remembrance of him. And thanne thei seyn that he is ravissht into another world, where he is a gretter lord than he was here. (183)

Cotton emphasizes the charlatanry of this secret burial practice, exposing to scorn the religious error of a people who could perpetrate such a falsehood in the name of religion.

The European reader is allowed to feel somewhat superior, as well: surely no European Christian could be fooled by such parlor tricks. The passage takes an overt ideological stand, and resonates with earlier debunkings in the *Book* of the "falsehoods" believed by the Muslims: that Mohammed's claim to speak with the angel of God is no more than a cover story for a very earthly, uninspirational case of epilepsy, for example. Egerton's lack of this material may be merely accidental, or it may be evidence of a redactor's impulse toward the "tolerance" for which the *Book* is so oft applauded. In any event, the Egerton text tends toward the maintenance of a kind of psychological distance: interested in reporting and proving, but less so in speculating and judging.

The account of the Amazons again reinforces this pattern. In Egerton the women simply arm themselves and take over the kingdom when they hear that most of the men have been killed in battle against the king of Scythia: "And, when the qwene and other ladys of that land herd tell that the kyng and the lordes ware thus slayne, thai gadred tham togyder with ane asscent and armed tham wele and tuke with tham grete company of wymmen and slewgh doune clenly all the men that ware left amanges tham" (77). Egerton suggests no possible reason for their actions, offering objective fact as much as possible (although in this case the lack of stated motivation may have the effect of worsening one's perception of the Amazon women, implying that they have been waiting for just such an opportunity). But the Insular version, and Cotton following it, are careful to establish motive, interpreting the slaughter as a terrible exercise of upperclass power, prompted by grief: "And whan the queen and alle the othere noble ladyes sawen that thei weren all wydewes, and that alle the rialle blood was lost, thei armed hem and as creatures out of wytt thei slowen all the men of the contrey that weren laft, for thei wolden that alle the wommen weren wydewes as the queen and thei weren" (113).

These are only short examples of a widespread pattern in which Egerton emerges as a more laconic, perhaps more encyclopedic text, in which the transfer of historical, geographical, and cultural information is perceived as more important than the interpretation of that information.

Such a view might be bolstered by an examination of what Egerton adds to its sources, as well as what it omits. Egerton's notable interpolations include such details as an account of how merchants make pepper seem fresher than it is, the Chaldean alphabet, and a second version of the Saracen alphabet which, the narrator says, he has seen variously depicted in different books. It is consonant with Egerton's more "encyclopedic" nature that it should betray an interest in how things are done, a description of process, as well as in transmitting the languages of other peoples to the European audience.[57] Egerton also betrays a consistent concern with establishing external authority, citing "auctoritees" more frequently than Cotton to back up its assertions. In the section on diamonds, for example, Cotton follows the Insular model fairly closely:

> And yif you lyke to knowe the vertues of the dyamand, as men may fynden in the lapidarye that many men knowen noght, I schalle telle you as thei beyonde the see seyn and affermen, of whom alle science and alle philosophie cometh from. (116)

Egerton, on the other hand, interpolates named sources: "I sall tell yow as Ysidre libro 16 Ethicorum, capitulo de cristallo, and Bertilmew De Proprietatibus Rerum, libro 16, capitulo de adamante, saise" (79). And in Egerton it is "Ysidorus" too who tells us of how "marchands sophisticatez peper, when it es alde" (84).

There are plainly substantive differences here: differences that alter every aspect of our reading, from what we come to know about the world, to how we think of "Sir John Mandeville," to what we perceive as some of the essential threads of the book: its religious and cultural attitudes, its sense of its own authority, its relationship to a changing audience. Yet either text has been used to stand for *The Book of John Mandeville* as a whole. While the texts are certainly similar to a high degree, their differences must be fully understood before informed generalizations can be made.

The large number of extant manuscripts and incunabular editions of the *Book* make the task of studying its multiplicity a somewhat daunting one. Even if one focuses solely on the English versions (insofar as one usefully may) the problem is complex. But because *The Book of John Mandeville* is multiple by nature, native to a world of scribal transmission, redaction, and conflation, it demands an approach that takes into account not only its original text or a limited number of "best texts," but all the variant texts produced by that world. Not only does such an approach keep us

---

[57] C. W. Moseley suggests in his Egerton edition that the alphabets (of which Egerton has six to Cotton's four) may be a kind of truth-claim in their own way, an "additional means of convincing his readers of the seriousness of his material" (*Mandeville's Travels*, 191).

from error, but it opens possibilities so far almost unglimpsed. In addition to the obvious textual comparisons that might be undertaken, a variety of other projects offer themselves. We might compare marginalia over a range of texts from those like Cambridge MS Gg. I. 34 (Defective) that have none (perhaps because it has no margins) to British Museum MS Arundel 140 (Defective), in which the marginal notes constitute an informal glossary and running commentary: declaring some stories, for example, simply "a tale" and others "a good tale." We might look at the different passages chosen for illustration in different texts, an area of study that has hardly been broached.[58] Further, we might more fully engage the reception-oriented questions of why the *Book* was converted into such widely different forms over the course of its transmission. In short, we could study the manuscripts completely, not merely as names or branches on a genealogical tree but as important parts of a medieval system of texts.

There is nothing to prevent such a move but our own preconceptions. We are encouraged by the meticulous and "scientific" nature of manuscript genealogy to see the groupings and subgroupings it produces as the logical outgrowth of text production, but we must realize that logic can produce a vast array of schemata to explain the same material, depending on what it chooses to emphasize and deemphasize. The Defective version is merely a construct, a model to help us understand manuscript lineages: we can acknowledge these texts' ancestries without discarding their singularities. It is sometimes useful to speak of the Defective texts as a unit because they do, in fact, share the "Egypt Gap," just as we sometimes speak of Cotton and Egerton as a unit, as the French- and English-derived texts in English that do not share it. But with the Defective texts as well as with Cotton and Egerton, it is necessary that we be able to separate them too, to look within the classification to the individual texts that make up the class. If we want to get to know the *Book*—the whole work, not just

---

[58] Because Cotton and Egerton have no illustrations, and editions have made the Augsburg woodcuts the more-or-less "official" illustrations to the *Book*, the often striking illustrations of the Defective manuscripts have yet to be studied. The Augsburg woodcuts stem from Anton Sorg's 1481 edition of the Velser translation. For information on their relationship to the English *Book*, cf. Josephine Bennett, "The Woodcut Illustrations in the English Editions of *Mandeville's Travels*," *Papers of the Bibliographical Society of America* 47 (1953): 59–69. Deluz's *Livre*, Appendix 5.5, includes a catalog of illustrations and marginalia for selected manuscripts and editions—a useful resource for those who would study the manuscript art.

The Defective version contains three illustrated and one decorated manuscript (cf. Appendix I), among which British Library MS Harley 3954 is especially remarkable. I hope to make a preliminary study of this text's illustrations available soon with my "Picturing the East: The Harley 3954 Illustrations to *The Book of John Mandeville*" (Kohanski, forthcoming in *Allegorica*). Royal 17C is also richly, though less formally, illustrated. Its depiction of rabbits (kangaroos?) playing the bagpipes in the margin of a passage on Christ and the coming of judgment [c. 26ʳ] continues to fuel my leisure hours with speculation.

the few texts that have been singled out for our attention—then it is no longer to our benefit to neglect the study of textual variance. Making the Defective texts available for scholars to study is central to the goal of understanding the *Book* as a medieval, and therefore multiple, work. It is my hope that this edition of Pynson will advance that goal by making one important Defective text more freely available for study, and helping to promote interest in the other texts called "Defective."

NOTES TO THE TRANSCRIPTION

THE BOOK

The Pynson print, usually dated to 1496, is of importance to scholarship on *The Book of John Mandeville* largely for its role as archetype for other printed versions, but also for its role in bringing the Defective version of the *Book* "officially" into the public eye. Manuscript evidence, as well as Pynson's reliance on a Defective source, suggest that the Defective version was widely known in manuscript. The release of the Pynson edition authorized that version by committing it to print. It was almost certainly the earliest printed edition of the work in English and provided the basis for every other edition until 1725, when a direct transcription of the Cotton manuscript was printed "for J. Woodman and D. Lyon and C. Davis" and subsequently became the new archetype for editions to follow.

Pynson is based on a Defective manuscript,[1] now lost, and survives in a single copy held by the British Library (G 6713), and in a fragment held by the Bodleian Library (Arch. G d. 31 (1)). The edition is bound a-g^8, h-i^6, k^4 with thirty blackletter lines to a full page. It is unillustrated, and untitled. The extant copy has been called by the British Library *Maunduyle's Boke of Wayes to Jerusalem*, and lacks sig. a8, c1, and c8. Sig. a1^{r-v} is blank: thus the text begins at sig. a2^r. While most modern scholars refer to the book as *Mandeville's Travels* or *The Travels of Sir John Mandeville*,[2] I have chosen *The Book of John Mandeville* for two reasons. First, Pynson's colophon reads "Here endeth the boke of Iohn Maundvyle." Not only is

---

[1] A B-text of the Defective version, according to M. C. Seymour, "The Early English Editions of *Mandeville's Travels*," *The Library* 5th ser. 19 (1964): 203.

[2] Important recent exceptions are both Higgins and Deluz, who have also chosen the more medieval *Book*. Deluz (*Livre*, 31) notes that "Travels" did not enter the English title until 1568, while Higgins remarks sensibly that the book can hardly be thought of as "Mandeville's Travels" when "we never see Sir John on the road" (*Writing East*, 64).

this the most common medieval 'title' for the work, but it also leaves agreeably open the issue of what, precisely, this "book" is. Second, *Mandeville's Travels* as title suggests an itinerary, a narrative movement of the speaker from point A to point B (an expectation rarely upheld in versions of the *Book*), as well as encouraging the overtones of the *Bildungsroman* of which Bennett made so much. As I have argued, the *Book* is, for me, more encyclopedic, understood by its earliest audiences as an informative work, a learned work, which enforced (essentially) the learned auctoritees on the Orient, while garnering for itself a more immediate form of authority based in presumed authorial experience. The title *The Book of John Mandeville* leaves, at least, more cognitive space in which readers may work to make their own determinations on such matters.

Until the discovery of the Pynson print, Wynkyn de Worde's 1499 edition was for many years considered the first English edition of the *Book*. In a note bound into the British Library's copy, Sir Francis Freeling remarks, "I rather think this edition of Pynson's must have been the first printed in this country. W. de Worde published an edition in 1499 & again in 1503—both with Wood Cuts. An imperfect copy of the latter is in the possession of Mr. Douce." A second note (probably Thomas Grenville's) lends its support:

> Dibdin seems to agree with Sir F. Freeling in considering this book of the 15th century & therefore prior to that of W. de Worde of 1499 which was esteemed the first edition.
>
> No other copy being as yet ascertained I readily purchased it tho' it wants a7 [sic]—c1—&c8.
>
> The text varies very much from Este's edition, but I have never found that of W. de Worde to collate it with that edition.

In fact, de Worde's 1499 edition agrees closely with Pynson, upon which it is based. It is, however, modernized somewhat, corrects the occasional obvious error, and includes many of the small amenities that Pynson lacks: a table of contents, woodcuts, chapter headings, rubrics. Essentially it is Pynson with minor editing, and de Worde's 1503 and 1510 editions are substantially so as well. Thomas East, however, in his 1568 edition, conflated de Worde with a Defective manuscript to produce a significantly altered text, albeit with Pynson still at its root.[3]

As the first English edition of the *Book*, the text that made the work broadly available for the first time, Pynson must be considered an important vehicle for its transmission to the general public, yet the Pynson print has up to now been available for the modern scholar only in the Exeter

---

[3] Cf. M. C. Seymour, "Early English Editions," 202–7 and Appendix II of this edition.

University Press facsimile edition. More than one scholar, wishing to embark upon the kind of comparative textual study I have advocated here, has dolefully remarked upon the lack of available editions. I have therefore attempted to supply the pressing need for a more approachable text of Pynson, which I hope may induce scholars to pay the edition the attention it deserves. It goes almost without saying that further editions, especially parallel-text editions of the Defective manuscripts, would be a great boon to variance- and reception-based study of the *Book*. If this edition can act, too, as a stepping-stone toward that goal, I shall be well pleased.

THE TRANSCRIPTION

My goal in transcribing the Pynson print has been to produce a transcription both accurate and readable. I have normalized "u" and "v", for the convenience of the reader. In addition, I have silently expanded abbreviations, of which there are many, to make the text as accessible as possible. Where symbols were unfamiliar or occurred only once in the text, rendering them difficult to judge by context, I have relied on Cappelli's *Elements of Abbreviation* to verify my expansions. It has proven an invaluable source.

The paragraphing of the original has been reproduced here as closely as possible, so that the distribution of material across various texts and printings can be conveniently studied. A new paragraph has been begun wherever Pynson's text ends short on a line and begins again on the next. In certain cases, the visual paragraphing has been unavoidably a matter of judgment. The Pynson text is of course right-justified and when lines stop noticeably short it is easy to interpret that a new visual paragraph is called for. But when a line stops only one or two characters short of the margin it is more difficult to judge. The text does, however, include many lines whose spacing has clearly been tightened or loosened to achieve right-justification, so that if a line stops short by even a little, one must entertain the possibility that a new visual paragraph is intended. I have tended to break the paragraph rather than not since the evidence suggests that the justification could be maintained if desired.

A small number of pages end a line or more short: $f2^r$, $h4^r$, $i4^r$, and $i6^v$ each have only 29 lines, while $i6^r$ has only 27. In such cases it is sometimes difficult to judge whether a textual break should be construed. $f2^r$, $h4^r$, and $i6^v$ each end in mid-sentence: thus I have not introduced paragraph breaks in these instances. $i4^r$ and $i6^r$, however, do end at stopping places, although the verso pages continue the same topics (the humbling of Alexander and the gold-digging ants). In these two cases I have chosen to begin a new paragraph, based on the space in the text.

Where a section is clearly set off in Pynson by additional space or by a large initial, I have echoed the practice here. Owing to the oversized capitals and the exigencies of modern printing, a space between paragraphs does occasionally appear in this text where it does not in Pynson—on pages 3, 40, 49, 59, and 66. The paragraph symbols (¶) translate the paraphs in the text.

I have chosen not to modernize the puctuation of this edition, as to do so would have introduced substantive changes, often preferring, for example, one interpretation of a passage over another, where the original punctuation or lack thereof allowed multiple possibilities to coexist. The original punctuation has been maintained, including the slashes that are used throughout Pynson's text in much the way we use commas today. While some readers may find these distracting, they have been retained in the modernized edition so that they may offer whatever assistance they can to those navigating the text. Pynson also uses a broken slash to hyphenate words continued on the following line, for which the slash is sometimes substituted in the original. In such cases I have omitted the slash, as I have regularly omitted the hyphen. Readers will note that many sentences lack end punctuation.

The original capitalization has been maintained, as it may be of value to scholars. Again, to normalize would have been to interpret what I sought rather to transmit, so that others might interpret for themselves.

The signature markings that appear at the bases of some pages in the text are included in brackets. The first page of each signature after sig. a is marked (bi, ci, di, ei, fi, gi, hi, ii, k) but the third page of each signature is also marked in sigs a through i as aii, bii, cii, etc.: a confusing situation that has yet to be clearly explained. The proper signature notation for each page of text is supplied in bold at the beginning of that page, for ease of reference. Where the page breaks in the middle of a word, I have simply put the signature notation at the end of that word, to facilitate reading. The daggers in the text supply the place of the term "*sic*"; I have placed them near the obvious minor errors in the text, such as words with missing or incorrect letters, or repetition of words, so that such abnormalities should not be mistaken for typographical errors in the transcription.

Pynson's chapters are set off by the large initials with which they begin. I have supplied a marginal index to the chaptering of the Cotton manuscript, the chapter breaks of which are marked in the text by the symbol ≠. This stands as well for modern editions of Egerton which, because it is without chapters, is generally chaptered according to Cotton's example. It will be immediately noticeable that the chaptering of Pynson differs significantly from that of Cotton. In addition, I have supplied marginal references to the text, for the assistance of those seeking to compare Pynson with manuscripts of the *Book* that may not share Cotton's chaptering. In studying such manuscripts, it is often most convenient to navigate as one might with a topographical map: by finding one's position with reference to highly visible features. Thus, if one can locate, for example, the Assassins' Paradise or the Trees of the Sun and Moon in the text, one can more easily find one's place. It is not my intention to afford a continuous marginal directory of the book, but rather to provide the occasional familiar landmark for the traveler in its pages. I have rendered these marginal references in modern English, to ensure that they not be mistaken for an original feature of Pynson's edition.

As modest aids to reading and interpretation, I have also supplied references for the biblical quotations, bracketed in the text, and have included a combined index and glossary to proper names at the back of this volume.

THE TYPE

Pynson's type is of interest, in that it incorporates several forms of many letters. There are, for example, two forms of capital W—one tall, one broad—interspersed evenly throughout the text. I have rendered both simply as capital W. Likewise, an angular capital C and a rounded one are used interchangeably. A barred capital H appears twice (d3^r, "Helyseus" and d5^v, "Hyllary"). A strange, squat d, with a very short ascender, appears in the text once (b5^v, "and they ar stronge men"). A form of l, with a horizontal cross through its center, occurs four times (a2^r, "hel"; b2^v, "right wel"; b4^r, "metal"; b4^v, "castel"). An unusual r, with a long descender and a loop on the bar, occurs once (b2^r, "in this maner"), and throughout the text there are two forms of lower case r, a full and an abbreviated form. The abbreviated form looks rather like a minim facing left, and tends to occur at the ends of words. I have rendered both simply as "r."

In addition, occasional e's and t's include a flourish, a short tail rising from the top that has no function as an abbreviatory mark. This is most probably simply a different kind of type, but occurs mainly on the top lines of certain leaves (e4^v, e7^v, g7^v, g8^v, h2^v, h6^v, i2^v, k2^r), just as in some manuscripts the letters on top lines are embellished with tall ascenders. There are two instances in which t with this flourish appears to stand for "ter": in the words "Englen**ter**" (a6^r) and "dough**ter**" (g6^r). This may be a holdover from manuscript hands, a signal that could still be used to show abbreviation in Pynson's day, but had most often become merely an embellishment. Similar to these are the d-flourishes in the text. Formed like the abbreviated r, they occur on e4^v ("englon**d**") and e7^v ("envyron**d**")— attached to a final d, but clearly with no function as letters or symbols.

There are six instances of type set upside down: on a4^v ("that overthwart was made of palme"), e5^v ("at the seven dayes ende"), e8^v ("shulde be gyven frely"), f5^v ("and men woete nat the cause"), i2^r ("lete other men have their maydenhede"), and i4^v ("and serve hym mekely and trewly").

The Book of John Mandeville

Prologue ≠   For as moche as the Lande over the see/ that is to say the holy lande that men call the lande of hetynge/ amonge all other landes it is mooste worthy lande and soveraigne of other landes/ and it is blessyd and halowed and sacred of the precious blode of oure lorde iesu cryst. In the whyche lande it lyked hym to take flesshe and blode of the virgyn mary/ and to environ that lande with his owne fete. And there he Wold do many myracles/ and preche and teche the feythe/ and the lawe of us cristen men as unto his childre. And therfore he wolde suffre many reproves and scornes for us. And he that was kynge of heven/ and of erthe/ of eyre/ of see/ and of all thynges that are conteyned in them wolde all oonly be callyd kynge of that lande whan he sayde. Rex sum iudeorum [cf. John 19:19-21]. I am kynge of Iewes. For that tyme was that lande of Iewes/ and that lande had he chosen before all other landes as for the best and the most vertuous and for the most worthy of the worlde/ and as the Phylosofer saythe thus. Virtus rerum in medio consistit.[1] That is to say the vertu of thynges is in the myd. and in that lande he Wolde lede his lyfe and suffre passion and dethe of the Iewes for us and for to delyver and bye us fro the paynes of hel/ and fro dethe wythouten ende. the Whyche was ordeyned to us for the synne of oure fader Adam. and for oure owne synnes also. For as hym self he had none evyll deserved: for he thought never evyll. ne dyd never evyll. And he that was kynge of glory and ioy myght best in that place suffre dethe. For he that woll do any thynge that he woll be knowen openly. He woll do crye it openly in the myddyll place of a towne/ or of a [a2ᵛ] cyte so that it may be knowen to all partyes of the Cyte. So he that Was kynge of all the world wold suffre deth for us at Ierusalem that is in myddis of the worlde so that it myght be knowen to men of all parties of the world

---

[1] Aristotle (*Nicomachean Ethics*, II: 6) and Cicero ("On Duties," I: 25), among others, speak of the virtue of the middle way.

howe dere he bought man that he had made to his owne lykenesse for the greate love that he had to us: for more worthy catell ne might he have set for us than his owne blessyd body and his owne precious blode/ the whych he suffred for us. A dere god what love he had to his subgettis. Whan he that had done no trespas wolde for trespassours suffre dethe. Right ought men to love and worship and drede and serve suche a lorde and worshyp and prayse such a holy londe that brought forth suche frute thorough the whych every man is saved but if it be hys owne defaute. This is the lande hight to us in heritage/ and in that lande he wolde dye as sesed to leve it to his children. For the Whiche every goode crysten man that may and hathe Wherof shulde strength hym for to conquere oure ryght heritage and chase oute the ylke trowand for We ar called cristen men of crist oure fader. and if we be right childre of crist we owe for to chalenge the heritage that oure fader left us and do it oute of straunge mens handis. But now pride/ covetise/ and envy/ hath so enflamed the hertis of lordes of the Worlde that they are more besy for to disherite their neyghbours than for to chalenge or conquere ther right herytage before sayde. And the comon people that Wolde put their bodyes and catell for to conquere oure heritage/ they may nat do withoute lordes for assemble of the people Wythoute a cheef lorde is as a flocke of shepe that hathe no shepeherde the whiche departe asonder/ [a3ʳ] and wote never wheder that they shulde go. But wolde god that the worldly lordes were at good accorde/ and Wyth other of their comon people wolde take thys holy vyage over the see. I trowe well that Wythin a lytell tyme oure right heritage before sayde shulde be reconsyled and put in the handes of the right eyres of Iesu cryst: and for as moche it is longe tyme that there was no generall passage over the see. And many men desyre to heere speke of the holy londe. and have thereof greate solace/ and comforthe. ¶ Iohn Maundevyle knyght. Thoughe it so be that I be nat worthy that was borne in englonde in the towne of saynt Albone and passed the see in the yere of the Incarnacion of oure lorde iesu crist M.CCCxxxii on the day of saynt Myghell and hyderwarde hathe be longe tyme over the se and have sene and gone thorowe many landes and many provynces/ and kyngdomes and Iles and have passed thorough Turky/ thorough/ Ermony the lytell and the greate thorough Tartary Thoroughe Percy/ thorough Syry/ thoroughe/ araby/ thorough Egypt the hygh and the lowe. thorough lyby thoroughe Caldee/ and a great party of Ethyope/ thorowe Amozome. thoroughe Inde the lesse and the more. a greate party. and thorough many other Iles whych are aboute Inde Where many dyvers maners of folke dwell of dyvers lawes and shappes/ of whyche londes and Iles I shall speke more playnly/ and I shall devyse a party of thynges what they are whan tyme shall be/ after it may come to mynde/ and specyally for theym that woll and are in purpos for to vysite the holy cyte of Ierusalem and the holy places that ar theraboute/ and I shall tell the [a ii] [a3ᵛ] Wey that they shall holde thyder for I have many tymes passyd and ryden it wyth good company/ and of many lordes.

Cotton ch. 1

≠ IN the name of god almyghty. He that woll passe over the se: he may go many weyes bothe on londe and see after the countrees that he comethe fro/ and many of theym come all to one ende: but trowest nat that I woll tell all the townes and cytes and castellys that men shall go by. for than shulde I make to longe tale/ but all only somme countres/ and moost pryncypall steddis that men shall goo thoroughe to go the right wey. ¶ Fyrste if a man come from the west syde of the Worlde as Englonde/ Irlande/ wales/ Scotlonde/ Norwey/ he may go if he woll thorough almayne/ and thorowe the kyngdome of hungery that marchys too the lande of poyalme and to the londe of pannony/ and of Allesey. And the kynge of hungery is a right greate lorde/ and a myghty/ and holdeth greate and moche londe. for he holdeth the londe of hungery and of allesy. Savoy Comame a greate party of Bulgary: that men calle the londe of Bugers/ and a greate party of the kyngdom of rosse and that lasteth to the londe of Nyflond and marchis unto Pruysse. and men go this† thorough the londe of Hungry thorough a cyte that men call Chyppron/ and thoroughe the castell of Newburgh/ and by the ille towne that is towarde the ende of hungry/ and men by the ryver of Daunby/ this is a full greate ryver and gothe into almaygne. under the hyllys of lumbardy and it taketh into hym xl. other ryvers/ and it renneth thorough hungry and thorowe Gresses. and thoroughe Tracy/ and gothe into the see so [a4ʳ] stalworthly and with so greate strength that the water is fresshe xx. myle within the see. and afterwarde go men to Belgrave and entre into the londe of Bugers and there passe men a Bredge of stone that is over the ryver Marroke/ and men pas thorugh the londe of Pynteras and com to Grece to the cyte of Sterny and to the cyte of affynpayn and sythyn to the cyte of Constantynople that was somtyme called Bessamorn and there dwelleth comonly the emperoure of grece there is the best churche of the worlde/ and the fayrest and it is of saynt Sophy/ and before this churche is an Image of Iustinian the emperoure gilt/ and it is upon an horse and crowned/ and it was wonte to hold a rounde appyll in his hande/ and men say there that it is a token that the emperoure hath lost a greate party of his londe/ for the appyll is fall oute of the ymages hande and also that he hath loste a great party of his lordship/ For he was wonte to be emperoure of romayn/ of grece and all assy the lesse of Surry and of the londe of Inde/ in the whych is Ierusalem/ and of the londe/ of Egypt/ of Percy and Araby/ but he hathe lost all but grece/ and that londe that he holdethe all only/ and men wolde many tymes put the appyll in the ymages hande but it wold nat holde it This appyll betokenethe the lordshyp that he had over all the Worlde. And the other hand he holdeth lyfte up ageyne the west in token for to manasse mysdoers. This Image standeth upon a pyller of marble at Constantynoble. ≠ there is the spounge and the rede of the whiche the Iewes gave oure lorde drynke gall on the crosse and there is one of the nayles that cryst was nailed with to the crosse.

[a4ᵛ] Somme men wene that halfe of the crosse of crist be in cypre in an abbey of munkes that men call the hyll of the holy crosse/ but it is nat so. for that crosse that is in cypre is the crosse on the whyche Dysmas the good theef was hangyd but all men wote nat that. and that is yll done but for getynge of the offringes they say that it is the cros of oure lorde iesu criste. And ye shall understande that the cros of oure lorde was made of foure maner of trees as it is conteyned in this verse. In cruce sit palma cedrus cipressus oliva.[2] For the pece that went right up from the erthe unto the hede was of cypres and the pece that went overthwart to the which the handes were nayled was of palme: and the stocke that stoode within the erthe/ to the whyche they had made a morteys was of cedre/ and the table above his hede that Was a fote

---

[2] Cf. Jacobus of Voragine, *The Golden Legend*, 2 vols., trans. William Granger Ryan (Princeton, N.J.: Princeton University Press, 1993) I: 278. "Ligna crucis palma, cedrus, cypressus, oliva." Paul Hamelius (*Mandeville's Travels*, 2: 25n) offers a lengthy note on other analogues to this passage.

and a halfe longe on the whyche the tytle was wreten in Ebrewe/ in grewe/ and in laten that was of olyve. And the iewes made the cros of these foure maner of trees for they trowed that oure lorde iesu crist shulde have hanged upon the cros as long as the crosse myght laste. and therfore made they the fote of cedre. for cedre may nat in erthe ne in water rotte. and they wolde it shulde have last longe/ and for they trowed that the body of crist shulde have stonken. that pece is made of cypre for it is well smellynge/ soo that the smell of his body shulde nat greve to men that come forby. and that overthwart was made of palme/ for in the olde testament it was ordeyned that whan any had the vyctory he was crowned with palme/ and for they trowed that they had the victory of Iesu crist/ therfore they made the pece that Went overthwart of palme/ and the table of the tytle they made [a5ʳ] of Olyve. for olyve betokenethe pees. as the story of Noe wytnesseth. whan the dove brought the braunche of olyve that betokenyd pees made betwene god and man Also the Iewes trowed to have had pees whan crist was dedde. for they sayde that he made discorde and stryfe amonge theym. And ye shall understande that oure lorde Was nayled to the cros lyinge. and therfore he suffred the more peyne. Also in Grece and the crysten men that dwell over the see say that the tree of the crosse that we call Cypresse was of that tree that adam ete the appyll and soo fynde they Wretyn. and they say as their scripture seyth that adam was sycke/ and sayde to his son Seth that he shulde go to paradyse and pray the aungell that kepethe paradyse that he wolde sende hym of the oyle of the tree of mercy for to anoynt with his membres that he myght have heele. And Seth went but the aungell wolde nat late hym come in at the dore. but sayde unto hym that he myght nat have of the oyle of mercy. but he toke to hym foure braunches of the same tree that hys fader etee† the apple/ and bad hym as sone as his fader was dede that he shulde put these graynes under his tonge/ and grave hym/ and he dyd so. and of these foure braunches sprange a tre as the aungell sayde that shulde bere a frute thoroughe whyche frute adam shulde be saved.

And whan Seth came ageyne he fonde hys fader nere dede/ and he dyd wyth the graynes as the aungell badde hym. of the whyche came foure trees. of whyche a crosse was made that bare goode frute. That is to say oure saveoure Iesu cryst. Thoroughe whome adam and all that came of hym were saved and delyvered from dethe [a5ᵛ] Withouten ende/ but if it be their owne defaute. This holy crosse the iewes hydde under the erthe under the roche of mount calvary. and it lay there two hundred yere and more unto the tyme that saynt Elyne fonde it: the whyche saynt Elyne was the moder of Constance the emperoure of rome. and she was doughter of kynge Alle that was kynge of englonde that than Was called the greate Bretaygne whom the emperoure toke to wife for hir greate fayrenesse whan he was in that countre. And ye shal understonde that the crosse of oure lorde was in lengthe/ viii. cubites. and that overthwart had in length .iii. cubytes and a halfe. A party of the crowne of oure lorde ihesu wherwithe he was crowned/ and of the nayles/ and the spere hede and many other relyques ar in fraunce in the chapell of the kynge of fraunce and the crowne lyethe in a vessell of crystell well dight and richely. for a kynge of fraunce bought theyse relyques somtyme of the Iewes. to whom the emperoure layde theym to wedde for a gret somme of sylver. And all if it be so that men say that this crowne be of thornes. ye shall understonde that it was and is of Ionkes of the see that was whyte that pryckethe as sharpe as any thornes. for I have sene and behold many tymes that of Parys and that of Constantynople.

for they were bothe of one made of Ionkes of the se but men have departed theym in two peces. the whyche one party is at parys/ and the other party is at Constantynople. And I have one poynt therof that semethe a whyte thorne and that was gyven to me for greate frendshype. for there is many of theym broken and fallen in the vessell to shewe the crowne to greate men that com thedyr.

[a6ʳ] And ye shall understand that oure lord in that night that he was taken he was led into a gardeyne/ and there he was examyned sharply. and there the Iewes scorned hym and made hym a crowne of braunches of albespyne that grew in the same gardeyne: and sette it on his hede so fast that blode ranne downe by many places of his vysage: and his necke and his shulders. and therfore hathe the albespyne many vertues/ for he that bereth a braunche of it upon hym/ no thunder/ ne no maner tempeste may dere hym ne none house that it is in may none evyll gost come in no place there it is. And in that same garden saynt Peter denyed oure lorde thryes.

¶ Afterwarde was oure lorde ledde before the bysshope and the mynysters of the Lawe in another gardeyne of anne there he was examyned also. and scorned and after ageyne

The Crown of Thorns

wyth a white thorne that men call barbarens that grewe in that gardeyne and that hath as many vertues. ¶ And afterwarde he Was ledde into a gardeyne of Cayphas and there he was crowned of one Englenter[3] and afterwarde he was ledde into a chaumber of Pylates/ and there he was examyned/ and crowned. and the Iewes sette hym in a chayre and cladde hym in a mantill and than made they a crowne of Ionkes of the see/ And they knelyd unto hym saynge. Ave rex iudeorum [Matthew 27:29; Mark 15:18; John 19:3]. That is to say in Englysshe. Heyle kynge of Iewes. And the crowne of the wyich one half is at parys/ and the other at Constantynople the which crist had upon his hede whan he Was done on crosse and therfore men shall Worshype that most and holde it more Worthy than any of the other. And that spere shafte hathe the emperoure of almaygne. [a6ᵛ] But the hede is at parys and many tymes sayth the emperoure of Constantynople that he hathe the spere hede. And I have often sene it but it is gretter than that of parys. ≠ Also at constantynople lyeth saynt anne oure ladis moder whom saynt Elyne made brynge from Ierusalem. And there lyethe also the body of saynte Iohn crysostom that was bysshop of constantynople. And there lyeth also saynt luke Evangelyst for his bones were brought fro Bethany. where he was graven and many other relyques are there. And there is of the vessellis of stone as it were marble the whych men call Idryons that evermore droppe water. and fyll theym sylfe eche yere. And ye shall wete that constantynople is a right fayre cyte/ and a gode and a well walled. and it is thre cornered/ and there is an arme of the see that men call hellespount/ and somme call it the bouche of constantynople. and somme call it the brache of saynt george. and this water enclosethe two partyes of the cyte/ and upwarde to the see upon the water Was wonte to be the greate cyte of troyse in a full fayre playne/ but that cyte was destroyed wyth theym of grece And there ben many Iles that men call Calastre calcas Certege/ Tesbyria/ Minona/ Faxton/ Molo Carpate and lempne. and in this yle is the mount Athos that passeth the clowdes/ and

Cotton ch. 3

---

[3] Among other extant editions and manuscripts, this word appears variously, usually as either "Eglenter" or "Englentine." As mentioned in the notes, I have expanded the abbreviation, "t" with a superior flourish, to "ter" on the authority of the same abbreviation in what is clearly the word "doughter" later in the text.

there is many speches/ and many countrees that are obeysaunt to the emperoure that is to say. Turcople/ Pyncy/ Narde/ Comange/ and many other Trachy and macydone/ of whyche Alysander was kynge. In this countre was arystotyll borne in a Cyte that men call strages. a lytell fro the cyte of Trachy/ and at strage lyethe arystotyll/ and there is an aulter upon hys [a7ʳ] tombe and there make they a greate fest every yere as he Were a saynt and opent† hys auter they holde their greate counseylis and assembles and they trowe that thorough inspyracion of god and hym they shall have the better counseyle. In this countre ar right hygh hylles towarde the ende of Macidone is a greate hyll that men call Olymphus that departeth Macidone and Trachy/ and it is highe up to the clowdes/ and the other hill that men call Athos is so highe that the shadowe of hym rechethe unto Olymphus that is nere lxxvii myle bytwene. And above that hill is the eyre so clere that men may fele no wynde there And therfore may no beest lyve there so is the eyre drye. And men say in these countres that Phylosofers somtyme wente up on those hyllys/ and helde to their noses a spounge moyst wyth Water for to have eyre for the eyre Was so drye. And above in the powder of the hyll they Wrote letters Wyth their fyngers. and at the yeres ende they came ageyne and fonde those letters the which they had wreten the yere before wythoute any defaute. And therfore it semeth well that those hilles passe the cloudes to the pure eyre. And at Constantynople the Emperours paleys is right fayre and Well dighte/ and therin is a fayre paleys for iustynge/ and it is on stages and eche man may Well se and none greve other. and under these stages ar stables vouted for themperours hors/ and all the pillers ar of marble. and within the church of saynt Sophy/ an emperoure wolde have layde the body of hys fader Whan he was dedde/ and as they made the grave they fonde a body in the erthe/ and upon that body lay a greate plate of fyne golde/ and therupon was wreten in Ebrewe/ in [a7ᵛ] Grewe and laten letters that sayde thus. Iesus cristus nascetur de virgine maria. et ego credo in eum. That is to say Iesu crist shalbe borne of the virgyn mary and I trowe in hym. And the date was it was layde in erthe ii. M. yere before oure lorde was born. And yet is that plate in the tresory of the churche. and men say that it was Ermogynes the wyse man. And all if it be so that men of Grece be cristen/ yet they vary from oure feythe. for they say that the holy gost cometh nat oute of the son but all

<small>Mounts Olympus and Athos</small>

only of the fader. and they are nat obeysaunt to the churche of rome ne to the pope/ and they say that their patriarkes have as moche power over the se as the pope hathe on this syde the see. And therfore pope Iohn the xxii sent letters to theym howe crysten feithe shuld be all one and that they shulde be obeysaunt to a pope that is cristis vyker in erthe to whome god gave playne power for to bynde and to assoyle/ and therfore they shulde be obedyent to him. and they sent hym dyvers answers and amonge other they saide thus Potentiam tuam summam circa subiectostuos firmiter credimus. Superbiam tuam summam tollerare non possumus. Avariciam tuam summam saciare non intendimus. Dominus tecum sit. quia dominus nobiscum est. vale This is to sey. we trowe well thy power is greate upon thy subgettis. we may nat suffre thy pryde. we are nat in purpos to staunche thy grete covetyse. lorde be wyth the for lorde is wyth us. Fare well. and other answere myght we nat have of theym. And also they make their sacrament of the auter of therf brede/ for oure lorde made it of therf brede whan he made his maunde/ and on sherthursday make they their bredde in tokenynge of the maunde/[4] [b1ʳ] ≠ were wonte to holde that place/ but in the tombe of seynt Ion is no thynge but Manna. for his body was translatyd into paradyse. and Turkes holde nowe that cyte and that churche and all assy the lesse/ and therfore is assy the lesse called turky/ and ye shall understonde that saynte Iohn dyd make hys grave there in hys lyfe/ and layde hym selfe therin all quycke/ and therfore somme sayn that he dyed nat/ but he restethe there to the day of dome/ and therfore sothely there is a greate marveyle for men may se there apertly the erthe of the tombe many tymes stere and move as there were a quycke thynge under. And from Ephesym men go thorough many yles in the se unto the cyte of Pateran where saynt Nycholas was borne/ and so to marca where he was chosen to the bysshoppe/ there growethe right good wynes and stronge/ that men calle wyne of marca. and fro thens se men Iles of Grece the whyche the emperoure gave somtyme to Ionays. And than passe men thorough the Iles of

Cotton
ch. 4
begins in
missing
sig.

---

[4] The text here misses sig. a8, which probably included information on Greek Orthodox customs and the way from Constantinople to Patmos and Ephesus. The church of St. John at Ephesus is the subject of the text when it resumes here at b1ʳ.

The Dragon-woman of Lango

Cophos and lango of the whyche Iles Ipocras was lorde/ and som say that in that Ile of lango is Ipocras doughter/ in maner of a dragon that is a hundred fote longe as men sayn for I have nat sene it. and they of the Iles call hir the lady of the countre/ and she lyeth in an olde castell and shewethe hir thryes in the yere. And she dothe no man no harme/ and she is thus chaunged fro a damsell to a dragon thorugh a goddesse that man call Deane/ and men say that she shal dwell so unto the tyme that a knyght come that is so hardy that dare go to hir and kysse hir mouth/ and than shal she turne ageyne to hir owne kynde and be a woman/ and after that she shall nat lyve longe. [b i]

[b1ᵛ] And it is nat longe sythen a knyght of Roodes that was hardy and doughty sayde that he wolde kysse hir and whan the dragon began to lyft up his hede ageyne hym and he sawe it was so hydious he fledde awey. and the dragon in his angre bare the knyght on a roche and of that roche she kest hym into the see and so was he lost. Also a yonge man that wyst nat of that dragon went oute of a shyppe and went thoroughe the yle tyll that he cam to a castell/ and cam into the cave and went so longe till he fonde a chamber/ and than he sawe a damsel that kempt hir hede and loked in myrroure and she had moch tresoure aboute hir and he trowed she had ben a comon woman that dwelled there to kepe men. and he obeyde unto the damsell. and the damsell sawe the shadowe of hym in the myrroure/ and she turned towarde hym/ and asked hym what he wolde and he sayde he wolde be paramoure or lemman. And she asked hym if he were a knyght. and he sayde nay.

And she sayde than myght he nat be hyr lemman. But she badde hym go ageyne to his felawes and make hym knyght and come ageyne on the morowe. and shulde come oute of the cave: and badde hym come and kysse hyr than on the mouthe/ and she bad hym have no drede/ for she shulde do hym no harme if all hym thought she were hydious to se. she sayde it was done by enchauntement. for she sayde that she was suche as he sawe hir than/ and she sayde that if he kyst hir he shulde have all that tresoure and be hir lorde. And lorde of those yles. and he departed fro hir and went to his felawes to ship and made him knyght/ and came ageyne upon the morowe for to kysse the damsell. And whan he sawe hir come oute of the cave [b2ʳ] in forme of a dragon he hadde so greate drede that he fledde too the shyp/ and she folowed hym/ and whan she sawe that he tourned nat ageyne/ she begane to crye as a thynge that had moche sorowe/ and she tourned ageyne and as sone the knyght dyed. and sythen hythertowarde myght no knyght se hir but he dyed as sone. But whan a knyght cometh that is so hardy to kysse hir/ he shall nat dy but he shall turne that damsell into hir right shappe/ He shall be lorde of the countre before sayde. And fro thens men come to the yle of rodes. the whyche the hospitelers holde and governe/ and that tooke they somtyme fro the Emperoure. and it Was wonte to be called Colles/ and so colles the turkes call it yet. ¶ And saynt Paule in his Epystelis wryteth to theym of the yle of Colocenses.

This yle is nere viii. hundred myle longe from Constantynople. ≠ and from this yle of rodes men go into Cypre where ar many vynes that first ar redde. and after a yere they wexe all whyte/ and those vynes that are moost whyte are moost cleere and beste smellynge and as men pas by this wey by a place where was wont to be a grete cyte that men calle Sathalay/ and all the countre was lost thorough foly of a yonge man for he hadde a fayre damosell that he loved well/ and she dyed sodeynly and was done in a grave of marbil/ and for the great love that he had to hir. he went on a night to hir Tombe and openyd it/ and went and lay by hir/ and whan he had done/ he went his wey. and whan it came to the ende of ix monethes a voyce cam unto hym and sayde in this maner of wyse. Goo unto the tombe of that same woman that thou haste lyne by/ and opyn it and beholde well that that [b2ᵛ] thou haste goten of hir: and if thou lette for to goo thou shalt have a greate harme/ and he went and openyd the tombe and there flewe oute a hede right hydous to se the whyche as swythe flewe above the cyte and the countre and sone the cyte sanke downe and there is many perilous passages fro Rodes to Cypre is nere v.C. myle and more/ but men may go to Cypre and come nat at Rodes

Cypre is a gode Ile and greate and there are many gode cytees and there is an archebysshop at Nycosy and iiii other bysshops in that londe. And at famagost is one of the best haven on the see that is in the worlde and that ar crysten men and sarasyns and men of all nacions. and in cypre is the hyll of the holy crosse/ and there is an abbey of monkes/ and there is the crosse of the gode theefe Dysmas as I have sayde before. And somme wene that there is the halfe of the crosse of oure lord but it is nat so and they do wronge that make

Cotton ch. 5

The Hideous Head of Sathalay

men to byleve so. In Cypre lyethe saynt Gononon af† whom men of that countre make greate solemnyte/ and in the castell of Amours lyeth the body of saynt hyllaryon/ and men kepe it full worshypfully. and besyde famagost was saynte Bernarde borne men hunt with the pampeons that are lyke to leopardes and they take wylde bestis right wel and they ar somwhat more than lyons and they take more sharply wylde bestys than houndes. In cypre is a maner that lordes and other men ete upon the erthe/ For they make dyches in the erthe all aboute the hall depe to the knee/ and they do peyne them and whan they woll ete they go there in and sytte there/ this their maner for to be more fresshe for that londe is more hote than it is here. And at greate [b3ʳ] festis/ and for straunge men they sette formes and bordes as men do in this countre/ but theym were lever syt in the erthe. Fro Cypre men go by londe to Ierusalem/ and by the see/ and in a day and in a nyght he that hathe gode wynde may come to the haven of Tyre that nowe is callyd Sure/ and also it is at the entre of Surry. there was somtyme a fayre cyte of crysten men. but sarasyns have destroyed it in greate party/ and they kepe that haven right well for drede that they have of crysten men. Men myght go right to that haven and come nat in Cypre but they go gladly to cypre to rest theym on the londe. or ellis to bye thynges that they have neede of to their lyvynge. Upon the see syde men may fynde many rubies and there is the well of the whyche holy wrytte spekethe. Fons ortorum et puteus aquarum vivencium [Canticles 4:15]. That is to say The well of gardeyns and dyches of waters lyvynge in the cyte of Tyre sayde the woman to oure lorde

Beatus venter qui te portavit et ubera que suxisti [Luke 11:27] That is to say Blessyd be the body that bare the/ and the pappes that thou souke and there oure lorde forgave too the woman of Canane hir synnes and before was wonte to be the stone on the whyche oure lorde sate on/ and preched. And on that stone was founde the churche of saynt Saveoure. Upon that see is the cyte of Saphen or Sarept or Sodom. there was wonte to dwell Elyas the prophete/ and there was reysed Ionas the prophete the wydowes son. And fyve myle fro Saphen is the Cyte of Sydon of the whyche Cyte dydo that was Eneas wyf after the destructyon of Troy/ and that foundyd the cyte of Cartage in Affryke and nowe is it callyd Didonsart [b ii] [b3ᵛ] Dydon is Beruth/ and fro beruth to Sardena is iii. iournes and from Sardena is fyve myle to Damas

WHo so Woll go lenger upon the see and come nere to Ierusalem he shall go fro Cypre by see to port Iaffe. For that is the next haven to Ierusalem. for fro that haven is nat but a dayes iourney and an halfe to Ierusalem. And that haven is callyd Iaffe and the towne affe. After one of Noe sonnes that men called Iapheth that founde it. And nowe is it callyd Iops and ye shall understonde that is the eldeste towne of the Worlde for that was made before Noes flode/ and there be bones of a geaunt syde that ben .xl. fote longe. And who so arryvethe at the first haven of Tyre or of Surrey beforesayde may go by londe if he woll to Ierusalem. and he gothe to the cyte of Acon in a day that was callyd Tholomayda. and it was a cyte of crysten men somtyme. but it is nowe all destroyed. and it is on the se And from Venys it is to Acon by se two thousande and foure score myles of lambardy/ and from calabre/ or fro Cycyle it is to Acon. M.ccc. myles of lumbardy: and the Ile of Grece is right in the mydwey. and besyde this cyte of Acon towarde the see at vi. score forlonges on the ryght syde towarde the North. there is the hyll Carme where Elyas the prophete dwellyd. and there Was the ordre of carmes first founde. This hyll is nat right greate ne highe. And at the fote of this hyll Was somtyme a goode cyte of crysten men that was called Cayphas. For Cayphas foundyd it but it is nowe all wastyd.

[b4ʳ] And at the lyft syde of the hyll is a towne that men calle Saffre. and that is sette upon another hyll. There was saynt Iames and saynt Ion borne. and in the worshyp of theym is there a fayrechurche.† And for Tholomayda that men call nowe Acon. to a greate hyll that men call Ekale de Tyrreyes is a hundred forlonges. and besyde the cyte of acon renneth a lytell ryver that men call Belyon/ and there nere is the fosse of Mymon all rounde that is an hundred cubytes or shaftmontis longe/ and it is all full of gravell shynynge of suche men make gode verres and clere..† And men come from ferre in a shyppe/ and by lande wyth cartes to take of that gravell. and if there be never so moche taken therof on a day/ on the morowe it is as full ageyne as ever it was. and that is great merveyle. and there is evermore wynde in that fosse that styrethe alwey the gravell and makethe it trouble.

And if a man put or do therin any metal as sone as it is in as sone it waxethe glasse. and the glasse that is made of this gravell if it be done ageyne into the gravell/ it tornethe ageyne to gravell as it was before. and som saye that it is a swolowe of the see gravell.

Also from acon before sayde go men thre iournes too the cyte of Phylistyen that nowe is callyd gaza that is to say cyte ryche/ and it is right fayre and full of folke and it is a lytell upon the see

And from that cyte brought Samson the stronge gates upon an high lande whan he was taken in that cyte and there he slewe the kynge in his paleys and many a thowsande more wyth hym. For he made a house to falle on theym. and fro thens shall men go to the cyte of Cesare [b4ᵛ] and so to the castel of pylleryns and so to Askalon/ and than to Iapheth. and so unto Ierusalem.

ANd who so woll go thorough the londe of Babylone where the Soudan dwelleth to have leve to go more sykerly to go thoroughe the churches and countrees/ and for to go to mount Synay byfore he came to Ierusalem/ and than turne ageyne by Ierusalem he shal go fro Gasa to the castell Dayr. And after a man cometh oute of Surry and goth in wildernes where the wey is ful sondy. and that wyldernesse lasteth viii. iourneys where men fynde all that theym nedethe of vytayles. and men call that wyldernes Archellek/ and whan a man cometh oute of this deserte he entrethe into Egypt/ and they call Egipt Canopat/ and in a nother langage men call it Mersyne. and the first goode towne that men fynde is callyd Beleth/ and it is at the ende of the kyngdome of Alape. And fro thens men come to Babylony and to kayre ≠ and in Babylony is a fayre churche of oure lady. where she dwellyd vii. yere whan she was in the londe of Iewes for dreede of kynge herode. And there lyethe the body of saynt Barbara virgyn. and there dwellyd Ioseph whan he was solde of his brether. and there made Nabugodonozor put their children in fyre. For they were of ryght trouthe the whiche children men callyd Anania Azaria Mysael as the psalme of benedicite saythe. But Nabugodonozor callyd theym thus. Sydrac/Mysael/ Abdenago. that is to sey. God glorious/ god victorious/ god over all kyngedoms. and that was for myracle that he made godde son/ as he sayde goo with those chyldren thorough the fyre.

Cotton ch. 6

The Court of the Sultan	[b5ʳ] There dwelleth the Soudon/ for there is a fayre see in a castell stronge/ and well sette upon a Roche. In that Castell is dwellynge alwey to kepe the Castell/ and to serve the soudan more than viii thousande persones of folke that take all their necessaries of the court of the sowdan. I shulde well knowe for I dwellyd wyth hym soudeour in his warres a great whyle ageyne the Bedoyns and he wolde have weddyd me to a great pryncys doughter right rychely and I wolde have forsaken my trouthe. And ye shall understand that the Soudon is lorde of v. kyngdoms the whyche he hathe conquered/ and goten to hym by strength. And this arre they of Canopate that is Egypte the kyngdom of Ierusalem wherof David and Salon were kynges: the kyngdome of Surrey. of the whych the cyte of Damas was the chef/ kingdom of anaple in the lond of Dameth/ and the kyngdom of arab was to one of the thre kynges that made offerynge to oure lorde whan he was borne. and many other londes he holdethe in his hande/ and also he holdethe Calaphes that is a greate thynge to the
Cotton ch. 7 wholly within "Egypt Gap." Cotton ch. 8 begins in "Egypt Gap."	Soudan/ that is to say amonge theym Roys Ile⁵ ≠ and this vale is full colde. and than men goo up on the mount of saynte Katheryn/ and that is moche hygher than the mounte Moyses. And there as saynt katheryn was graven is no church ne chapel ne other dwellynge place/ but there is an hyll of stones gedred togeder aboute the place there she was graven of aungellis. there was wonte to be a chapell. but it is all casten downe. and yet lye a greate part of the stones there.
	And all it be so that the Collet of saynte katheryn say that it is all one place where oure lorde gave the law to Moyses. [b5ᵛ] And there saynt katheryn was graven. ye shall understonde that it is all in a countre or ellys in a stedde that bereth all a name. For they are called both mount Synay. but it is a greate wey betwene theym and a greate vale.
Cotton ch. 9	≠ NOwe sythen a man hathe vysited this holy place of saynt katheryn. and he woll turne to Ierusalem/ he shall first take leve at the monkes and recommaunde hym specyally to their prayers. and those same monkes gyve wyth goode wyll to pylgryms vetayles to pas wythe thorough wyldernes to Surry and that lastethe wel xiii: iournes. And in that wylder-

---

⁵ This is the site of the "Egypt Gap."

The Bedouins

nesse dwell many arabyns that men call Bedoynes and ascopardes. these ar folke that are full of all maner of yll condicyons and they have no houses but tentys whyche they make of beestys skynnes as of camellys and other bestis/ the whyche they ete and therunder lye they. and they dwell in places where they may fynde Water as on the redde see. For in that wyldernesse is greate defaute of water and it falleth oft where a man fyndeth water one tyme he fyndeth it nat another tyme/ and therfore make they no howses in those countrees. These men that I speke of they tyll nat the londe for they ete no brede. but if it be any that dwell nere a goode towne/ and they rost all their fysshes and flesshe upon hote stones ageyne the son. and they ar stronge men and well fightynge and they do no thynge but chase wylde bestis for theyr sustenaunce/ and they sette nat by theyr lyves. and therfore they drede nat the Soudan nor none other prynce of all the worlde

[b6ʳ] And they have oft werre wyth the Soudan. and that same tyme that I was dwellynge wyth hym they bare nat but a sheelde/ and spere for to defende theym wyth. And they holde none other armours. but they wynde their hedes and their neckes in a great lynen clothe/ and they are men of full yll kynde. and whanne men are passed this wyldernesse toward Ierusalem they come to Bersabe. that was somtyme a fayre and a lykynge towne of crysten men and yet is there somme of their churches and in that towne dwellyd somtyme abraham the Patryarke. This towne of bersabe foundyd urrey wyfe of whom Davyd engendred Salon the wyfe† that was kynge of Ierusalem and of xii. kyndes of Israel and he reigned xl yere. and from thens go men to the vale of Ebron that is fro thens nere xii. myle. And somme call it the vale of Mambre: and also it is called the vale of Teres/ for as moche as adam grete in that vale a hundred yeere the detthe of his son abel that caym slough And Ebron that was somtyme the pryncipall cyte of Phylistiens/ and there dwellyd Geauntes and there it was so fre that men toke alle fleers of all other places that hadde done yll In Ebron Iosue Calofe and their felaweshyp came firste to aspye howe they myght wynne the lande of promyssyon. In Ebron davyd reygned first vii yere and halfe and in Ierusalem he reigned xxxiii yere and halfe. And there ar the graves of Patryarkes adam/ abraham/ Iacob and theyr wyves/ Eve/ Sara/ Rebecca/ and they are in the hyngynge of the hylle/ and under theym is a right fayre churche kyrnelde after the facyon and maner as it were a castell. The whyche churche the sarasyns keepe ryghte [b6ᵛ] well and they have that place in greate worshyp. For the holy patryarkes that lyethe there/ and they suffre no crysten men ne Iewes come in there. but they have specyall grace of the soudan. for they holde crysten men and Iewes but as houndes that shulde come in no holy place.

And they call the place spelunke/ or double cave/ or double grave for one lyethe on another. and the sarasyns cal it on their langage. Caryatharba that is to say the place of patryarkes. and Iewes call it arboth. And in that same place was abrahams howse/ and that Was the same the whiche sate in his dore/ and sawe thre persones and worshypped one. as holy wrytte Wetnesseth saynge.

Tres vidit et unum adoravit.⁶ That is to say he sawe iii. and worshypped one/ and hym toke abraham to his house. And right nere to the place is a cave in a Roche where adam and eve dwellyd whan they Were dryven oute of paradyse/ and there gate they their chyldren. And in that same place was adam made as some men say/ for men callyd somtyme that place the felde of Damasse. For it was in the lordshyp of Damasse/ and fro thens he was translatyd into paradyse as they say. And afterward he was dryven oute of paradyse and put there a geyne/ for the same day that he Was put into pararise† the same day he was dryven oute. for as sone he synned.

There begynneth the vale of Ebron that lasteth nere to Ierusalem. and the aungel bad Adam that he shulde dwell with his wyfe. and there they engendred Seth of the whiche kyn Iesu cryste was borne.

¶ And in that Vale is a feelde where men drawe oute of the erthe a thynge the whyche thynge men in that countre [b7ʳ] call chambyll and they ete that thynge in stedde of spyce and they bere it to sell and men may nat make it so depe ne so wyde but that it is at the yeres ende full ageyne up to the sydes thorough the grace of god. And two myle from Ebron is the grave of loth that was abrahams brother. and a litell from ebron is the mount Marbre of the whyche

---

⁶ Not biblical but patristic. Ambrose, "De fide," I: 13, 80 has "Abraham quoque tres vidit, et unum adoravit (Gen. xviii, 2)" (*Patrologiae Cursus Completus. Series Latinae*, Ed. J. P. Migne, 221 vols. [Paris, 1844–64], 16: 547 B); See also Augustine, "Sermo 46," *Patrologiae Latinae* 40: 1325, line 37; Pseudo-Ambrose, "Hymnus ad Sextam," *Patrologiae Latinae* 17: 1179, line 20). Genesis 18:2 is apparently the "holy writ" referred to.

The Dry Tree

the vale toke his name. and there is a tree of oke that sarasyns call Dyrpe that is of Abrams tyme/ that men call drye tree. and they say that it hathe ben from the begynnynge of the worlde and was somtyme greene/ and bare leves unto that tyme that oure lord dyed and so dyd all the trees in the worlde/ or ellis they fayled in their hertes/ or ellys they faded/ and yet is many of thoose in the worlde. And somme prophesies say that a lorde prynce of the west syde of the worlde shall wynne the londe of promyssion/ that is the hooly londe wyth the helpe of crysten men. and he shall do synge a messe under the drye tree. and than the tre shall waxe grene and bere frute and leves/ and thorough that myracle many sarasyns and iewes shalbe tourned to crysten feyth/ and therfore they do greate worshyp therto and kepe it ryght besyly. And all if it be drye it bereth a greate vertue. for certeynly he that berethe a lytell therof on hym it heleth of the fallynge evyl and many other vertues. and therfore it is holden ryght precious. Fro Ebron men go to bethleem on halfe a day for it is but fyve myle and it is a perylous wey and thorugh wodes full lykand. But bethleem is a lytell cyte longe/ and narowe and well wallyd and enclosyd wyth a dyke and it was wonte to be called Effrata. as hooly wryttte† sayth. Ecce audivimus eum in effrata [Psalm 132:6]. That is to say. [b7ᵛ] Lo we herde hym in effrata towarde the ende of the cyte towarde the est is a right fayre churche. and a gracious/ and it hathe many toures and pynnacles and kyrnellys full straungely made/ and within that churche is .xliiii. of marble pylers great and fayre. and betwene thys chuche† and the cyte is the felde Floridons/

Story of the First Roses

and it is called the feld florysshed. For as moche as a fayre mayden that was blamed with wronge that she had done fornycacion. for the whyche cause she was demyd to the dethe and to be buryed in that place to the whyche she was ledde/ And as the Wode beganne to brenne aboute hir she made hir prayer to oure lorde as she was nat gyltye of that thynge. that he wolde helpe hir that it myght be knowen to all men. And whan she had thus sayde she entred the fyre and as soone was the fyre oute. and thoose braunches that were brennynge bycam redde roses/ and those braunches that were nat kyndled becam whyte rosers full of whyte roses/ and thoose were the fyrst roses/ and rosers that any man sawe/ and thus was the mayden saved thoroughe the grace of god. And therfore is the felde called the feld of god florysshed/ for it was full of rooses. Also besyde the queere of that churche at the righte syde as men come downeward .xii. grees is the place. where oure lord was borne that is nowe full well dight of marble and full rychely depeyntyd of golde sylver and asure/ and other colours. and a lytell thens by thre pacys is the Crybbe of the oxe/ and the asse. And besyde that is the place where the sterre fell that ledde the thre kynges Iasper Melchior and Balthasar. But men of grece call the kynges thus. Galgalath/ Saraphy/ Galgalagh. Theyse iii. kynges [b8ʳ] offred to oure lorde. Encenfe†/ gold and myrre/ and they cam togeder thorough myracle of god for they mette togeder in a cyte that men call Chasak. that is liii. iournes fro Betheleem/ and there they were at betheleem the fourth day after they hadde sene the sterre. And under the cloyster of this churche xviii. grees at the righte syde of the Charnel of the Innocentis where their bones lye/ and before that place where crist was born is the tombe of saynt Ierom that Was a prest and a cardynall that translatyd the byble and the sauter fro Ebron to latyn. and besyde that churche is a churche of saynt Nycholas where oure lady restyd hir whan she was delyvered of chylde. And for as moche as she had so moche mylke in hir pappes that grevyd hir she mylked it oute upon the redde stones or marble. so that yet may the traces be sene whyte upon the stoones. and ye shall understonde that all that dwell in betheleem ar crysten men and there are fayre wynes all aboute the cyte and greate plente of wyne for their bokes that machomete betoke theym. the whyche they calle Alkaron. And somme call it alkaron. and somme call it Massap. and som call it harme forbedeth theym to drynke wynes: for in that boke machomete cursethe all those that drynke of that wyne and all that sell it for somme men sayde ones that he slow a good heremyte whyche he loved moch in his dronkenes And therfore he cursed the wyne/ and theym that drynke Wyne. but his malison is turned to hym self as holy writ saythe.

Et in verticem ipsius iniquitas eius descendet [Psalm 7:16]. That is to say in englysshe: His wyckednes shall descende in hys owne hede. And also the Sarasyns bryngethe forth no [b8ᵛ] gryse ne they ete no swynes flesshe/ for they say it is brocher† too man and that it was forboden in the olde lawe. Also in the londe of Palestyne/ ne in the londe of egypte they ete but lytell veale and beefe/ but it be so olde that it may nomore travaile ne work nat for it ts† forbode but for they kepe theym for tyllynge of their londe. Of thys cyte of bethleem was davyd the kynge borne/ and he had syxty wyves and thre hundred lemmas: Fro bethleem. to Ierusalem is two myle/ and in the wey to Ierusalem. halfe a myle from bethleem is a churche where the aungell sayde to the shepeherde of the berynge of cryste. and in that way is the tombe of Rachell/ that was Iosephs moder the patriarke and she dyed as sone as she had borne beniamyn and there she was graven/ and Iocob hir husbonde sette xii. greate stones upon hir in tokenynge that she hadde borne xii: children. In this wey to Ierusalem ar many churches crysten by the whyche men goo to Ierusalem.

Cotton ch. 10

≠ For to speke of ierusalem ye shall understonde that it standeth fayre amonge hylles/ and there is nouther ryver ne well but water comethe by condyte fro Ebron. and ye shall wete that men callyd it first Iebus and sythen Was it called Salomee unto the tyme of kynge davyd: and he sette these two names Samen and called it Iebusalem. and than came Salon/ and called it Ierusalem and so is it callyd yet. And aboute Ierusalem is the kyngdom of Surrey/ and therby is the lond of Palestyne and Ascalon/ but Ierusalem is in the londe of Inde/ and it is called Indee.[7]

[c2^r] worldes hathe wrought heele in the myddys of the erthe. And also upon the Roche where the crosse was fyxed is wryten wythin the roche. Gros guist basis thou pestes thoy thesmoysy[8] That is to say in laten. Quod vides est fundamentum tocius mundi et huius fidei. and it is too say. that thou seest is grounde of all the world and of this feythe. And

Christ's Age at Death

ye shall understonde that oure lord whan he dyed was xxxii. yere olde. and thre monethes/ and the prophesy of david sayth that he shulde have .xl. yere whan he sayth thus. Quadraginta annis proximus fui generacioni huic [cf. Psalm 95:10] That is to say. Fourty yere Was I neyghbour to this kynde. and thus shulde it seme that prophesy were nat sothe/ but it is. For in olde tyme men called yeres of x. monethes: of the whyche marche was the firste. and december the laste. But Gayus Cesar that was emperoure of rome dyd sette to

---

[7] The text here misses sig. c1, which probably contained a brief description of the lands surrounding Jerusalem and the beginning of the discussion of the Church of the Holy Sepulchre. "Inde/Indee" here refers not to India, but to Judea.

[8] Apparently garbled Greek. Cf. Hamelius, *Mandeville's Travels*, 2: 59n.

these two monethes Ianuary and February and ordeyned the yere of xii. monethes. that is to say ccc. dayes wythoute lepe yere. the propyr cours of the sonne. And therſpret† after the accomptynge of ten monethes to the yere he dyed in fourty yere: and after oure yeres of xii. monethes is xxxii. yere and thre monthes. Also within mounte calvary at the right syde is an auter where the Pyller lyethe that oure lorde was bounde too whan he was scourged/ and there besyde at foure fote ar foure stones that alwey droppe water. and somme say that those stones wepe for oure lordes deth. and nere this auter in a place xlii degrees depe was found the very cros by assent of saynt Elyn under a roche where Iewes had hydde it/ and it was assayed for they fonde thre crosses. one of oure lorde and two of the two theves

[c2ᵛ] And saynt Elyne assayed theym on a dede body that rose as sone as the very crosse was layde on. And therby in the vale is the place where the foure nayles of our lorde was hydde. for he had two nayles in his handes/ and two in his fete. And of one of these nayles the emperour of Constantynople dyd make a brydell for his hors to bere hym in batayle. for thorough vertu therof he overcam his ennemys. And whan all londes of assy/ turky/ damazyne more and the lesse/ surrey/ and Ierusalem/ araby/ persy/ and Messopotany/ the kyngdom of alappe/ egipt the hygh and the lowe/ and other kyngdoms many unto welle[9] lowe in Ethyope/ and alsoo unto Inde the lesse that than was crysten. and there was in that tyme many gode men. and holy heremytes of whom the bokes of the fader lyfes speketh/ and they ar nowe in paynemes and sarasyns handes but whan god Woll ryght as these londes are lost thorough synne of crysten men soo shall they be wonne ageyne by cristen men thorough helpe of god. And in the myddis of this church is a compas in the whyche Ioseph of aramathy layd the body of oure lord whan he had taken hym of the crosse. And that compasse men say it is in myddys of the Worlde. and that churche of the sepulcre on the northe syde is the place where oure lorde was done in pryson in many places/ and there is a party of the cheyne with the whyche he was bounde. And there he apperyd first

---

[9] Most of the first vowel in the word is missing here. I supply "e" as the most likely choice.

to mary magdalen whan he was rysen/ and she trowed that he hadde been a gardyner in the churche of the sepulcre was wonyd to be chanons of the ordre of saynt kenet/ and they had a pryoure but the patryarke was their soveraigne. and withouten the doores [c3ʳ] of the churche at the right syde as men goo up .xviii. degrees sayde oure lorde to his moder. Mulier ecce fi ius✝ tuus. That is to say woman beholde thy son. Deinde dicit discipulo. Ecce mater tua. That is to say. Than sayde he to his discyple. Beholde thy moder. And this word he sayde upon the crosse/ and upon these degrees wente oure lorde whan he bare the crosse upon his shulder and under these degrees is achapell✝ where prestis synge/ but nat after oure lawe. and alwey they make ther sacrament of the auter of bred saynge Pater noster. and other thynges/ as with the whiche thynge they say the wordes of whom the sacrament is made. for they knowe nat of addicyons that many popes have made/ but they synge in gode devocyon. and there nere is the place where oure lorde restydde hym whan he was wery for berynge of the crosse. And ye shall understonde that before the churche of the sepulcre is the cyte moost wake/ For the greate playne that is betwene that cyte and the churche on the est syde without the wallys of the cyte is the Vale of Iosaphat that cometh to the wallys. In that vale of Iosaphat withoute the cyte is the churche of saynt stephyn where he was stoned to dethe. and therby is the gate gylted that may natte be openyd. Thoroughe that gate oure lorde entred on palme sonday upon an asse and the gate openyd ageyn him whan he wolde go to the temple/ and yet are the steppis of the asse sene in thre places the whyche are full of harde stones. Before the churche of the sepulcre two hundryd pacys is a greate hospytall of saynt Iohn of the whyche hospytalers halfe their foundement/ and to go towarde the est fro the hospitall is a right fayre church that men call [c ii] [c3ᵛ] Nostre Dame de vatynz/ and there was mary Cleofe/ and mary magdeleyne and drewe their here whan oure lorde was done to dethe. ≠ And fro the churche of the sepulcre toWarde the est at xviii. pacys is temple domini that is a fayre house and it is all rounde and right high. and coveryd with leede. and it is well panyd wyth whyte marble. but the sarasyns woll suffre no cristen men ne Iewes come therin. for they say that so foule men shulde nat come into that holy place/ but I cam in there and in other places where I wolde. for I had letters of the Soudan with his greate Seale. and

Cotton ch. 11

Temple Domini

comonly other men have but of his signet: and men bere his letter with his seale before theym hangynge on a spere/ and men do greate worship therto and knele ageyne/ it as we do ageyne goddis body/ for those men that it is sent to/ befoore they take it. they enclyne theym first therto. and sythen they take it/ and layde it upon their hedys and afterwarde they kysse it/ and than rede all enclynynge with greate worshyp/ and than they profer theym to do all that the brynger woll/ and in this temple domini. were wonte to be chanons regulers/ and they had an abbotte to whom they were obedyent/ and in this temple was Charlemayne whan the aungell brought hym the prepuys of oure lorde whan he was circumcised. And after kynge charles dyd bere it too parys. And ye shall understonde that is nat the temple that salamon made/ for that temple lasted but a thousande/ an hundred and two yere. For Tytus Vaspasiane son that was emperoure of rome that layde syege aboute Ierusalem for to discomfite the Iewes for they hadde doo cryst to dethe withoute love of the emperoure/ and whan he had take [c4ʳ] the cyte he dyd bren the temple and kest it down/ and toke all the Iewes and dyd of theym to dethe .xi.C.M. and the other he dyd in pryson/ and solde of theym thretty for a peny/ for they sayde that they bought iesu cryst for xxx pens. And sythen gave Iulyan apostata leve to the Iewes to make the temple of Ierusalem for he hated crysten men/ and yet he was crysten. but he forsoke his lawe and whan the Iewes hadde made the temple/ came an erthe quaue† as god wolde that kest downe all that they hadde made. Sythen Adryan emperoure that was of them of Troys made Ierusalem ageyne and the Temple in the same maner that Salamon made it and wolde that no Iewe shulde dwell there but all crysten men/ for if all it were so that he was nat crystened he loved crysten men/ more than any other men. save men of his owne feythe. And this emperoure dyd enclose and wall the churche of the holy sepulcre within the cyte that before was fer with oute the cyte/ and he wolde have chaunged the name of Ierusalem and callyd it Helyam/ but that name lasted nat longe. And ye shall wete that the sarasyns do greate worshyp to that temple/ and they say that place is ryghte holy/ And whan they go theder in/ they go barefote and knele many tymes downe.

¶ And whan my felowes and I came theder in we dyd of oure harneyse/ and cam barefote into the temple/ and thought that we shulde doo as moche: or more than they that were mystrowynge. and this Temple is thre score and thre cubytes of wydnesse and as moche of length and of heyght vi. and twenty and fyve cubytes/ and it is wythin all aboute of pyllers of marble

[c4ᵛ] And in myddes of the temple is a stage of xxiii. degrees of height. and goode pyllers all aboute/ Thys place the Iewes called it. Sancta sanctorum. That is to say. Holy of holyes/ and in that place cometh none but only theyr prelate that maketh their sacryfice. and the folke standethe all aboute in dyvers stages after they are of dignyte and of worshyp/ and there is foure entres to that temple and the dores are of cypres well dight/ and within the est dore Oure lorde sayde here is Ierusalem. ¶ And on the Northe syde within the dore is a stannke. but it rennethe nat: of the whyche holy wrytte speketh/ and sayth thus. Vidi aquam egredientem de templo.[10] That is to say. I sawe water comynge oute fro the temple. And upon the other syde is a roche that men called somtyme Moriach but after was it called Belet or the hutche of god wythe the rylikes of Iewes. Thys arke or hutche gart Tytus loode with the relykes to greate rome whan he had dyscomfyted all the Iewes. In that same arke was the ten commaundementis/ and of arons wonde/ and of Moyses wonde with whiche he departyd with the redde see whan the folke of Israel passed thorough on fote drye/ and wyth that wonde he dyd many wonders/ and there was a vessell of golde full of Manna/ and clothynge and ornamentes. and the tabernacle of Aron: and a table square of golde With xii precious stones/ and a bost of Iasper grene With foure fygures/ and viii. names of oure lord within/ and vii candylstickes of golde/ and foure censers of golde/ and an aulter also of gold/ and foure lyons of golde. Upon the whyche they hadde Cherubyn of golde twelve span longe/ and a tabernacle of golde/ and also [c5ʳ] twelve trompettis of sylver/ and a table of sylver/ and seven barly loves. and all other relykes that were before the Nativyte of Ihesu. Also upon this Roche slepte Iacob whan he sawe aungellys goo up and downe by a stey†. and sayde vere locus iste sanctus est/ et ego ignorabam [Genesis 28:16]. That is to say Forsothe this place is holy and I wyst nat. And Iacob helde the aungell styll that chaunged his name and callyd hym Israel. and in that place sawe David the aungell that

---

[10] Antiphon for the blessing of water in Paschaltide. Cf. Ezekial 47:1.

sharethe folke With a swerde/ and put it all bloody in the shethe. And in this Roche was saynt Symeon/ whan he resceyved oure lorde in to the temple. and on this Roche he set hym whan the Iewes wolde have stoned hym/ and the roche ryved in two/ and in that ryft he hyd hym. and a sterre came downe and gave hym light. And on this roche sate oure lady and lerned hir sauter. and there forgave oure lorde the synnes to the woman that was founde and taaken in aduoutrye. and there was oure lorde Iesu cryste circumcysed/ and there the aungell denounsed the Nativite of saynt Iohn baptyst. and there offred first Melchysedech bredde and wyne and water to oure lorde in tokenynge of the sacrament that was for to come./ And there felle david praynge to oure lorde/ and the aungell that he wolde have mercy of hym and of the folke/ and oure lorde anon herde his prayer/ and therfore wolde he make the temple in that place/ But oure lorde Iesu cryst forbadde hym by an aungell for he hadde done treason/ whanne he dyd sle Ury a gode knyght for to have his wyfe.

¶ And therfore all that he hadde ordeyned for too make the Temple he betoke it unto Salamon hys son. And [c5ᵛ] he made it and he prayed oure lorde that all those that prayed in that place devoutly and with good hert that he wolde here that prayer and graunt that they asked righwysly† and oure Lorde grauntyd it. And therfore Salamons son caliyd it temple of counseyle and helpe of god withoute the dores of that temple is an autere where/ Iewes were wont to offre dowves and tyrtilles/ and in that temple was zachary slayne. and on the pynnacle the Iewes sette saynt Iame on the erthe that first was bysshoppe of Ierusalem. a lytell fro this temple on the right syde is a churche coveryd wyth lede that is called the scole of salamon: And towarde the southe is the temple Salon/ that is full fayre and a greate place. and in this place dwelle knyghtes that are called templers/ and that was the foundement of.† and of their ordre. and in that Temple Domini dwell chanons. Fro this temple towarde the est at xxvi pace in a corner of the cyte is the bathe of oure lorde and this bath was wonte to go to paradyse. and besyde is oure ladyes bede. and nere there is the tembe of saynt Symeon/ and withoute the cloyster of the temple towardes the northe is right a fayre churche of saynt An oure lady moder. There was oure lady conceyved. and before that churche is a greate tre that began to growe that same nyght. And as men go downe fro that churche. xxii. grees lyeth Ioachym oure ladyes fader in a tombe of stoone. and there nere was layde somtyme saynt an/ but saynte Elyn dyd translate hir into Constantynople.

¶ In this churche is a well in maner of a Cysterne that is callyd Probatica piscina. That hadde fyve entringes/ And in that Cysterne was wonte an aungell to descende [c6ʳ] and stere the water/ and what man that bathed hym first therin after the movynge was made hole that was syke What sykenesse so ever he hadde And there was the man in the palsy made hole. that was syke xxxviii. yere And oure lorde sayde unto hym in this maner of wyse.

¶ Tolle grabatum tuum et ambula [Mark 2:9; John 5:8]. That is to say in englysshe Take thy bedde and goo. ¶ And there besyde was the hous of pylate. and a litell thens was the hous of heraude the kynge that dyd slee the Innocentis. Thys Heraude was a full wyckyd man and a fell. For he dyd first and formest sle his wyfe whyche he loved full welle And for the greate love that he had to hir whan she was dede he behelde hyr and went oute of his wyt and so was he longe tyme. and afterwarde he came ageyne to hym selfe. And sythen he dyd sle his owne children that he had goten of that wyfe. and after he made sle the other of his wyves. and a son that he hadde goten of that same wyfe and he dyd all the yll that he myght.

<small>Herod the Great</small>

¶ And whan he sawe that he shulde dye he sent for hys suster and all the greate lordes of that countre. and Whan they were there he putte all the lordes tn† o toure and sayde to his suster He wyste well that the men of the countre shulde make no sorowe for hym whan he were dede.

And therfore he made hir for to swere unto hym that she shulde do smyte of the hedes of his lordes everychone after hys dethe. and than shulde men of all the countre make sorowe for his dethe. and ellys they wolde nat sorowe And thus he made his testament. But his suster fulfyllyd it nat. as that thynge that parteyned unto the lordys for as sone as he was dede she delivered the lorde† oute of [c6ᵛ] the toures and sent everychone home to their houses and tolde theym what hir brother wolde she hadde done wyth theym. And ye shall understonde/ that in that tyme was thre herodes of greate name. ¶ This of whom I speke men called hym Herode ascolonyte/ he that dyd smyte of saynt Iohns Baptyst hede was Herode antipa. and herode agryppa dyd sle saynt Iames. Also ferthermore in the cyte is the churche of the saveoure/ and there is the arme of saynt Iohn Crysostom. and there is the more party of saynt stephens hede. And on the other syde towarde the Southe as men go to mount syon is a fayre churche of saynt Iames where his hede was smyten of/ and there is mount Syon/ and there is a fayre church of god and of oure Lady where she was dwellynge/ and dyed/ and there was somtyme an abbey of chanons regulers. and fro that place she was borne of the apostles unto the Vale of Iosaphat. And there is the stone that the aungel bare to oure lady fro mounte Synay. and it is of that colour that the roche of saynt katheryn is of/ and there besyde is the gate where oure lady whan she was wyth chylde wente to Betheleem. Also at the entre of mount Syon is a chapell and in that chapell is that stone great and large wyth whiche the sepulcre Was covered whan cryst was layde therin. the whyche stone thre Iewes sawe turned upwarde whan they cam to the sepulcre and there they fonde an aungell that sayde to theym that cryste was rysen fro deth to lyfe. And there is a lytell pece of the pyller/ to the whyche oure lorde was scourged. and theere was Anne house that was bysshop of the Iewes in that tyme/ and in that same place forsoke saynt Peter oure lorde thryes [c7ʳ] before the kocke crewe. and there is a party of the table on the whyche god made his maunde with his discyples/ and yet is there the vessell with water/ and therby is the place where saynt stephen was graven/ and theere is the auter where oure lady herde the aungellis synge messe. and there apperid cryst firste to his discyples after his resurrection whan the gates were sperde/ and sayde. Pax vobis [John 20:26]. That is to say. Peas to you. And on that mounte apperyd cryst to saynt Thomas/ and bad hym assay hys wounde. and than trowed he firste and sayde. Dominus meus et deus meus [John 20:28]. That is to say. My lorde/ and my god/ in that same chapell behynde the hygh aulter Were all the appostlis on wytsonday. whan the holy goost descendyd on theym in lykenesse of fyre/ and there made god Paske with his disciples. And there slepte saynte Iohn the Evangelyst on oure lordes kne/ and sawe slepynge many prevy thynges of heven. The mount syon is within the cyte and it is lytell higher than the other syde of the cyte and that cyte is stronger on that one side than on the other for at the fote of mounte synay† is a fayre castell and stronge/ on mount syon was davyd kynge Salon and other many graven/ and there is the place where saynte Peter wept full tenderly whan he had forsaken oure lorde and a stone cast from that is another place where oure lorde was Iuged/ for that tyme was there cayphas hous/ also betwene the temple Salamon and mounte Syon is the place where crist reysed the mayden fro deth to lyfe. Under mount syon toward the vale of Iasaphat is a well that men calle Natatoyr Sylo there was oure lord washen after he was baptysed. and nere there is the tere†/ on [c7ᵛ] the whyche Iudas hangyd hym selfe for despayre whan he had solde cryst/ and therby the synagoke where the bysshop of Iewes and sarasyns came. som to holde counseyle/ and there Iudas cast the xxx. pens before theym and sayde peccavi/ tradens sanguinem iustum [Matthew 27:4]. That is to say I have synned deceyvynge rightwys blode. And on the other syde of mount Syon toward the southe a stone cast is the feld that was bought with those thretty pens for whan cryst was solde that men call Acheldemak/ that is to say the felde of blode/ in that felde is many tombes of cristen men. for there be many pylgrymes graven. and also in Ierusalem toward the west is a fayre churche where the tree grewe of the whyche the crosse was made/ and there nere is a churche and that a fayre Where oure lady mette wyth elysabethe whan they were bothe wyth chylde and saynt Iohn styred in his moders wombe and made worshyppe to oure lorde his maker. and under the aulter of the churche is a place where saynt Iohn was borne/ and therby is the castell of Emaux. And two myle fro Ierusalem is the mount ioy that is a fayre place and lykynge and there lyethe Samuel the prophete in a fayre tombe and it is called mount ioy. for there many pylgryms first see Ierusalem/ and in the myddell of the vale of Iosaphat is a lytell ryver that is called Torrens Cedron/ and overthwart this ryver lay a tre of the which the cros was made that men yode over. Also in that vale is a churche of oure lady and there is the sepulcre of oure lady and oure lady was of age whan she dyed lxxii. yere. and there nere is the place where oure lorde forgave saynte Peter all his synnes and mysdedis that he had done.[11]

[d1ʳ] fastyd fourty dayes/ and the ennemy of hell bare cryste

---

[11] The text here misses sig. c8, probably including further description of the Church of Our Lady, the Mount of Olives, and the Mount of Galilee, with reference to the sacred history enacted there.

and sayde to hym thus. Dic ut lapides isti panes fiant [Matthew 4:3]. That is to say that these stones be made loves. and there is an ermytage where dwell a maner of crysten men that men call Georgyns/ for saynt george converted theym. And upon that hyll dwellyd Abraham a greate whyle. Also as men go to Ieryco. In the wey sate many sycke men cryinge Iesu fili david miserere nobis [Matthew 20:30, 31]. That is too say. Ihesu david son have mercy on us. ≠ Also two myle fro Ierico is flom Iordan. and ye shall wete the dedde see departeth the londe of Indee/ and of araby/ and the water of that see is full bytter/ and thys water castethe oute a thynge that men call aspaltum as great peces as an horse. and Ierusalem is cc. forlonges from this see/ and so it is called the dedde See. for it renneth nat. no man/ ne beest that hathe lyfe that is therin may lyve/ and that hathe ben proved many tymes. for they cast therin men. that are demyd to dethe/ ne no man may dwell ne drynke of that water/ and men cast yron therin it comethe up ageyne. And if a man cast a fether therin it gothe too the grounde/ and that is ageynst kynde. And there groweth trees that bere frute of fayre coloure and seme rype. but whan a man brekethe theym or cutte in theym he fyndeth nought in theym but coles of asshes in tokenynge that thoroughe vegeaunce† of god. These cytees were brent with fyre of helle. and somme men call that lake. the lake of the alphitedde/ and somme call it the flome of the devyll/ and somme the flome of stynkande. for the water is stynkyng There sanke these fyve cytees thoroughe wreche of god/ That is to say/ Sodom/ Gomor/ Aldema/ Solome/ and [d i] [d1ᵛ] Segor. For the synne of Sodom that reigned in theym but Segor thorough the prayere of Loth was savyd a greate whyle for it sate on a hyll and yet appereth moche therof above the water/ and men may see the walles in clere wedyr. And there Loth dwellyd a grete whyle and was made dronken of his doughters and lay by theym. they trowed that god shulde have destroyed all the world as he dyd with Noes flode. And therfore they lay by their fader. for men shulde be borne of theym into the worlde. And if he had nat be dronken/ he hadde nat lyen by them And at the right syde of this se dwellyd lothis wyfe a stone of salte for that she loked ageyne whan the cyte sanke downe. ¶ And ye shall understonde that Abraham had a son that he called Isaac/ and he was circumcysed whan he was of viii. dayes olde. and therfore the Iewes dyde circumcyse theym at the age of .viii.

Cotton ch. 12

The Dead Sea

dayes/ and he hadde another son that was called Ismael and he was of xiiii yere of age whan he was circumcysed on a day. and therfore the sarasyns dyd circumcyse theym at xiiii. yere olde And into that dede see renneth the Flom Iordan and maketh ende there. And this Flom Iordan is no great ryver but there is moche gode fysshe therin. and it comethe from mount Lybany. for two welles that men call Ior and Dane. and of theym it takethe the name. and upon the one syde of that ryver is mount Gelboe. and there is a fayre playne: And on that other syde men go by mount Lybane to the Desart of Pharao/ These hylles departe the kyngdom of Surry and the countre of Phenys. On that hyll growe Cedres that bere longe apples Whych ar as moche as a mannys hede

[d2ʳ] ¶ This flom Iordane departeth Galyle: and the londe of Idones and the londe of Botron/ and it renneth into a playne that men call Meldane in Sermoys and in that playne is the temple Iob. In this flom Iordan oure lorde was baptysed. and there was the voyce of the fader herde saynge. Hic est filius meus dilectus in quo mihi bene complacui ipsum audite [Matthew 3:17; Luke 9:35]. That is to say. here is my son that I love in whom I am well payde here hym and the holy goost descendyd on hym in lykenesse of a dowve and so was there in his baptysynge all the Trynite. And thorough the flom Iordan passed the chyldren of Israel all drye and they sette stones in the myddes of the Water in token of greate myrecle. and also in that flom Naaman of Surry bathed hym that was a mesell and he was hole. and a lytell thefro is the cyte of hay. the Whych Iosue assayled and toke. Also in the Flom Iordan is the vale of Mambre. that is a fayre vale and a plenteuous.

ANd ye shall understonde that for to go fro the ded see afterwarde oute of the Marche of the lond of promyssion is a stronge castell that men call Carras/ or Sermoys. That is to say Reale mount in frenche.

This castell dyd make a kynge of fraunce that men callyd Baudewyn that had conqueryd all that Londe/ and put it into crysten mennys handes to kepe and under that castell is a fayre towne that men call Sabaoth. theraboute dwell many cristen men under trybute. And than go men to Nazareth of the whyche oure lorde hadde hys name/ ¶ And from Ierusalem unto Na arethe† is thre [d2ᵛ] Iornes. Men go thoroughe the provynce of Galyle thorough Ramatha thorough Sophym and thoroughe the highe hyll of Effraym where/ Anna Samuel/ Moder the prophete dwellyd and there was the prophete borne/ and after his dethe he was graven at mount Ioy/ as I have sayde/ And after came men to Sybola where the Arke of god was kepte under Hely the prophete. There made the folke of Ebron their sacrafyce to oure lord and there spake oure lorde first unto Samuel and there mynystred god the sacrament/ and there nere at the lyft syde is Gabaon and rama beniamin of the whyche holy wryte spekethe. And than come men to Sychem/ that somme men callyd Sicar. This is in provynce of Samarytanes. And there was somtyme a churche/ but it was cast downe and it is a fayre vale and plenteuous. and there is a gode cyte that men call Neople. and from thens is a dayes iourney to Ierusalem/ there is the well where oure lorde spake to the woman Samaritane. Sychem is ten myle fro Ierusalem and it is callyd. Neople that is to say the newe towne. and there nere is the temple Ioseph Iacob son that governed Egypt fro thens were his bones brought and layde in that temple and theder came Iewes oft in pylgrymage with greate devocion/ and in that cyte was Iacobs doughter ravysshed. For whan hir brother slewe many men. And there nere is the Cyte of Garryson where the Samarytans make that sacryfice.

On this hyll wolde Abraham have sacrifyed his sonne Isaac. and there nere is the vale of Dotaym. and theere is the Cesterne where Ioseph was casten of his brethern before that they solde hym. and it is two myle to Sycar [d3ʳ] fro thens men come to Samary. that men call Sebast. and that is cheef cyte of that countre. and of that cyte were the xii. kyndnes of Israel. but it is nat so greate as it was. There was saynt Iohn graven betwene two prophetes Helyseus and Abdon but he was heded in the castell of Makaryn besyde the dedde se. and he was translated of his disciples and graven at Samary but there dyd Iulius apostata take his bones and bren theym for he was that tyme emperour/ but the fynger with the whyche he shewed oure lorde: saynge. Ecce agnus dei [John 1:29]. That is to sayde. beholde the lambe of god. myght nat be brente. and saynt Tecle the virgyn dyd seynt Iohns hedde the baptyst be closed in a wall. but the emperoure Theosody dyd take it oute. and he fonde it lappyd in a clothe all blody/ and so he dyd bere it to Constantynoble and there is yet the one halfe of the hede/ and the other is at Rome. in the churche of saynt Sylvester..† and the vessell in the whiche the hede was layde whan it was smytten of is at Geene/ and men of geen do it greate worshype. Some say that saynt Iohns hede is at Ameas in pycardy/ and somme say it is saynt Iohns hede the bysshop. I Wote nat but god wote. From Sebast to Ierusalem is xii. myle. and betwene the hylles of countrees is a welle that men call Fons Iacob that is to say Iacobs Well that chaunged foure tymes in the yere his Coloure. for somtyme it Was redde and somtyme clere somtyme thycke and men that dwell there are called Samaritans. and they Were converted thorough the apostles/ and their lawe varyeth from crysten lawe and sarasyns lawe also. and fro Iewes. and paynymes that they trowe well in one god that [d ii] [d3ᵛ] all shall deme. and they trowe the byble after the letter and they lappe their hedes en redde lynnen clothe for difference of other. for sarasyns lappe their hedes in whyte clothe/ and crysten men that dwell there in blewe cloth or blo. And Iewes in yelowe And in this countre dwelle many Iewes paynge tribute as cᵣysten men done. and if they woll wete the letter

The Hebrew Alphabet

of the Iewes they ar suche/ and the names of their letters as they call them. Alpha. for a beth. for b. gimel. c. he. d. van. e. zay. f. ex. g. ioth. i. karph. k. lamp. l. men. m. sameth. o. ey. p. phe. q. lad. r. coth. s. fir. t. soun. v. than. x. lours. y. Nowe shall ye have the fygures.∵ 𝔇𝔦𝔭𝔥 𝔱𝔰 𝔇 𝔈 𝔖 𝔦𝔫𝔥 𝔎

Cotton ch. 13

𝔑/ 𝔣𝔠𝔤𝔥𝔫𝔡𝔦𝔈.¹² ≠ ¶ And fro thst countre that I have spoken of. men go to the playns of Galyle. and leve the hylles at the one syde. and Galyle is of the provynce of the londe of promyssion/ and in that provynce is the lond of Naym and Capharnaym and Corosaym/ and at besayda was saynt Petyr and saynt Andrewe borne. of Corosaym shall antecryst be borne/ and as somme say he shalbe born in babylony. Therfore sayth the prophete. ¶ De babilonia columba exiet que totum mundum devorabit.¹³ That is to say. Of babylon shall a dowve come oute that shall devoure all the Worlde. And this antecryst shalbe norysshed in Besayda and he shall regne in Corosaym. and therfore sayth holy wryt

---

¹² The line breaks, in Pynson's edition, between 𝔑 and 𝔣 in the list of Hebrew letters. The slash may be meant merely as a hyphen, or may be part of the alphabet.

¹³ *Columba*: dove is apparently an error for the more usual *coluber*: serpent. The passage may refer loosely to Genesis 49: 17 or, as Hamelius suggests, it may be a piece of anti-Papal sentiment current at the time: "the Roman Church . . . was by heterodox sects in the Middle Ages called the impure Babylon of Revelation" (*Mandeville's Travels*, 2: 74n).

thus. Ue tibi corosaym. Ue tibi Besayda [Matthew 11:21; Luke 10:13]. That is to say. wo be to the corosaym. Woo be to the Bsayda. and the Chan of galyle also is there foure myle from Nazareth. Of that cyte was the woman of chananee of whom the gospell speketh/ and there oure lorde dyd the fyrst myracle at the weddynge of Archetryclyne [d4ʳ] Whan he converted water into wyne. And fro thens men go unto Nazareth that was somtyme a greate cyte. but nowe is there but a lytell towne/ and it is nat wallyd. and there Was oure lady borne: the name toke oure lorde of this cyte/ but oure lady was goten at Ierusalem. at Nazareth toke Ioseph oure lady to wyfe. whan she was of xiiii. yere of age. and there the aungell salued hir sayng Ave maria gratia plena dominus tecum [Luke 1:28].[14] That is to say heyle mary full of grace lorde be with the. and there was somtyme a greate churche. and nowe is there but a lytell closet to resceyve the offerynges of pylgrymes. and there is the well of gabryell where oure lorde was wonte to bathe hym whan he was lytell at Nazareth was oure lorde norysshed. And Nazareth is to say. floure of gardeyne. and it may well be called so. for there was norysshed the floure of lyfe that Was oure lorde Iesu cryst. At halfe a myle from Nazareth is the blode of oure lorde. for the Iewes ledde hym upon an highe roche to cast hym down and slee hym/ but Iesu cryst passed thorough theym and lepe on a roche where his steppes are yet sene. and therfore say somme whan they drede theym of theves or ellys of ennemyes. they say thus. Iesus autem transiens per medium illorum ibat [Luke 4:30]. And they say also these verses of the saulter. thre tymes. Irruat super eos formido et pavor in magnitudine brachii tui. Domine fiant immobiles quasi lapis donec pertranseat populus tuus domine et populus iste quem redemisti.[15]

¶ And so whan all this is sayde a man may goo wythoute any lettynge. ¶ And also ye shall understonde and knowe that oure blessed lady bare chylde whan she was [d4ᵛ] of xv yere of age. and she lyved with hym xxxii. yere. and thre monethes. and after his passyon she lyved xxii. yere. And from Nazarethe to mount Thabor is thre myle. and there oure lorde

---

[14] With the addition of "maria."
[15] Not from the psalter, but from Exodus 15:16.

transfured hym before seynt Peter saynt John and saynte Iame. and there they sawe goostly oure lorde and moyses and Hely the prophetys.

And therfore sayde saynt Peter Bonum est hic esse faciamus tria tabernacula [Matthew 17:4; Mark 9:4-5; Luke 9:33] etcetera. That is to say. It is gode to be her.e† make we thre tabernacles. and oure lord iesu cryst badde that they shulde say it to noo man unto the tyme that he was rysen from dethe unto lyfe. and upon the same hyll shall foure aungellys sowne theyr trompettes. and reyse all men that are dede unto lyfe. and than shall come in body and soule unto the Iugement. but the Iugement shalbe in the vale of Iosaphat on pase day. at suche tyme as oure lorde rose from deth to lyfe. And also a myle from mount Thabor is the mount Ermen. and there was the cyte of Namy. before the gates of that cyte oure lorde raysed the Wydowes son that hadd nomore chyldren. and from thens men go to a cyte that men calle Tyborne that syttethe on the see. of Galyle. and all if it be called the see Galyle. it is no see ne arme of the See for it is but a staumble of fresshe Water. and it is more than a hundred forlonges longe and fourty brode. and therin is many gode fysshes. and on the same see/ but chaungeth the name after cytees that stande therupon yode oure lorde dryefote/ and there sayde he to petyr whan he came on the water and was nere drownyd. Modice fidei quare dubitasti [Matthew 14:31]. That is to say Thou of lytell trowthe. why haddest thou doute. In this cyte of Tyborne is the [d5ʳ] table that cryste ete of with his discyples after his resurrection/ and they knewe hym in brekynge of brede as holy writte saythe. ¶ Et cognoverunt eum in fractione panis [Luke 24:35]. That is to say they knewe hym by brekynge of brede. And ye shall understande that Flom Iardon begynnethe under the hyll of Lyban/ and there begynnethe the londe of promyssion and it lasteth unto Bersabe of lengthe to go towarde the Northe and the southe. and in brede it holdeth ix. score myle. and of brede from Ierico unto Iaffe it is fourty myle: ¶ And ye shall understond that the londe of Promyssion is in the kyngdom of Surrey. and it lastethe unto the wyldernesse of Araby. And I do you to wete that amonge the Sarasyns in many places dwell crysten men under tribute and they are in dyverse maners/ and dyvers maners of monkes/ and they ar all crnstened†/ and have dyverse lawes/ But they all trowe Well in oure lorde god the fader and in the son/ and in the holy goost. but yet they

Jacobite Christians

fayle in the articles of oure feyth And they are callyd Iacobynes. For saynt Iames converted theym to the feyth. and saynt Iohn baptysed them And they say that men shall only shryve theym unto god and nat unto man. for they say that god badde nat man shryve hym unto another man. And therfore sythe Da[16] in the sauter in this maner of wyse

¶ Confitebor tibi domine in toto corde meo [cf. Psalm 9:1; Psalm 111:1] etcetera.

That is to say in englysshe. Lorde I shall shryve me unto the in all myn herte. ¶ And in another place he saythe thus ¶ Delictum meum cognitum tibi feci [Psalm 32:5]. ¶ That is for to say. My trespas I have made knowen unto the And in another place. ¶ Deus meus es tu et confitebor [d5ᵛ] tibi [cf. Psalm 118:28]. That is to say thou art my god and I shall be shryven of the. and in another place. Quoniam cogitatio hominis confitebitur tibi [cf. Psalm 94:11]. That is to say. For thoughte of man shalbe shryven to the. and they can well the byble. and the sauter. but they legge it nat in laten. but in their owne langage. and sayth that David and other prophetes say it. But saynt Austen and gregory say. Qui scelera sua cogitat et conversus fuerit veniam sibi credat.

That is to say. Who so knowe his synne/ and turned/ he may trowe to have forgyvenesse. and saynt gregory saythe thys Dominus pocius mentem quam verba considerat. That is to say. oure lorde takethe more kepe to thoughte than to worde..† And Hyllary sayth. Longorum temporum crimina ictu oculi perient si corde nata fuerit temptatio.[17]

That is to say. Synnes that are done of olde tyme shal perysshe in twynkelynge of an iye if despysinge of them be borne in a mannys herte. and thus say they. Men shall shryve theym to god all only by theyse auctorytees. And this was the shryft in the first tyme. But saynt Peter/ and the apostles and popes that came sythen have ordeyned/ that men shall shryve theym to prestes: men as they are. and this is their skyll. For they say that a man that hath a sykenesse/ men

---

[16] "Da" appears at the end of a line, with the broken slash Pynson uses as a hyphen, but the name (David) is not completed on the following line.

[17] The words of Augustine, Gregory, and Hilary here are generally supposed to stem from Jacques de Vitry's account of the Jacobites, but the reference is unclear. There may also be a connection to Hayton the Armenian, ch. 14. Albert Bovenschen (262n) annotates this passage comprehensively.

may gyve hym no gode medycyne. but they knowe the kynde of the sykenesse. and so say they a man may gyve no covenable penaunce. but if he knowethe and understonde the synne. For there is a maner of synne that is grevouser to a man than too a nother. and And† therfore it is nedefull that a man knowe and understonde the kynde of synne. ¶ And therfore is other men that men call Surryens. they helde the lawe of Grece/ [d6ʳ] and they have longe beerdys. and there is other that men call Georgyens whom saynt George convertedde. and they do more worshyp to halowes of heven than other do and they have theyr crownes shaven. The clerkes have rounde crownes. and lewde men have crownes square And they holde the lawe of Grekes/ and other is there that men call crysten men of gyrdinge/ for as moche as they were gyrdeles underneth. Som outher hatte Nestorynes somme aryens. somme Nubyens. som Gregours. som Indyns that are of the londe of Preter† Iohn. and everichone of these have somme articles of oure trouthe. But eche of theym vary from other. and of their variaunce were to moche for to tell

Cotton ch. 14

≠ NOwe syth I have tolde you of many maners of men that dwell in countrees before sayde. Nowe woll I turne ageyne to my way. For to turne upon this syde nowe he that Woll turne fro the londe of Galyle that I spake of. to come on this syde he shall go thorough damas that is a fayre cyte and full of goode marchaundyses/ and it is thre Iournes from the see/ and v. Iournes fro Ierusalem. but they cary marchaundyses upon Camelles/ Mules/ hors/ and Dromederies: and other maner of bestes. This cyte founded Helyseus Damaske. that was abrahams servaunt before that Iosyas was borne/ and he wenyd to have be abrams eyre and therfore he called that cyte after his name damas. In that place slowe Caym his brother Abel. And besyde damas is the mount of Syry. and in that cyte is many a physycien/ and that holy man saynt Poule was a phesycyen to save mennys [d6ᵛ] bodyes in hele. before that he was converted. and sythen he was a phesicyen of soules. and men come by a place fro Damas that is callyd Nostre dame de sardemarke. that is fyve myle from damas. and it is on a roche/ and there is a fayre churche and there dwell monkes and nonnes crysten in the churche. behynde the high auter. In the vale is a table of tree on the whyche the Image of oure lady was depeyntyd that many tymes was tourned into flesshe but the ymage is nowe sene but a lytell.

but ever more thorough grace of god the table droppeth oyle as it Were an Olyve. and there is a vessell of marble under the table to receyve the oyle. therof they gyve to pylgrymes for it heleth of many sykenesses/ and he that kepethe it clenly a yere. after the yere it turneth into flesshe and blode ¶ Betwene the cyte of Darke and the cyte of Raphane is a ryver that men call Sabatory. for on the saturday it renneth fast and all the weke ellys it standeth still and renneth nat/ or lytell: And there is another ryver that on the nyght freseth fast. and upon the day no frost is sene. And so goo men by a cyte that men call Beruch/ and there men gone into the see that shall go into cypre. and they arryve at port of Sur or of Thirry and than go men to cypre or ellys men go or may go from the port of Thirry right and come nat at cypre/ and arryve at som haven of Grece. and than come men in these countrees by wayes. that I have spoken of before

¶ Howe a man may go ferthest and lengest
in those countrees as herafter ben rehersed

Several Routes to Jerusalem

[d7ʳ] NOwe have I tolde you of weyes/ by the whyche men go ferthest and lengest as by Babylony/ and mounte Synay/ and other places many/ thoroughe the whiche londes men turne ageyne to the londe of promyssyon. ¶ Nowe wolle I tell you the wey to Ierusalem. For somme men woll nat passe it. somme for they have nat to spende. somme for they have no company/ and many other causes resonables. and therfore I shall tell you shortly howe a man may go with lytell costage and short tyme. A man that cometh from the londes of the weste he gothe thoroughe fraunce: burgoyne/ and lumbardy/ and to Venys/ or to Geene/ or som other haven/ of those marches and take there a shyp and go by see unto the Ile of Gryff/ and so arryveth he in Grece/ or ellys at port myroche/ or Valon/ or Duras/ or som other haven of those marches/ and go to londe for to rest hym/ and gothe ageyne to the see and arryveth in Cypre/ and comethe nat in the Ile of rodes/ and arryveth at Famagost that is the chef haven of Cypre or ellis at lamaton/ and than entre ship ageyne and passeth beside the haven of Tyre. and come nat to londe/ and so passeth he by all the havons of that cost unto he come to Iaffe that is the next haven to Ierusalem. for it is xxviii. myle betwene. And froo Iaffe men go to the cyte of Ramos/ and that is but litell thens and it is a fayre cyte/ and besyde Ramos is a fayre churche of oure lady where oure lorde shewed hym unto hyr in this lykenesse that betokened the trynite. And there nere is a churche of saynt George where his hede was smyten of. And than to the castell of Chmay/ and than unto mount Ioy: and fro thens pylgrymage to Ierusalem. [d7ᵛ] And than to mount Modyn and than to Ierusalem. At mount Modyn lyeth the prophete Machabe/ and over Ramatha is the towne of Donke Wherof Amos the prophete was.

For as moche as many men may nat suffre the savoure of the see. but is lever to go by lande if all it be more peyne. A man shall goo to one of the havens of lombardy as venys or another. and he shalpasse into grece to port myroche or another/ and shall go to Constantynople. and shall passe the water that is called the Brace of saynt george that is a an† arme of the see And from thens he shall come to pulverall/ and sithen to the castell of Synople. And fro thens shall he go unto Capadoce/ that is a greate countre Where is many grete hylles. and he shall go thorough Turky. and to the cyte of Nyke the whyche they wan fro the emperoure of constantynoble/ and it is a fayre cyte and well wallyd/ and there is a ryver that men call the lay. and there goo men by the alpes of Mormant. and by vales of Mallebriuz and the vale of Ernax. and so to antyoche the better/ that sytteth on the rychay. and theraboute is many good hylles and fayre and many fayre wodes and wylde bestis And he that woll go another way he gothe by the playnes of Romayn costande the romayn see. On that coste is a fayre castell that men call floraghe. And whanne a man is oute of the hylles he passethe thoroughe the cyte of Moryache and Artoyse where is a greate brydge upon the Ryver. of ferne that men call fassar. and it is a greate ryver beringe shyppes/ and besyde that cyte of Damas is [d8ʳ] a ryver that cometh fro the mount of Lybany that men call alban at passinge of this ryver saynt Eustache lost his two sonnes Whan he had lost his wyffe. and it goothe thoroughe the playne of archades. and so to the redde see. and so go men to the cyte of Phenne and so to the cyte of Ferne. And antyoche is a fayre cyte and well wallid for it is two myle longe. and at eche pylour of the brydge is a gode toure. This is the best cyte of the kyngdom of surry. Fro antyoche men shall go to the cyte of Locuth/ and than to Geeble. and than to Tortouse. And therby is the londe of Cambre where is a straunge castell that men call Manbek. And fro Tourtouse men go to trypelle on the see. and upon the see men go to Dacres. and there is two weyes to Ierusalem. on the lyft way men go first unto Damas by flom Iordan. on the right syde men go thoroughe the londe of Flagine/ and so to the Cyte of Cayphas/ of whiche Cayphas was lorde/ and somme calle it castell pellerinz/ and from thens it is foure dayes Iourne to Ierusalem. and they go thoroughe Cesary Phylyp and Iaffe and Rames and Emaux. and so to Ierusalem

NOwe have I tolde you somme wayes by londe/ and by water. howe men may go to Ierusalem. If all it be so that there be many other wayes that men goo by after countrees that they come fro. Nevertheles they turne all to one ende/ yet is there a wey all by londe too Ierusalem and passe no see from fraunce or flaunders but that wey is full longe and a perylous and of gret travayle/ and therfore fewe go that wey. he that shal go that wey he goth [d8ᵛ] thoroughe almaigne and Pruysse. and so unto Tartary This tartary is holden of the greate Cane of Whome I shall speke afterwarde/ for theder lasteth his lordshyppe And the lordes of this Tartary yelde hym Trybute. this is a full evyll londe and sondy and lytell frute berynge. for there groweth lytell goode of corne or wyne ne benes ne pesen. but bestes are there greate plente/ and therfore ete they but flesshe Withoute brede/ and they soupe the bret† and they drynke mylke of all maner of beestes. They ete cattes and all maner wylde bestes/ Ratons and myce/ and they have lytell wode/ and therfore they dight their mete with hors mylke and other bestes Whan it is drye. Prynces and other lordes ete but ones on the day/ and right lytell and they be right foule folke and of evyll kynde and in somer there is many tempestis and thundres that sleth many folk and bestes and right sodeynly is it there greate colde and as sodeynly is it right hote. The prynce that governeth that londe that they call Raco dwelleth at a cyte that men call Orda and forsoth there woll no gode man dwell in that londe for it is gode to sowe in thornes and wedes/ and other gode none as I herde say for I was nat that wey but I have ben in other londes marchynge theron/ as the lond of Rossye and Nyflande/ and the kyngdom of Grecon/ and lectowe. and the kyngdom of Graften and many other places but I Went never that wey to Ierusalem. and therfore I may nat Well tell it. for

I have understonde that men may nat well goo that wey/ but in wynter for Waters and marrays that are there that a man may nat passe but he have frost right harde and fast snowynge above. for were nat the snowe there myght no man go

[e1ʳ] And ye shall understonde that a man shall go thre iournes fro Pruysse to passe this Wey tyll he come to the londe of Sarrasyns that men dwell in. And all if it be that crysten men every yere passe there they cary their vetayle With theym. for they shulde fynde no thynge there. but a maner of thynge that they call Soleys/ and they cary/ their vytalles upon the yce on sledes and chariettes with oute wheles. and as longe as their vetels last they may dwell there/ but no lenger. And whan spyes of the countre see cristen men come they renne to the townes and cry right loude. kera kera kera. and as sone they kepe theym And ye shall understonde that the frost that there is and the yce is harder there than here. and every man hathe a stewe in his house. and therin ete they and done all thynges that they may..† and that is at northe syde of the world Where it is comonly colde. for the sonne commeth/ ne shynethe but a lytell in that countre/ and that londe is in som place so colde that there may no man dwell. And on the southe syde of the worlde is in som place so hote that there may no man dwell for the sonne gyveth so greate hete in those countrees

Cotton
ch. 15

Beliefs of
the Saracens

≠ For as moche as I have tolde you of the Sarasyns and of their lawes. If ye woll I shall tel you a party of their lawe and of their trouthe. after their boke that they call alkaron sayth somme call that boke Mesap. som harme in diverse langage of countrees the which boke machomete gave theym in the whyche he wrote amonge orher† thynges as I have oft redde and sene that they that are gode shall go to paradyse.

and the evyll to hell/ and that trowe all sarasynes and if [e i] [e1ᵛ] a man aske of what paradyse they mene/ they say it is a place of delyces where a man shall fynde all maner of frutes in all tymes and waters and ryvers rennynge with mylke and hony/ Wyne and fresshe water/ and they shal have fayre houses and gode as they have deserved. And those howses ar made of precious stones gold and silver and every man shall have x. wyves and all maydens. and he shall every day ones have to doo with theym and shall evermore be maydens. Also they speke oft and trowe of the virgyn mary and say of the Incarnacion that mary was lerned of aungellis/ and that Gabryell sayde to hir that she was chosen before all other fro the begynnynge of the worlde/ and that wytnesseth well their boke.

And that Gabryell tolde hir of the incarnacion of Ihesu cryst. and that she conceyved and bare a chylde mayden. And they say/ that cryst spake as sone as he was korne.† and that he was a very and a holy prophete in word and dede/ and meke and rightwys to all/ and wythoute any Wyte. And they say that whan the aungell sayde hyr of the Incarnacyon she hadde grete drede for she was right yonge. And there was one in that countre that medlyd with sorcery/ that men called Takyna that with enchauntmentes coude make hym lyke an aungell/ and he wente oft and lay with maydens/ and therfore was mary ferd for the aungell and wenyd in hir mynde that it hadde be Takyna that wente with the maydens: and she coniured hym that he shulde say unto hir/ if he was that eche Takyna. and the aungell badde hyr have noo drede/ for he was certeyne messenger of Iesu cryst.

[e2ʳ] ¶ Also their boke sayth she hadde chylde under a Palme and than was she shamed/ and grete/ and sayde/ that she Wolde be dede. and as sone the chylde spake and conforted hir and sayde to mary. Ne timeas maria [cf. Luke 1:30]. That is to say. Be nat adred mary. and in many other steddes sayth their boke alkaron. that Iesu crist spake as sone as he was borne. and the boke sayth that Iesu crist was sente fro god almyghty to be ensample to all men and that god shall deme all men/ the gode to heven and the wycked to hell and that Iesu cryst is the best prophete of all other/ and nerest to god/ and that he was very prophete that gave the blynde syght and helyd mesellis and reysed dedde men and went all quycke to heven. and if they may fynde a boke with gospellis and namely Missus est angelus [Luke 1:26]. they do it greate worshyp/ they fast a monethe in the yere. and they ete nat but on the nyghtys/ and than they kepe theym fro their wyves/ but they that are seke ar nat constreyned to that. And that boke speketh of Iewes/ and sayth they ar wycked folke for they woll nat trowe that Iesu crist is of god. and they say that the Iewes lye on oure lady/ and hyr son Iesu cryst saynge that they dydde hym nat on crosse. and for sarrasyns trowe so nere oure feyth/ they are lyghtly converted whanne men preche the lawe of Iesu cryst/ and they say they wote wele by their prophesies that their lawe of machomete shall fayle as doth the lawe of Iewes. and that cristen mens lawe shal last unto the worldes ende.

¶ And if a man aske theym wherin they trowe. and they say that they trowe in god almyghty the whych is maker of heven/ and of erthe/ and other thynges. And withoute [e2ᵛ] hym is no thinge done/ and the day of dome when every man shalbe rewarded after his desert/ and that all thynge is soth that cryst sayde thorough mouthes of his prophetes. Also Machomete bad in his alkaron that ylke man shulde have two wyves or thre or foure. but nowe take they nyne. and as many lemmans as theym lyke. and if any of their wyves do amys ageyne their husbondes. he may dryve hir oute of his house/ and another but hym behoveth yeve hir of his goodes. Also Where men speke of the fader and son and holy goost. they say that they are. thre persones and nat one god. For their alkaron spekethe nat therof/ ne of the trynite. but they say that god spake or elles was he domme. And god hath a goost or elles were he nat in lyve. and they say that goddes worde hath a greate strength. and so sayth their alkaron. and they say that abraham and moyses were well wyth god for they spake with hym/ and Machomete was right messanger of god. and they have many gode articles of oure feythe And those that understande the scriptures and prophesyes for they have theym. And the gospell and the byble is wreten in their langage/ and so wote they well of holy writ but they understonde it nat. but after the letter and so do the Iewes/ for they understonde nat the letter gostly. and therfore sayth saynt poule. Littera occidit spiritus autem vivificat [2 Corinthians 3:6]. That is to say. Letter sleeth/ and gost maketh quycke. And the sarrasyns say that the Iewes ar wiked for they kepe nat the lawe of Moyses/ the which he toke to theym. And also crysten men ar yll. for they kepe natt the commaundementis of the gaspellys that Iesu Cryste sent unto theym. And therfore I shall telle you that the [e3ʳ] that the† soudan tolde me upon a day in his chaumber he dyd voyde oute all maner of men/ lordes/ knyghtys/ and other and for he wolde speke with me in counseyle. and he asked me howe crysten men governed theym in oure countre. and I sayde to hym right well thanked be god and he sayde sykerly nay/ for he sayde oure prestis made no force of goddis servyce. for they shulde gyve ensaumple to men to do well and they gyve yll ensample. And therfore when the people shulde go on the

The Sultan's Speech

holy day unto the church to serve god. they go to taverne to be in gloteny all the day/ and the nyght/ and ete and drynke as beestes that wote nat whan they have Inough. and also crysten men he sayde aforsed theym to fight samen/ and everychon to begyle other/ and also they are so proude that they Wote nat howe they may cloth theym/ nowe longe nowe short nowe streyte/ nowe wyde/ on all maner of wyse. They shulde he sayde be symple/ meke and sothefast and do almes as iesu cryst dyd in whom they trowe. And they are he sayde to covetous that for a lytell sylver they sell their chyldren theyr susters and theyr wyves/ and one takethe another mannys wife and none holdeth his feyth to other And therfore sayde he For their synnes hathe god gyven these londes to oure handes/ and nat thorough oure strengthe/ but all for your synnes/ For we wote well forsothe whan ye serve well youre god that he woll helpe you so that no man shall wynne ageyne the londe whan they serve their god well. but while they lyve so fouly as they do. we have no drede of theym/ for their god shall nat helpe them. and than I asked hym howe he knewe the state of crysten men so. and he sayde that he knewe well both of [e ii] [e3ᵛ] lordes and of comons by his messangers which he sente thorough all countrees as it were marchauntis with precious stones and other marchaundises to knowe the maner of every countre. And than he dydde call ageyne all the lordes into the chamber/ and than he shewed me. iiii. that were greate Lordes in that countre that devysed me my countre and other as in cristendome all as they hadde be men of the same countre/ and they spake french right well and the soudan also. And than had I greate marvayle of this great sclaunder of our feyth. and so they that shulde be tourned by oure goode ensaumples to the feyth of Iesu cryst/ they are drawen awey thorowe oure evyll lyvynge. and therfore it is no wonder if they calle us evyll/ for they say sothe/ but the sarrasyns are trewe for they kepe truly the commaundementes of their alkaron that god sent theym by his messangere Machomete/ too Whom they say seynt gabryell the aungell spake oft and sayde hym the wyll of god. And ye shall understond that Machomete was borne in Araby/ and he was first a pore knave and kept horse and went after marchaundyse. And so he cam ones into Egypt with marchaundise and Egypt was that tyme crysten/ and there was a chapelle besyde araby and there was an Eremyte/ and whan he come into the chapell that was but a lytell house/ and a lowe/ assone the entre began to be as greate as it were of a paleys gate/ and that was the fyrste myracle that the sarrasyns say that he dyd in his youthe. After began Machomete to be wyse and ryche. and he was a great Astronomer/ and sythen was he keper of the londe of the prynce Corodan and governed it full well/ in the whych maner [e4^r] that whan the prynce was dede. he weddyd the lady that men called Quadryge. And Machomete fell oft in the fallynge evyll. wherfore the lady was wrothe. that she had taken hym to hir husbonde and he made hir to understonde that every tyme that he fell so. he sayde that gabryell the aungell spake to hym/ and for the great brightnes of the aungell he fell downe. This Machomete regned in araby the yere of oure lorde. syx hundred xx. and he was of the kynde of Dysmael that was abrahams son. that he gate of Agar and other ar properly called Sarrasyns of Sarra/ but somme are called Moabites/ and som amonites after two sonnes of Loth. And also Machomete loved well a gode man an heremyte that dwellyd in wyldernesse a myle from mount Synay. in the wey as men go fro araby to Caldee and ynde a dayes iourne fro the se where marchauntes of Venys came. and machomete went so oft to this heremyte that all his men were Wroth for he hard gladly the heremyte preche/ and dyd his men wake all the nyght. and hys men thoughte they wolde this heremyte were dedde. So it befel on a night that Machomete was full dronken of gode wyne and he fell in slepe/ and his men toke Machometes swerde out of his shethe whyles he lay and slepte. and therwyth they slewe the heremyte. and afterwarde they put the swerde up ageyne all blody. And upon the morowe Whan they fonde thys heremyte thus dedde/ he was in his mynde very angry and right wroth/ and wolde have done his men unto the deth/ but they all with one accorde and with one wylle/ sayde that he hym selfe hadde slayne hym Whan he was dronken. And they shewed hym his owne swerd [e4^v] All blody and than trowed he they sayde sothe/ and than he cursed the wyne and all those that droken† it. And therfore sarrasyns that ar devoute drynke no wyne openly. they shalbe reproved but they drynke gode beverage and swete and norysshynge that is made of Calamels/ therof is sugour made. Also it befalleth somtyme that crysten men became sarrasyns/ outher thorough poverte or symplenesse or wyckednesse. And therfore larcheslevyn whan he receveth theym seyth thus. Laeles ella Machomete ro cs† ella.

THE PYNSON EDITION 45

That is to say. There is no god but one and machomete his messanger. And sythen I have told you a party of their lawe and of their customes I shall say you of their letters. that they have with their names First they have for A almoy beth-ath for b cathi c ephoti for d delphoy e fothy f garophin g hechun h iocchi i kathi. k lothnn l malach m nahalot n or-thy o. choziri p zoth q. rutholat r routht s solathi t chatimus v yrithom x mazot ȝ zatepin ⁊ iohetus ₉ these are the names. These foure letters they have yet more for diversite of their langage for as moche as they spake so in their throtes as we have A in oure langage and speke in englond Two letters may than they have in their abc. That is to say y and ȝ the Which are called thorn and zowx[18]

Cotton ch. 16

≠ ANd sythen I have devysed before of the holy londe and countrees theraboute and many wayes theder/ and to mounte Synay to Babilon. and other places of the whyche I have spoken.

¶ Nowe I woll tell and speke of yles/ and of dyverse [e5ʳ] bestes and dyvers folke/ for in those countres is many divers folke. and countres that are departed by the fowre flodes that came oute of paradyse terrestre. For Mesopotany and the kyng-dom of Caldee and araby ar betwene two flodes Tygre and Eufrate. And the kyngdom of Mydy and Perse ar betwene two flodes Tigre and Nyke† and the kyngdome of Surrey and Palastyne/ and Fnnes† ar betwene Eufrate and the see medi-teran/ and it is of length from Maroch on the se of Spayne unto the greate se/ and so lasteth it beyonde Constantynople. thre thousand and fourty myle of lombardy. And to the oc-cean see in ynde is the kyngdom of Sychy. that is alle closed amonge hylles and ye shall understonde that in tho countres ar many yles and londes of the whyche it were to moche to tell all: but of somme I shall speke more pleynely afterward. Fer he that woll go to Tartary or persy or Caldee/ or ynde. he entrethe the see at Geene or Venyse or at another haven and so passeth by the see and arryveth at Trapazonde that is a gode cyte. that somtyme. men called le port de pounce. There

---

[18] The sign used for "zatepin" here is the sign Pynson uses for "and" throughout the edition. The subscript "9" for "iohetus" is, in superscript, the common abbreviation for "-us" at the ends of words. The figure 3 here is used, rather confusingly, both for the Hebrew letter "mazot" and for the English letter yogh, which Hebrew is said not to include.

is the kyngdome of persans and Medoyns and other marches
In this cyte lyeth saynt Athanas that was bisshop of Alysaunder that made the Psalme Quicunqz vult This man was a
greate Doctoure of divinyte/ and of the godhede/ he was accused unto the pope of Rome that he was an heretyke

Saint
Athanasius

And the Pope sent for hym and put hym into pryson and
whyle he was in that same pryson he made this Psalme and
sent it unto the pope/ and sayde if that he was heretyke than
were that heresy/ for that was his trouth and his byleve And
whan the Pope sawe that he sayde. therin was [e5ᵛ] all oure
feyth. anone he dyd delyver hym oute of pryson. And he commaunded that psalme to be sayde every day at pryme and so he
helde athanas for a goode crysten man: but he Wolde never
go unto his bysshopryche for they accused hym of heresy.

¶ Topazonde Was somtyme holden of the Emperour of
Constantynople/ but a great man that he sent to kepe that
countre ageyne the Turkes/ and helde it too hym selfe and
called hym selfe Emperoure of Topazonde.

The Castle
of the
Sparrowhawk

¶ And from thens men go thoroughe lytell armony In that
countre is an olde castell that is on a Roche that men call
the castell of Spernere. and there men fynde an hawke syt-
tynge upon a perke ryght well made/ and a fayre lady of fary
that kepeth it.

¶ And he that woll wake this same hauke seven dayes/
and seven nyghtis. and somme say that it is but thre dayes
and thre nyghtes. alone withyouten any companye/ and wythouten slepe. This fayre lady shall come unto hym at the sev-
en dayes/ or thre dayes ende. and shall graunte unto hym the
fyrste thynge that he woll aske of worldly thynges. and that
hath oft be proved.

¶ And so upon a tyme it befell that a man whyche that
tyme was kynge of Ermony that was a ryght doughty man
waked upon a tyme. and at the seven dayes ende/ the lady
cam unto hym/ and bad hym aske what he wold for he hadde
wele done his devoure/ And the kynge answered and sayde
that he was a greate lorde and in gode peas/ and he was
ryche so that he wolde aske no thynge but all only the body
of the fayre lady to have his wyll of hir. ¶ Than this fayre-
lady† answered/ and sayde to [e6ʳ] hym that he was a fole for
he wist nat what he asked for he myght nat have hir/ for he
shuld nat aske but worldly thynge and she was nat worldly
and the kynge sayde he wold nought ellys. and she sayde to
hym syth he wold nat ellys aske she shulde graunt hym soure

thynge and to al that came after hym/ and sayde unto hym. Syr kynge ye shall have warre withoute peas alwey unto the ix. degre: and ye shalbe in subiection of youre ennemyes/ and ye shall have greate nede of gode and catell. and sythen that tyme all the kynges of Ermony have ben in warre/ and nedefull and under tribute of sarrasyns. Also a pore mans sons woke the a† tyme/ and asked the lady that he myght be ryche and happy in marchaundyse/ and the lady graunted hym. but she sayde hym that he had asked his undoynge. for greate pryde that he shulde have therof. But he that shall wake hathe nede to kepe hym from slepe. for if he slepe he is lost that he shall never be sene. but that is nat the right wey. but for the mervayle. And from Topazonde men go to greate armony to a cyte that men call Artyron that was wonte to be a gode cyte. but turkes have destroied it. for there neyther groweth no wyne ne frute. From this artyron men go to an hyll that is called Sabyssatoll. and there nere is a nother hylle that men calle ararach. but the Iewes calle it Thano where Archa Noe rested/ and yet is on that hyll/ a man may se it fro ferre in clere weder/ and the hyll is twelve myle of heyght/ and somme say they have be there at. and put their fyngers in the holes where the fends[19] went oute whanne Noe sayde in this maner of wyse. Benedicyte.

But they note well for no man may go on that hyll for [e6ᵛ] Snowe that is alwey upon that hylle both Wynter/ and somer. that no man may go up and never yode syth Noe was. A monke thoroughe grace of god brought a planke that is yet at the abbey at the hyll fote/ and he had greate desyre to go upon that hyll/ and aforsed hym therto/ and whan he was at the thyrd part upward he was so wery that he myght no ferther and he rested him and slept and whan he awoke than he was downe at the hill fote and than prayde he to god devoutly that he wolde suffre hym go upon the hyll. and the aungell sayd unto hym that he shulde go upon the hyll/ and so he dyd. and sythen that tyme noo man came there. And therfore men shall nat trowe suche wordes. And fro thens men go to a cyte that is called Tanziro/ and that is a fayre cyte and gode. Besyde that cyte is an hill of salt/ and therof eche man take what he woll. there dwell many crysten men

---

[19] Possibly "fende." The letter is difficult to discern.

under trybute of Sarrasyns. fro thens men go by many townes and castellys and many towarde ynde. and come to a cyte that men call Cassage that is a fayre Cyte. and there met the thre kynges togeder that went to make present to oure lorde in Bethelem. fro that cyte men goo to a cyte that men calle Cardabago. and Paynemes say that crysten men may nat dwell there but they dye sone and they wote nat the cause. And from thens men go thorugh many countrees cytes and townes that were to longe to tell/ to the cyte of Carnaa that was wont to be so great that the wall aboute was of xxv. myle/ the Walle sheweth yet. but it is nat nowe in habyte with men. and there endeth the londe of the emperoure of Percy:

Cotton ch. 17

≠ On the other syde of that cyte of Carnaa men entre into the [e7ʳ] londe of Iob. that is a gode londe and greate plente of all frutes/ and men call that londe the londe of Swere In this lond is the cyte of Thomar. Iob was a paynym and also he was Cofraas son/ and he helde the Londe as prynce therof/ and he was so ryche that he knewe nat the hundreth of his gode. and after his povert god made hym rycher than he was before. For after he was kynge of Idumea: and sithen kinge of ysan. and whan he was kynge he was callyd Iobab and in that kyngdom he lyved Clxx yere/ and so he was of age whan he dyed ccxlviii. in the londe of Iob is no defaute of no thynge that is nedefull to a mannys body. There ben hylles where men fynde manna. and manna is called aungellys bredde that is a white thinge right swete and moch swetter than sugoure or hony. and that cometh of the dewe of heven/ that falleth on the herbes/ and there is† coagles and wex whyte and men do it in medecynes. for riche men. Thys londe marcheth to the londe of Caldee that is a gret londe. and there is full fayre folke and well apeyraled and women ar right layth and evyll cladde and they go bare fote/ and bere a yll cote large wyde and shorte unto the kne: and longe sloves downe to the fote/ and they have great here/ and longe hyngynge aboute their shulders. After the lond of Caldee is the londe of Amo-

The Amazons

sony that is a londe where is no man but all women as men say. for they woll suffre no man lyve amonge theym ne to have lordspyp† of theym. For somtyme was a kynge in that londe and men were dwellynge there as dyd in other countrees. and had wyves/ and it befell that the kynge had a gret warre with theym of Sychy and he was called Solopenco/ and [e7ᵛ] he was slayne in batayle/ and all the gode blode of hys londe. And this quene whan she herde that/ and other ladyes of that londe that the kynge and the lordes were slayn they gadred theym togeder and slowghe all the men that were left in their londe amonge theym/ and sithen that tyme dwelled no man amonge them. And whan they woll have any man to ly by theym they sende for theym into a countre that is nere to their londe/ and the men come and ar there viii. dayes or as the woman lykes and than goo they ageyne. and if they have men chyldren/ they sende theym to their faders whan they can ete and goo. and if they have mayde chyldren they kepe theym and if they be of gentyll blode they brenne the left pappe away for berynge of a shelde. and if they be of lytell blode they bren the right pappe away for shotynge. For those women of that countre ar gode warreours and ar oft in sonde with other lordes/ and the quene of that londe governeth well that londe. This londe is all envyrond with water. Besyde Amozonde is the londe that† turmagute that is a gode londe and profitable. And for goodnesse of that lond kynge Alysaunder dyd make a cyte there that he calledde alysaunder/ On the other syde of Caldee toward the southe syde is Ethyops a greate londe In this londe on the southe ar the folke right blacke. In that syde is a well that on the day the water is so colde that no man may drynk therof. and on the night it is so hote that no man may suffre to put his hande in it. In this londe the ryvers and al the waters ar trobolous and somdell salt for the grete hete. And men of that londe are lightly dronken and/ have lytell appetyte to mete/ and they have comonly the flyx [e8ʳ] of body and they lyve nat longe. In Ethiope are suche men that hath but one fote. and they go so fast that it is a greate marveyle/ and that is a large fote that maketh shadowe and covereth the body fro the sonne and in ethyope is a cyte of Saba of the whiche one of the thre kynges that sought oure lorde was kynge.

FRo Ethyope men go into ynde thorough many divers countrees and it is called ynde the more. And it is departed in thre partyes that is to say. ynde the more that is a full hote londe/ and ynde the lesse is a temperet londe. and the third party that is towardys the northe. there is right colde. so that for greate colde/ and frost and yce the water becometh crystall. and upon that groweth the gode dyamande that is lyke a troble coloure and that dyamande is so harde that

Diamonds

no man may breke it Other dyamandes men fynde in Araby that are nat so gode that ar more nesshe. and somme are in Cypre/ and in Macydony men fynde also dyamandes. but the best are in ynde. And somme ar founde many tymes in a mas that cometh oute where men fynde golde fro the myne. whan men breke the masse in peces. and somtyme men fynde somme of gretnesse of a pese and somme lesse/ and those are as harde as those of ynde

And all if it be that men fynde good dyamandes in ynd upon the roche of crystall. also men fynde gode dyamandes upon the roche of adamande in the see. and on hylles as it Were hasyll nottes: and they ar all square and poynted of their owne kynde/ and they growe both togeder male and femmall and ar norysshed with the dewe of haven/ and they engender comonly and bringe forth smal childre that [e8^v] multyplye and grewe all the yeres. I have many tymes assayed that if a man kepe them with a litell of the roche and Wete theym with many dewes oft sythes they shalle growe ylke a yere. and the small shall wexe great/ and a man shall bere the deamand in his lyft syde/ and than is it of more vertue/ and for the strength of their growynge is towarde the northe/ that is the left syde as men of those countrees say. To hym that berethe the deamande upon hym it gyveth hym hardynes it kepeth his lymmes of his body/ it gyveth vyctory of ennemys if a mannys cause be right/ and hym that bereth it in gode wyll it kepeth hym fro strife fro ryot fro yll dremes/ and sorceryes and enchauntementes. Also no wylde best shall greve hym ne assayle hym. And also the Deamande shulde be gyven frely withouthoutent covetyse/ and byinge/ and than it is of more vertue. it heleth hym that is lunatyke. and that is travayled with a devyll. and if venym or poyson be brought in presence of the deamand as sone it moysteth and begynneth to wex swete. and men may wel polyce them to make men trowe that they may nat be polisshed But men may assay them well in this maner. first shere with theym in diverse precious stones as gasyrs/ or other upon crystalle/ and than men take a stone that is called adamande. upon that adamande and lyeth a nedyl before that adamand/ and if the dyamande be gode and vertuous the adamand draweth nat the nedyll to hym whyles the dyamande is there. And this is the prove that they beyonde the se make. but it falleth somtyme that the gode dyamande loseth his vertue thorough hym that bereth it/ and therfore it is nedefull to make it

THE PYNSON EDITION   51

Cotton
ch. 18

cover his vertue ageyne [f1ʳ] or ellys it is lytell of value/ and there is many other precious stones.[20] ≠ and it is called ynde/ In that water men fynde elys of xxx. fote lynge. and men that dwell nere that water ar of evyll coloure and yelowe and grene. In ynde is more than v thousande Iles that men dwel in goode and greate beside those that men dwelle nat in. And in echone of those is greate plente of cytes and moch folke/ for men of ynde ar of that condicion that they pas nat oute of their londe comonly/ for they dwell under a planet that is called Saturne/ and that planet makethe his cours by the xii. signes in xx. yere and the mone passeth thorough the xii. signes in a moneth. and for that Saturne is of so late sterynge/ therfore men that dwell under hym/ and in that Clymate have no goode wyll to be moche styrynge aboute. And in oure countre is a contrary for we ar in a clymate that is of the mone/ and of lyght styrynge and that is the planet of way. and therfore it gyveth us wyll to moche movynge and styringe and go in to dyvers countres of the worlde. for it gothe aboute the worlde more lightly than another planet doth. Also men passe thoroughe ynde by many countrees unto the greate see Occian. And than they fynde the yle of Hermes wheder marchauntes of Venys and of Geene and other partyes of crystendome come to bye marchaundyse. but it is so warme there in that yle that mens ballokes hange downe to ther shankes for the great dyssolvynge of the body/ And men of the countre that knowe the maner do bynde theym up full streyte and anoynte them with oyntementis made therfore for to hlde† theym up/ or ellys they myghte nat lyve. ¶ In this londe and many other. men/ and [f i] [f1ᵛ] women ley theym all naked in ryvers and waters from undren of the day to it be passed none. And they lye all in water but the face. for the greate hete that is there. In this yle are the shyppes withoute nayles of yron or bond for roches of adamonde that are in the See woll drawe shyppes to theym. Fro this Ile men go by see to the Ile of Cana where is greate plente of corne and of wyne/ and the kynge of this Ile was somtyme so myghty that he held warre with kynge alysaundre. Men of this yle have dyvers lawes. for som worshyp

---

[20] Something is apparently missing from the text here, although it is not lengthy—a matter of perhaps a line, introducing India.

the sonne/ som the fyre/ and som nedyrs/ som the trees/ som the first thynge they mete in the mornynge. and som worshyp simulacres and ydollis but bytwene simulacres and ydols is no difference/ For som sacres† are ymages made to lykenesse of what thynge a man woll that is nat kyndly/ for som ymage hathe thre hedes/ one of a man and an horse/ and an ox or any other best that no man hath sene. And ye shall understonde that they that worshyp symulacres they worshyp them for worthy men that were somtyme/ as hercules/ and other that dydde many marveyles in their tymes. For they say they wote well they are nat gode of kynde that made all thyng but that they are well With god. for the marvayles that they do/ and therfor they worshyp theym. And so say they of the son for it chaungeth oft the tymes somtyme gyvethe greate hete to norysshe all thynges on erthe And for it is so greate profyte they wote well it is nat gode. but it is well wyth godde and that god loveth it more than any other thynge. and therfore they say gode skyll to worshyp it. ¶ And so they make skylles of other planettes/ and of fyre also for it is so profitable and nedefull

[f2ʳ] ¶ And of ydols they say that the Oxe is the holyest best that they may fynd here in erthe and most profytable than any other. for he doth many goodes and none ylle. And they wote wele that it may nat be withoute specyall grace of god/ and therfore they make their god of an Oxe. the one halfe. and the other halfe a man for man is the fayrest and the best creature of the worlde. And they make worshyp to nedders and other bestes that they mete firste at morowe and namely those bestis that have goode metynge after whom they spede well all day: the whych they have proved of longe tyme. and therfore they say that this gode metynge cometh of goddes grace/ and therfore have they do make ymages lyke unto those thynges that they may worshyp theym before they mete any thynge ellis. And yet are som crysten men that say that som bestis are better for to mete than som for hares and swyne and other bestes are yll to mete first as they say. ¶ In thys yle of Cana is many wylde bestes/ and Ratons of that countre are as greate as houndes here. and they take them wyth mastyfes/ for Cattes may nat take theym. From thens men come to a cyte that men calle Sarchis/ and it is a fayre and a gode cyte and there dwell many crysten men of goddys feyth/ and there be men of religion. Fro thens men come to the londe of Lombe. and there is the cyte of Polomes. and under that cyte is an hyll that men call Polombe. and therof taketh the cyte his name.

The Fountain of Youth

¶ And so at the fote of the same hyll is a righte fayre and a clere well that hath a full gode and swete savoure. and it smelleth of all maner sortes of spyces. ¶ And also at [f2ᵛ] eche houre of the day it chaungeth his savoure dyversly and who so drynketh thryes on the day of that well he is made hole of all sykenes that he hath. I have somtyme dronken of that welle. and methynketh yet that I fare the better. somme call it the well of youth. for they that drynk therof seme to be yonge alwey and lyve withoute greate sykenesse. and they say this well cometh froo Paradyse terrestre. for it is so vertuous. In that countre growethe gynger and theder come many goode marchauntes for spices. In this countre men worshyp the Ox for his grete symplenesse/ and mekenesse/ and the profyte that is in hym they make the Ox to travale vi. or vii. yere/ and than men ete theym. And the kynge of that londe hath evermore one ox with hym. and he that kepeth hym every day taketh his fees for the kepynge. And also every day he gadereth his uryne and his donge in a vessell of golde/ and bereth it to the prelete that they call Archiporta papaton. and the prelate bereth it to the kynge/ and maketh therupon a greate blessynge and than the kynge putteth his hande therin and than they calle it gaule/ and he anoyntethe his front and his brest therwith/ and they do it great worshyp. and say he shall be fulfylled with vertue of the ox before sayde/ and that he is halowed thorough vertue of that holy thynge as they say. and whan the kinge hath thus done than do other lordes and after them other men after they ar of degre/ whan they may have any remenaunte. An† this countre their ydols ar halfe man and halfe oxe. And in these ydols the wycked gost speketh to theym and gyveth answeres of what they aske/ before these ydollis they sle theyr childre many tymes and sprenge the blode on [f3ʳ] the ydols. and so make they sacryfyce. and if any man dye in that countre they brenne hym in tokenynge of penaunce that he shulde suffre no penaunce if he were layde in the erthe of etynge of wormes and if his wife have no chyldren they bren hir with hym/ and they say it is gode reoson† that she make hym company in the other world as she dyd in this/ and if she have children she may lyve with theym and she woll and if the wyfe dye before men brenne hir and hir housholde as if he woll. In this lond groweth gode wyne. and women drynke

Cotton
ch. 19

The Tomb
of Saint
Thomas

The
Juggernaut

wyne and men none. and women shave their berdes/ and men nat. ≠ Fro this londe men go many iourneys to a countre that men call Mabaron/ and this is a greate kyngdom. There in is many fayre cytees and townes. In this londe lyeth saynte Thomas in flesshe in a fayre tombe in the cyte of Calamy/ and the arme and the hande that he put in oure Lordes syde whan he was rysen. Whan cryst sayde to hym. Noli esse incredulus/ sed fidelis [John 20:27]. That is to say/ Be nat of wanhope but byleve. that same hande lyeth yet wyth oute the tombe bare. and with this hande they gave their domes in that countre to wete who hath ryght. and who nat. for if any strife is betwene two partyes they do wryte their right in two bylles/ and those bylles ar put in the hande of saynt Thomas/ and as sone the hande castethe away the byll that hath wronge/ and holdethe the other styll that hathe right/ and therfore they come fro ferre to have iugementis of causes that ar in doute. In the churche of saynt Thomas is a greate ymage that is a symulacre and it is Well dight with riche precious stones/ and perles/ and unto that ymage men come in pylgrymage [f ii] [f3ᵛ] fro ferre with greate devocion as cristen men go to saynt Iame. And there come som in pylgrymage that bere sharp knyves in their handes and as they goo by the wey/ they shere ther shankes and thighes that the bloode may come oute for the love of that ydoll And they say that he is holy that woll dye for that goddes sake. And som is there that fro the tyme that they go oute of their houses at eche thirde pas they knele to that they come to this ydol. and whan they come there they have ensence/ or suche other thynge/ to ensence the ydoll as we wolde do to goddes body/ and there is before that Mynster of this ydoll a ryver ful of Water. and in that vynere pylgrymes cast golde/ sylver/ precious stones and perles. without noumbre in stedde of offrynges. and therfore whan the mynster hathe nede of helpynge. as sone they go to that vyner and take that they have nede to helpynge of the mynster. and ye shall understond whan greate festes come of that ydoll as the dedycacion of the churche or of the thronynge of the ydoll all the contrey is assembled theder/ and men set this ydoll with greate worshyp in a chayre well dight with ryche cloothes and gode and other and lede hym with greate worshyp aboute the cyte. and before the chayre goth first in procession all the maydens of the countre two and two togeder. And after theym go the pylgrymes that are come fro ferre countrees of whyche pylgrymes som fall downe before the chayre and lateth all go over theym and so are they som slayne and som ar broken their armes and shankes and thys do they for love of the ydol/ and they trowe the more peyne that they suffre here for their ydoll. the more Ioye shalle they have in the other worlde. and a man shall fynde fewe [f4ʳ] crysten men that woll suffre so moche penaunce for oure lordes sake as they do for their Idol. And nygh before the chayre go all mynstrellis of the countre as it were withoute noumber with many dyvers melodyes/ And whan they ar come ageyne to the churche. they set up the Idol ageyne in his throne and for worshyp of the Idoll two men or thre ar slayne with sharpe knyves with ther gode wyll. And also a man thynketh in oure coutre† that he hathe a greate worshyp. And he have an holy man in his kyn. so say they there that those that ar thus slayn ar holy men and sayntes. and they ar wreten in their letany and whan they ar thus dede their frendes brenne their bodyes and they take the asshes and those ar kept as relikes and they say it is hooly thynge/ and that they have doute of no peryll whan they have those asshes. ≠ Fro this countre lii. iournes is a countre that men call Lamory/ in that londe is greate hete/ and it is custome syth that men and women go all naked and they scorne theym that ar clad. for they say that god made Adam and Eve al nakid and that men shulde have no shame of that/ that god made

and they byleve in god that made Adam/ and Eve/ and all the worlde/ and there is no woman weddyd but women ar all comon there/ and they forsake no man. And they say that god commaunded to Adam and Eve and all that came of theym saynge.

¶ Crescyte et multiplicamini et replete terram [Genesis 9:1; 9:7].

That is for to say in englysshe ¶ wex and be multyplyed and fyll the erthe/ and no man may say there. Thys is my wyfe. Ne woman say. This is my husbond. And whan they have chyldren they gyve to whom they woll. [f4ᵛ] of men that have delt with theym. Also the londe is alle comom† for that one man hathe in one yere another man hath it another yere. Also all the goodes/and cornes of the countre ar in comon/ for there is no thynge under lok and as riche is one man as another. but they have an yll custume/ they ete gladlyer mans flesshe than other Theder brynge marchauntes their children

Cotton ch. 20

The Isle of Lamory

> Cotton ch. 21

to sell/ and those that are fatte they ete theym. and the other kepe they tyll they be fatte and than are they eten. ≠ Besyde thys Ile is an Ile that men call Somober that is a gode yle. men of that Ile do marke theym in the visage with an hoote yron men and women for great nobley and to be know from other. for they holde theym self the worthyest of the worlde. and they have warre evermore wyth those men that ar naked that I spake of before. And there ar many other Iles and dyvers maners. of men of whyche it were overmoche for to speke of all. But there is a great Ile that men call Iana. And the kynge of that countre hath under hym vii. kynges for he is full mighty In that Ile groweth all maner of spices more plenteuously than in other places as gynger/ clowes/ canell/ nutmygges/ and other and ye shall understonde that the nutmygge bereth the maces/ all thynge therin is plente but wyne. The kynge of this londe hath a riche paleys: and the best that is in the worlde for all the greces in to his hall and chambers ben all of golde. another of sylver/ and all the walles ar covered and plated with golde and sylver. and in those plates ar wreten storyes of knyghtes and batayles and the pavement of the hall and chaumbres is of golde and of silver. and there is no man that wold trowe the ryches that [f5ʳ] is there: but if he had sene it. and the kynge of thys Ile is so myghty that he hath many tymes overcome the greate Chane of chatay that is the myghtyest Emperour that is in all the worlde for there is oft warre amonge theym for the greate Chane wolde make hym holde his lond to hym and for to go furth by see men fynde one Ile that is called Salamasse. and som call it paten. that is a great kyngdom with many fayre cytees. In this londe growe trees that bere mele. of which men make fayre bredde/ and whyte and of gode savoure/ and it semethe as it were of whete. And there is other trees that bere venym/ ageyne which is no medecyne. but one. that is to take of the leves of the same tre/ and stampt theym and temper wyth water and drynke it or elles he shall dye sodeynly for tryacle may nat helpe. And if ye woll wete howe the Trees bere mele I shall say you. men hewe wyth an hachet aboute the rote of the tre by the erth so that no berke be persed in many places and than cometh oute a lycoure thyk which they take in a vessell and put it to the sonne and drye it and whan it is drye they do it unto the mylle to grynde and so is it fayre mele and whyte/ and hony/ and wyne: and

> The Wondrous Trees of Salamasse

venym ar drawe oute of other trees in the same maner and do it in vessels to kepe. In that Ile is a ded see/ that is a water that hath no grounde/ and if any thynge fall therin it shall never be founde. besyde that see groweth greate cannes and under their rotes men fynde precyous stones of greate vertue. for he that bereth one of tho stones upon hym there may no yron dere hym ne drawe blode on him. and therfore they that have these stones fighte ful hardely for there may no quarel/ ne such thynge dere [f5ᵛ] theym: therfore they that knowe the maner of them they make their quarels withoute yron and so they sle theym And than is another Ile that men call Calonach that is a greate londe and a plenteuous of godes. And the kynge of that londe hath as many wyves as he woll. for he hathe a thousande and mo and lyethe never by one of them but ones. And that londe hathe a marvayle that is in no other londe. For all maner of fysshes of the see comethe a tyme of the yere every maner after other. and layethe theym nere the londe and on the londe somtyme and there they lye thre dayes. and men of the londe come theder and take of theym what they woll. and than go those fysshes awey/ and comethe another maner and lyethe other thre dayes and men take of theym. And thus doth every maner of fysshes tyll all have be there: and men have taken of everychone what they woll. And men woete† nat the cause why it is. But they sey there. that those fysshes come so theder to do worship to their kynge. for as the most worthy kynge of the worlde for he hath so many wyves. and geteth so many children of theym. ¶ And than is a nother Ile that men call Gaffolos. Men of thys Ile whan ther frendis ar seke that they trowe that they shal dye they take and hange hym up all quyk on a tre and say it is better that birdes that ar aungellis of god ete theym than wormes of the erth Fro thens men go to an yle there the men ar of yll kynd they noryssh houndes for to worow men and whan theyr frendes are syke that they hope they shall dye/ they do those houndes strangle them for they wol nat that they dy kyndly deth for than shuld they suffre to gret peyne as they sey and when they ar thus ded they ete their flessh for venyson [f6ʳ] ¶ A fro thens men go thorough many Iles by see unto an Ile that men call Melke/ there is full yll folke for they have none other delyte but for to fyght and sle men for they drynke gladly mannys blode whiche blode they call god. and he that may moost sle is of

The Self-Sacrificing Fish

moost name amonge theym. And if two men be at stryfe/ and they be made at one. theym behoveth to drynke eyther too other blode/ or ellys the accorde is noughte. Fro this Ile men go to an Ile that men call Tracota where all men are as bestes and nat resonable and they dwell in caves for they have no wytte to make theym howses. and they ete edders and they speke nat. but they make suche a noyse. had† edders have one to another/ and they make no force of rychesse/ but of a stone that hath fourty colours/ and it is called Traconyt after that Ile. but they knowe nat the vertue therof but they covet it for the greate fayrenes. Fro that Ile men go to an Ile that men call Natumeran that is a greate Ile and a fayre/ and men/ and women of that countre have hounde hedes and they ar resonable and worshyp an Ox for their god and they go all naked but a lytell clothe before their prevy membres they ar gode men to fight and they bere a greate targe/ with whych they cover all the body and a spere in their hande/ and if they take any man in batayle they send hym to their king which is a great lorde and devout in his feyth. for he hath aboute his nek on a cord iii. c. perles great and orient in maner of Pater noster of lambre and as we say Pater noster and Ave maria. right so the kynge sayth eche day iii. c. prayers to hys god before he ete/ and he bereth also aboute his nek a Ruby orient fyne and gode that is nere a fote and v. fyngers long [f6ᵛ] For whan they chese theyr kynge/ they gyve too hym that Ruby to bere in his hande/ and so they lede hym ridynge aboute the cyte/ and therfore he bereth that Ruby alwey aboute his necke. for if he bare nat the ruby/ they wolde no lenger holde hym kynge. and the great Chane of chatay hathe moche coveted this Ruby. but he myght never have it/ for warre ne for other catell. and this kynge is a full true and a rightwys man. for men may go safly/ and likerly thorough his londe and bere all that he woll. for noman is so hardy to lette hym. ≠ And than is another Ile that men call Dodym. that is a greate Ile. In this Ile ar many dyvers maner of men and have evyll maners for the fader eteth the son/ and the son the fader/ the husbonde the wyfe/ the wyfe the husbonde. And if it so be that the fader be syke or the moder or any frende the son gothe as sone to the preest of the Lawe/ and pray hym that he woll aske of the ydoll if his fader shall dye of that sykenesse or nat. And than the preest and the son knele down before the ydoll devoutly and asketh

The Land of Dog-Headed Men

Cotton ch. 22

hym/ and he answereth to theym/ and if he say that he shall lyve. than they kepe hym well. and if he say that he shall dye/ than come the prest with the son or with the wife or what frende it be unto hym that is seke/ and they lay their hande over hys mouthe to stoppe his breth/ and so they sle hym/ and than they smyte all the body in peces. and do pray all his frendes for to come and ete of hym that is dede/ and they make a greate fest therof/ and have many mynstrels there. ¶ And so Whanne they have all eten the flesshe. Than they bery and grave the bones/ and all those that are of his frendes that were nat there at the etynge of hym hath [f7ʳ] a greate shame and velany so that they shall never more be holden as frendes. And the kynge of this Ile is a greate lorde and myghty. and he hath under hym liii yles and eche of theym hath a kynge. and in one of these yles ar men that hath but one iye and that is in the myddes of their front and they ete nat but flesshe and fysshe rawe. and in another yle dwell foule men that have no hedes: and their iyen are in their shulders and their mouth is on their brest. And in another Ile ar men that have no hede ne iyen and their mouth is behynde in their shulders And other men is there that have a platte face withoute nose. and iyen but they have two smale holes in sted of iyen: and they have a plat mouth liples. In another Ile are foule men that have the lyppe above the mouthe so gret/ that whan they slepe in the sonne they cover all their face with the lyppe. In another Ile is folke that is both men and women and have membres of bothe for to engender with and whan they woll they use bothe on a tyme and the other another tyme. and they gete childre whan they use the membre of man. and they bere children whanne thet use the membre of woman. Many other maner of folke is in yles theraboute of whom/ it Were to longe tyme to tell all. And for to passe forth men come into an yle that men ar right small in. and they have a lytell hole in stedde of the mouthe. and they may nat ete/ but all that they shall ete or drynke they take it thorough a pype of a fether or suche a nother thynge.

For to go fro this Ile toward the see that is called occean toward the est many iournes/ a man shal fynde a kyngdom that is called Mancy/ and [f7ᵛ] this in ynde the most and the lest and moost delictable/ and of most plente of all godes that

Isles of Monstrous Races

is in power of man In this londe dwell cristen men and sarrasyns for it is a greate londe. therin is two thousande cytees greate and other many townes. In this londe no man goth on beggynge for there is no pore man/ and the men have berdes thynne of here as it were cattes. In this londe ar fayre women and therfore som men call that lond albany for the whyte folke. and there is a cyte that men call latorym and it is more than Paryse. In that Cyte is a fayre water berynge shyppes and in that londe ar birdes twyes so great as in any other place of the worlde/ and there is gode chepe of vetayles/ and there is plente of greate neddres. of whyche they make greate fest and ete theym at great solemnytees. For if a man make a greate fest/ and hadde gyven theym all the mete that he myght gete and he gyve theym no neddres he hath no thanke for all that he doth. ¶ In this countre are hennes whyte and they bere no fethers/ but wolle as shepe do in oure londe. and women of that countre that are weddyd bere crownes upon their hedes that they may be knowen by. In thys countre they take a best that is callyd Loyrys and they ken it to go into waters or vyners: and as sone he bryngeth oute of the water greate fysshes/ and thus take they fyssh as longe as they woll to that theym nedeth. Fro this cyte men go by many iournes ta† another greate cyte that is called Cassay/ that is the most cyte of the worlde. and that cyte is. l. myle aboute and there is in that cyte mo than xii. thosaund gates and eche gate is a gode toure where the kepers dwell to kepe it ageyne the great chan for it marcheth on his londe/ and [f8ʳ] on one syde of the cyte renneth a great ryver. and there dwel crysten men and other many. for there is a gode countre and plenteuous/ and there groweth right gode wyne/ that men call bygon/ this is a noble cyte where the kynge of Mancy was wonte to dwell. and there dwell religyous men crysten freres. and men go upon that ryver tyll they come to an abbey of monkes a lytell fro the cyte and there in that abbey is a greate gardeyne and fayre/ and therin is many maner of trees of dyverse frutes. In that gardeyne dwell many maner of bestes as baboynes/ apes/ marmosettes and other and whan the covent hath eten a monke taketh the relyf and do bere it into the gardeyne and smyteth ones with a clyket of sylver which he holde in his hande. and sone after comethe oute theyse bestes that I spake of and other many nere iii. thousand or iiii thousand and he gyveth theym to ete of fayre ves-

The Monks' Charity to the Apes

sellys of silver/ and whan they have eten he smyteth the clyket ageyn and they goo ageyne there they cam froo. And the monke sayth that those bestis ar soules of men that ar dedde and those bestes that ar fayre are soules of lordes/ and other ryche men/ and those that ar foule bestes ar soules of other comons. and I asked theym if it had nat be better to gyve that relef to pore men and they sayde there is no pore man in that countre. And if there were/ yet it were more almes to gyve it to those soules that suffre there their penaunce and may go no forther to gete their mete than to men that have wytte and may travayle for their mete.

Than come men to a cyte that is callid Chibens and there was the first syege of the kynge of Mancy. Iy† thys cyte is lx. brydges of stone as fayre as they may be.

[f8ᵛ] WHan men passe fro the cyte of Chybense they pas over a great ryver of fressh water/ and it is nere foure myle brode. and than men entre into the londe of the greate Chan. This ryver goth thoroughe the londe of pegmaus†/ there men ar of lytell stature for they ar but thre span longe and they are right fayre men gyf all they be lytell and they ar wedded whan they ar half a yere olde/ and they lyve but viii. yere/ and he that lyve viii. yere is holde right olde. These smale men travayle nat/ but they have amonge theym greate men as we are to travayle for theym. and have greate scorne of those grete men as we wolde have of geauntes that were amonge us. Fro this londe men go thorough many countres and cytees and townes tyll they come to a cyte that men calle Menk. In that cyte is a greate Navy of shyppes/ and they are as whyte as snowe of kynde of the wode that they ar made of and they are made as it were greate houses with halles and chaumbers and other esementys. From thens men go upon a ryver that men call Ceromosan

This ryver gothe thorough Chatay/ and doth many tymes harme whan it wexethe greate. ≠ Chatay is a fayre countre goode and ryche full of godes and marchaundises/ theder come marchauntis every yere for to fetche spyces and other marchaundises more comonly than they do in other countrees. And ye shall understonde that marchauntes that come fro Venys or fro Geene or other places of lumbardy or romayne/ they goo by see and londe. xi. monethes and more or they may come to Chatay. and towarde the est is an olde

The Pygmies

Cotton ch. 23

Cathay

cyte in the provynce of Chatay and beside that cyte the Tartarynes have made another [g1ʳ] cite that men call Cadom that hath seven gates and ever betwene two gates is a great myle. so that those two cytees the olde and the newe is aboute than xx. myle. In this cyte is the sege of the great chane in a full fayre place and greate of whiche the walles aboute it is two myle. and within that ar many fayre places/ and in the gardeyne of that paleys is a right greate hyll/ on the whych is another paleys/ and it is the fayrest that may be found in any place. and all aboute that hyll are many trees berynge dyvers frutes. and aboute that hyll is a great dyche and there ar nere many ryvers and vyners on eche syde. And in those are many wylde foules that he may take and go nat oute of the paleys. withoute the hall of that paleys is xxiiii. pillers of gold and all the walles ar covered with riche skynnes of bestes that men call panters Those ar fayre bestes and well smellynge/ and of the smel of the skynnes none evyll smell may come to the paleis those skynnes ar as redde as blode. and they shyne so ageyne the sonne that unnethes may men beholde theym. and men preyse those skynnes as moche as it were fyne golde. In myddes of that paleys is a place made that they call the mountoure for the greate chane that is made wel with pricious stones and greate perles hangynge aboute and at foure corners of that mountour ar foure nedders of golde/ and under that mountour and above ar condytes of beverage that they drynke in the emperours courte and the hall of that palys is richely dight/ and well. and first at the over ende of the hall is the throne of the emperoure right hye where he sitteth at mete at a table that is wel bordured with golde and that bordure is full of precious [g i] [g1ᵛ] stones and greate perles and the greces on the whych he gothe up ar of dyvers precious stones bordured with golde At the lyft syde of his throne is the sege of his wyfe a degre lower than he sitteth and that is of Iasper bordured with golde/ and the sege of his secounde wyfe is a degre lower than the firste and that is also of gode Iasper bordured with golde. and the sege of the thyrd wyfe is a degre lower than the secounde. for alwey he hath thre wyves Wyth hym where soo he is besyde these wyves on the same syde sitteth other ladyes on his kynne echone lower than other as they ar of degre. And all those that ar weddyd have a counterfete of a mannys fote upon their hedes a shaftmon longe and all made with

The Seat of the Great Khan

precious stoones. and above ar they made wyth shynynge fedyrs of Pecok/ or such other in token that they ar in subieccion to man and under mannys fote and they that ar nat wedded have none such. And the right syde of the emperoure sitteth first his son that shalbe emperoure after hym/ and he sytteth also a degre lower than themperoure in suche maner of seges as the emperoure sitteth/ and by hym sytteth other lordes of his kyn echone lower than other as they ar of degre

And the emperoure hath his table by hym/ one that is of golde and precious stones or of whyte cristall or yelowe bordered with golde. and eche one of his wyves hathe a table by hir selfe/ and under the emperours table sitteth iiii. clerkes at his fete that wryte all that the emperoure sayth be it gode or yll. And at greate festes above themperours table and all other tables In the hall is a vyne made of fyne golde that goth all aboute the hall and it hath many braunches of grapes like to grapes of the vyne. some are [g2^r] whyte som ar yelowe som red/ and som blacke. all the red ar of rubyes of cremas or alabaunce/ the whyte ar of crystall or byrall/ the yelowe ar of Topaces the grene ar of Emeraudes and crysolitis/ and the blake ar of quyches and gerandes. and this vyne is made thus of precious stones so propyrly that it semethe as it were a vyne growynge. And before the borde of the emperoure standeth greate lordes and no man is so hardy to speke to him but if it be mynstrellis for to solace the emperoure. and all the vessell that is served in his hall or chambers ar of precious stones and namely at tables where greate Lordes ete. that is to say/ of Iasper crystall amatyst or fyne golde/ and the cuppes are of Emeraudes Saphyres topaces pydos/ and other many maner of stones/ of sylver have they no vessell/ for they preyse sylver but lytell to make vessell of/ but they make of sylver greces pylleris and pavementes of halles/ and of chaumbers. And ye shall understonde that my felawe and I was in favoure with hym xvi monethes ageyne the kynge of Mancy of whome he made warre/ and the cause was for we had so gret desire to se the nobley of his court if it were such as we herde speke of and forsoth we fonde it more rych and more solempne than ever we herd speke of/ and we shuld never have trowed it had we nat sene it: but ye shal understond that mete and drinke is more honest amonge us than in those countres/ for all the comons ete nat but flessh of all maner bestes/ and whan they have al ete they wype ther handes on ther skirtis and they ete but ones on the day/ ≠ and ye shall wete why he is called the gret chan ye wote wel that al the world was destroyd with noes flode but noe and his wif and his childre Noe had iii sonnes sem cam and iaphet cam was he that[21] [g2ᵛ] sawe his faders balockes naked whan he slept and scorned it. and therfore was he cursed and Iapheth covered it ageyne. These thre bretherne had all the londe. Cham toke the best party estward. that is called assy. Sem toke affryke. and Iapheth toke Europe. Cham was the myghtyest and rychest of his brethern and of hym ar come the paen folke and dyvers maner of men of the yles some hedles/ and other men disfigured. and for this Cham the emperoure there calleth hym Cham and lorde of all. but ye shall understonde that the emperoure of Chatay is called Chane and nat cham. and for this skyll it is nat yet viii. yere gone that all Tartary was in subieccyon. and thrall to other nacions aboute/ and they were made herdmen to kepe bestes/ and amonge theym was seven lynages or kyndes. the first was called Tartary. that is the best. The secounde lynage is called Tanghot. The thyrd Eurace. the forth Valayre. the fyft Semeth. the vi. Menchi. the seventh Sobeth. These ar all holding of the greate chane of chatay. Nowe it befel so that in the first lynage was an olde man and he was nat ryche and men called hym Changuys. This man lay and slept on a nyght in a bed and there cam to hym a knyght al whyte syttinge upon a whyte horse and sayde to hym Chan slepest thou god that is almyghty sent me to the/ and it is hys will that thou say to the vii. lynages that thou shalt be ther emperoure for ye shal conquere all the londes that ar aboute you and they shalbe in your subiecconn as ye have be in theirs and whan morowe cam he rose up and sayde to the vii. lynages/ and they scorned hym and sayd he was a fole and the nyght after the same knyght cam to same lynage/ and bad theym [g3ʳ] of goddes behalfe to make Changuys their emperoure/ and they shulde be oute of all subiection/ and on the morowe they chase changuys to emperoure/ and dyd hym all worship that they myght do and called hym Chane as the whyte knyght called hym. and they sayde they wolde doo as

Cotton
ch. 24

Why He
Is Called
the Great
Khan

The
First Khan

---

[21] The words "cam was he that" appear on g2ʳ underneath the thirtieth line, off center, as if they had been forgotten and later filled in.

he bad theym/ and he made than many statutes and lawes
the which he called Isakan. and the firste statute was that
they shuld be obedient to god all myghty/ and trowe that he
shulde delyver theym oute of thraldom and that they shulde
calle on hym in all their myster. Another statute was that all
men that myght bere armes shulde be noumbred and to eche
x. shulde be a mayster. and a C. a mayster and to a thousand
a mayster/ and than he commaunded to all the grettest and
pryncypallis of the seven lynages/ that they shulde forsake all
that they had in herytage or lordshype and that they shulde
holde theym payde of that he wold gyve theym of his grace
and they dydde so. And also he bad theym that eche man
shulde brynge his eldest son before hym/ and sle his owne
son with hys owne handes/ and smyte of their hedes/ and as
sone they dyd his byddynge And whan he sawe they made no
lettynge of that he bad theym do. than bad he theym folowe
his baner. and than he put in subieccion all the londes
aboute hym. And it befell on a day that the chane rode wtyht†
a fewe men to see the londe that he had wonne/ and he
mette with a greate multytude of his ennemyes and there was
he cast down of his hors and his hors slayne. and whan his
men sawe hym at the erthe they trowed he had be ded and
fled. and the ennemyes folowed after/ and whan he sawe the
ennemyes were ferre he hyd hym in a busshe. for the wode
[g ii] [g3ᵛ] was thycke there and whan they were come a-
geyne froo the chasse they went to seke amonge the wode if
any were hyd there/ and they fonde many and as they cam to
the place there he was. they sawe a byrde sitte upon a tre the
whiche byrde men call an oule/ and than sayde they that
there was no man for that byrd sate there and so went they
away. and thus was the chane saved fro deth/ and so he went
awey on a nyght to his owne men which were fayne of hym.
And fro that tyme hyderwardes men of that countre have do
greate worshyp to that byrde and therfore before all byrdes of
the Worlde they worshyp that maner of bird. and than he assembled all his men and rode upon his ennemyes and destroyed theym. and whan he had Wonne all the londes that
were aboute hym he held theym in subieccion. And whan
the chane had Wonne al the londes to mount Belyan. the
whyte knyght came to hym in a vision ageyne/ and sayde
unto hym. Chane the wyll of god is that thou passe the
mount Belyan/ and thou shalt wynne many londes/ and for
that thou shalt fynde no passage. go thou to mounte Belyan

that is upon the see syde and knele ix tymes theron ageyne the Est in the worshyp of god and he shall shewe the a wey howe thou shalt passe. and the chane dyd so. and as sone the see that towched to the hyll withdrowe hym and shewed a fayre wey of nyne fote brode betwene the hylle/ and the See. and so passed he righte well wyth all hys men. and so he wanne the londe of chatay that is the most lond and grettest of the worlde. and for those ix. knelynges and the ix. fote of wey the chane and men of tartary have the noumbre of ix. in gret worship. and whan he had won the lond of [g4ʳ] Chatay he dyed/ and than regned after Cythoco Chane his eldest son/ and his other brother went to wynne them londes in other contres. and they wan the londe of pruys and of russy. and they dyd call them self chane. but he of chatay is the great chane the grettest lord of all the world and so he calleth hym in his letters and saith thus. Chan filius dei excelsi universam terram colencium summus imperator et dominus dominancium. That is for to say Chane goddes son Emperoure of all those that tyll all the londe and lorde of all lordes. and the wrytynge above his greate seale is Deus in celo. Chan super terram eius fortitudo omnium hominum imperatoris sigillum. That is to say thus God in heven. chan upon erthe his strength. The seale of the emperoure of all men/ and the wrytynge a boute his prevy seale is thus. Dei fortitudo omnium hominum imperatoris sigillum. That is to say the strength of god seale of the emperoure of all men. And all if it be so that they be nat crysten: yet themperour and the tartaryns trowe in god almyghty

Cotton
ch. 25

The Court
of the
Great Khan

NOWe have I tolde you why he is called the greate chane. ≠ Nowe shall I tell you of the governynge of his courte whan they make gret festes and the pryncipall foure tymes in the yere. the fyrst feste is of his berynge. the secound whan he is borne to the temple to be circumcised. the third is of his ydols whan they begyn to speke. and the forth whan the ydol begynneth firste to do myracles and at those tymes he hath men well arrayed by thousandis and by hundres and echone wote well what he shall do for there is first ordeyned iiii. thousande riche barons/ and myghty for to ordeyne the fest and to serve the Emperoure/ and all these barons have crownes of gold wel [g4ᵛ] dight with precious stones and perles and they ar cladde in clothes of golde and camathas as richely as they may be made/ and they may well have suche clothes for they ar there of lesse pryce than wollen cloth is here. And these iiii. thousande barons ar departed in iiii. partyes/ and eche company is clad in dyvers coloure right richely. and whan the first thousande is passed and hath shewed them/ than come the secounde thosand/ and than the thyrde/ and than the forth and none of theym spekethe a worde. And on o syde of the emperours table sytteth many phylosophers of many sciences. som of astronomy/ nygromancy/ geometry/ pyromacy/ and other many scyences. and som have before theym astrolabes of gold or of precious stones full of sonde or of cooles brennynge. som have orlages well dight and richely and other many instrumentes after their scyences. and at a certeyne houre whan they see tyme they sey to men that stande before them make pees. and than say those men with a loude voys to al the hall nowe be styll a whyle. and than sayth one of the phylosophers eche man make reverence and bowe and loute to themperoure that is goddes son and lorde of the world for nowe is tyme and houre. and than all men loute to hym/ and knele on the erthe. and than byddeth the phylosopher them ryse up ageyne. and at one other houre another phylosopher byd theym all put their fyngers in their erys and they do so. and at another houre byddeth another phylosopher that all men shall lay their hande on ther hede and they do so and than he byddeth theym take away and they do so. and thus fro houre to houre they byd dyvers thynges: and I asked pryvely what this shuld mene. and one of the maysters [g5ʳ] sayde that the loutynge and the knelynge on the erthe at that tyme hath this token. that all those men that knelyd so shall evermore be true to themperoure/ that for no gift/ ne hetynge they shall never be tratours/ ne fals to hym. And the puttynge of the fynger in the ere hath this token. that none of those shall here none yll be spoken of themperoure or his counsayle. And ye shall understonde that men dight no thynge/ clothes/ bred/ drynke/ nor non suche thynges to the emperoure but at certeyne houres that the Phylosophers tell/ and if any man reyse warre ageyne that emperoure in what countre so it be/ theyse phylosophers Wote it sone and tell the emperoure or his counseyl and he sendeth men theder for he hathe many men. And he hath many men to kepe byrdes as garfaukons/ sperhaukes/ faucons/ gentyls/ laners/ sacres/ popyniayes that ar spekynge/ and other many. x. thousande Olyfantes baboyns: marmosettis and other. and he hath many fysyciens of the which he hathe. CC. of theym that are crysten men. and xx. sarrasyns but he trusteth more in crysten men than in sarrasyns. and there is in the countre many barons and other servauntes that ar crysten and converted to the good feyth thorowe prechynge of goode crysten men that dwell there. but there are many that woll nat that men wete that they ar cristen. And he is a ful greate lorde for he may despende what he woll. and he hath in his chaumber a pyller of golde in the which is a Ruby and a carbuncle of a fote longe the whyche lyghtethe all the chamber upon nyght/ and he hath other many precyous stones and rubeis: but this is the most. Thys Emperoure dwelleth in the somer towardys the Northe in a [g5ᵛ] cyte that men call Sarduz and there is colde ynough and in wynter he dwelleth in a cyte that men call Camalach there is right hote londe and there dwelle he for the most party. And whan this greate chane shall ryde from one countre to another they ordeyne foure ostes of folke. of whych the first goth before a dayes iourney. for that ost lyeth at evyn where the Emperoure shall lye on the morowe and there is plente of vetayles. And another ost cometh at the right syde of hym and another at the lyft syde and in eche ost is many folke. and than cometh the forth ost behynde hym a bowe draught. and there is more men than in any of the other. And ye shall understonde that the emperoure rideth on no horse but if he woll wende to any place with pryve meyne/ but he rydeth in a charette with foure wheles. and therupon is a chamber made of a tre that men call lignum aloes that cometh oute of paradyse terrestre/ and that chaumber is covered with plates of fyne golde and precyous stones and perles and foure Olyfauntes and foure stedes gone there in. And v. or vi greate lordes riden aboute hym so that none other men shall come nere hym but if the emperoure call any. and that same maner with chariottes and suche ostes ridethe the Empres by another syde/ and the Emperours eldest son on the same array. and they have so many folkes that it is a greate marvayle to see. And also the londe of the greate Chane is departed in twelve provynces. and eche provynce hathe more than two thousande kynges. Also whan the emperoure rideth thorowe the countre. and he passeth thorough cytees and townes. eche man maketh a fyre before his hous and casteth therin ensence/ and other [g6ʳ] thynges that gyve gode smel to the emperoure/ and if men of religion that ar cristen dwell nere as the emperoure cometh they mete hym with procession with a crosse and holy water.

The Khan's Mode of Travel

and they synge Veni creator spiritus with a loude voyce. And whan he see theym come he comwaundethe to the lordes that ryde nere hym to make wey that the relygyous men may come to hym. and whan he se the crosse de† dothe of his hatte that is made of precious stones and greate perles. and that hat is so ryche that marveyle it is to tell. and than he lowteth to the crosse. And the prelate of the relygious men say orysons before hym/ and gyve hym the benyson with the crosse. and he lowteth to the benyson full devoutly. and than the same prelate gyvethe hym som froyte of the noumbre of ix. in a plate of gold for the maner is such there that no straunge man shalle come before the emperour but he gyve hym somwhat after the olde lawe that sayth. Nemo accedat in conspectu meo vanuis† [Exodus 23:15].[22] That is to say. No man come in my sight to me.† And than the emperoure byddeth these religyous men that they shall go forth so that men of his ost defoule theym nat. and those religious that dwell where themperesse or the emperours son cometh do in the same maner. for this gret chane is the grettest lorde of the worlde. for prester Iohn is nat so greate a lorde as he. ne the soudan of Babylon ne the emperoure of persy. In his londe a man hath a C wyves and som xl. som mo som les and they take of ther kyn to wyves all but ther moders sonnes and doughters ≠ and men and women have al o maner of clothing so that tehy† may nat be knowe but that women that ar wedded bere a token on ther hedes and they dwel nat with ther husbondes [g6ᵛ] but he may lye by whych that he woll. They have plente of all maner of bestes but swyne. forthose† Wol they non and they trowe well in god that made all thynge and yet have they ydols of golde and sylver/ and to these ydollis they offre the first mylke of their bestes. And thys empeperoure† the greate chane hath thre wyves. and the pryncypall wyfe was prestyr Iohns doughter/ The folke of this countre begyn to do all their thinges in the newe mone/ and they worshyp moch the sonne and the mone and those men ryde comonly withoute spores/ and they holde it greate synne to breke a bone with a nother and to cast mylke on the erthe or any other lycoure that men may drynke. And the most synne that they may do is to pys in their houses there they dwell/ and he that pisseth in his howse/ shalbe slayne/ and of

Cotton
ch. 26

Customs and
Observances
in the
Khan's
Empire

---

[22] The line in Exodus reads "vacuus," rather than "vanuis."

these synnes they shryve theym to their prestes/ and for their penaunce they shall gyve sylver/ and the place where men have pyssed shalbe halowed/ or ellys may no man come there. and whan they have do their penaunce. they shall passe thorowe a fayre fyre/ or two to make theym clene of their synnes. and whan they have eten they wype their handes on ther skyrtes for they have no bordclothes/ but it be right great lordes and whan they have all eten/ they putte theyr dysshes/ or doublers. nat wasshen in the potte or cawdron with the flessh that levethe whan they have eten unto they woll ete another tyme. and riche men drynke mylke of meres/ or asses/ or other bestes/ and other beverage that is made of mylke/ and water togeder for they have nother wyne ne ale and whan they go to warre they werre full wysely and eche man of theym berethe two bowes or thre. and many[23] [g7ʳ] arowes and a greate hachet/ and gentyll men have short swerdys/ and he that fighteth in batayle they sle hym/ and they ar ever in purpos to brynge all londes in subiecconn to theym for they say prophesyes say that they shalbe over come by shot of archers and that they shall turne theym to their lawe/ but they wote never what men they shall be and it is greate peryll to pursue the Tartaryns whanne they flee. for they Woll shote behynd and sle men as wel as before. and holde oyle of Oyle for a gode medycyne. and they have small iyen as lytel byrdes and they are comonly false for they holde nat that they hete. And whan a man shall dye amonge theym they steke a spere in the erthe besyde hym: and whan he draweth to the deth/ they go oute of the house tyl he be dede and than they put him in the erthe in the felde. And whan the Emperoure is ded they sette hym in a chayre in myddes of a tente. and they set before hym a table with a cloth and flesshe and other mete/ and a cuppe full of mylke of a mere/ and they set a mere with a fole by hym and an horse sadlyd and brydelyd/ and they lay upon the hors golde and sylver: and all aboute hym they make a greate grave/ and put hym in. And tent to all other thynges they put in the erth to geder/ and they say whan he cometh into another world he shall nat be withoute an house ne horse ne sylver and the mere shall gyve hym mylke and brynge forth more

---

[23] There is a space of approximately two letter-widths at the end of this line. Clearly, however, a paragraph break is not intended.

hors til he be well stored in the other worlde/ for they trowe that whan they ar ded they shal go into another worlde and ete and drynke and have solace wyth theyr wyves as they have here. ¶ And whan that he is leyde in the erthe no man shall be so hardy for to speke of hym before his frendes. [g7ᵛ] And than whan the emperoure is dede the. vii. lynages geder theym togeder: and they touche hys son or the next of his blode/ and they say thus we woll and we ordeyne and we pray that thou bo† oure lorde and oure emperoure and he enquyreth if ye woll that I regne upon you echone woll do that I byd hym. And if he bydd that any be slayne he shalbe slayne. And they answere all wyth one voyce/ all that ye byd shalbe done. Than sayth the emperoure fro nowe forth my word shalbe sherynge as my swerde. and than they sette hym in a chayre and crowned hym. and than all the gode townes sent hym presentes so that he shall have more than a cart full of golde and sylver and other many Iuellys that he shall have of lordes of precyous stones and golde withoute noumbre and horse/ and ryche clothes of camacas and tartaryns and suche other. ≠ This londe of Chatay in assy the depe. and the londe of chatay marcheth towarde the west upon the kyngdom of Sercy the which was somtyme to one of the thre kynges that went to seke oure lorde in Betheleem These men of Tartary drynke no wyne. In the londe of Corosaym that is at the northe syde of chatay is ryghte greate plente of gode but no wyne. the whych hath at the est syde a greate wildernesse that lasteth more than a hundred iourneis and the best cyte of that londe is called Corosaym. and therafter is the londe so called Men of this londe ar gode warreours and hardy. And therby is the kingdom of Comayn. This is the most and the grettest kingdom of the worlde/ but it is nat all inhabyte. for in one place of that londe is so greate colde that no man maye dwell there for cold. and in another place is so greate hete [g8ʳ] that no man may dwell there. and there ar so many feyghes that a man wote nat on what syde he may turne him In this londe ar but fewe trees berynge frute. In thys londe men lye in tentes and they brenne dunge of bestes/ for defaute of wode. This londe descendethe towardys Pruyse and rosy. and thorough this londe renneth the ryvere Echel that is one of the grettest ryvers of the world and it is frosen so harde eche yere that men fight theron in greate batayles on hors. and fote men more than an hundred thousand at ones. And a lytell fro that Ryver is the greate see of occian that

Cotton ch. 27

The Lands Around Cathay

they call Maure. And betwene this Maure and the Caspy is a full streyte passage too go towarde ynde and therfore kynge alysaunder dyd make there a cyte that men call alysaundre to kepe that passage so that no man may passe but if he have leve. And nowe is that cyte called Port de fear. and the pryncipall cyte of Comayn is called Sarachys. thys is one of thre wayes to go into ynde/ but thorough this way may nat many men go but if it be in wynter. And this passage is called Berbent. and another wey is for to go from the londe of turkeston thorowe persy/ and in thys wey ar many iournes in wyldernesse. and the third way is that cometh fro Cosmane and that goth thorowe the great cyte and thorowe the kyngdom of abachare. And ye shal understonde that all these kyngdoms and londes unto persy ar holden of the great chane of chatay and many other and therfore he is full greate lorde of men and of londes.

≠ NOwe have I devysed you the londes towarde the north to com fro the londes of chatay to the londes [g8ᵛ] of Pruys/ and Rosy where crysten men dwelle. Nowe shall I devyse to you other londes and kyngdoms in comynge downe fro Chatay to the grekes see where cristen men dwell. And for as moche as next the greate chane of chatay the emperoure of percy is the grettest lorde. therfore I shall first speke of hym and ye shall understonde that he hath two kyngdoms the one begynneth Estward and the kyngdom of Turkescon and it lesteth westward to the see of Caspy. and southward to the londe of ynde and this londe is gode and pleyne and well mannyd gode cytees. but two most pryncipall of the cytees ar called Bacirida and Sormagnant. The other kyngdom of percy lasteth fro the ryver of Physon unto the great Ermony and Northward unto the see of Caspy and southwarde to the londe of ynde. and this is a full plenteuous countre and goode. and in this cyte is thre pryncypall cytees. Nessabor/ Saphan/ and Sarmasse. and than is the lond of Ermony in whyche was somtyme thre kyngedoms/ This is a gode londe and plenteuous/ and it begynneth at percy and lasteth westward to Turky of lengthe and in brede it lasteth fro the cyte of alysaundre that nowe is called Port de feare unto the londe of Myddy. In thys Ermony are many fayre cytees but Canryssy is most of name. Than is the londe of Myddy that is full longe but nat brode. that begynneth Estwarde at the londe of percy and ynde the lesse and lasteth westward to the kyngdom of

Cotton ch. 28

The Kingdoms of Persia

Caldee and Northwarde to lytell Ermony. In thys Myddy ar many great hilles and lytel pleyne and there dwell Sarrasyns and another maner of men that men call Cordynz and karmen. Than is next the kyngedom [h1ʳ] of George that begynneth estward at a greate hyll that men call Abior. this londe lasteth fro Turky to the grete see and the londe of myddy and the great Armony. and in this londe ar two kinges one of Abcaz/ and another of George/ but he of george is in subieccion to the gret chan but the abeacaz hath a stronge countre and defendeth hym wel ageyne his ennemyes. And in this londe of abcaz is a great marveyle for there is a countre in that londe that is nere thre dayes iourney longe and aboute/ and it is called hamfon. and that countre is all covered with myrkenes so that it hath no light that no man may se there. and no man dare go into that countre for the myrkenes. and neverthelesse men of the countre therby say that they may somtyme here therin the voyce of men and hors whynynge and cockes crowe and they wote well that men dwell there/ but they wote nat what maner of men. and they say this myrkenesse cometh thorough myracle of god that he dyd for crysten men there. For there was a wycked emperoure that was of Poy. and he was called Saures and he pursued somtyme all crysten men to destroy/ and dyd theym make sacrifice to his false goddes and in that countre dwelled many cristen men/ the whych left all ther godes and catellys and riches and wolde go into grece and whan they were all in a great playne that men call Megon themperour and his men cam for to sle these cristen men/ and than the cristen men all set them on ther knees/ and prayed to god. and as sone cam a thycke cloude/ and overlapped the emperour and all his ost/ so that he myght nat go away and so dwell they in myrkenes/ and they came oute never sythe and the cristenmen went where they wold and therfor they myght [h i] [h1ᵛ] say thus. A domino factum est istud et est mirabile in oculis ntis[24] That is to say of oure lord is this done and it is wonderful in oure iyen. Also oute of this myrke londe cometh a ryver that men may se by gode token that men dwell therin. Than next is this londe of Turky that marcheth to gret armony. and therin

The Land of Murkiness

---

[24] "ntis" appears here with no mark of abbreviation, and so I have not expanded it to "nostris" in the transcription. The quotation is Psalm 118:23.

ar many countrees as capadoce saure Bryke/ quesicion/ Pytan/ and geneth/ In eche one of these ar many gode cytees/ and it is a playne londe/ and fewe hylles/ and fewe ryvers. and than is the kynge of Messopotayne that begynneth estward at Flom of Tygre at a cyte that men call Mosel. and it lasteth westward to the Flom of Eufraten to a cyte that men call Rochayz and westward fro high Ermony unto the wyldrnes of ynde the lesse and it is a gode londe and a playne/ but there is fewe ryvers and there is but two hylles in that londe. the one is called Symar and the other lyson/ and it marcheth to the londe of Calde. And ye shall wete that the londe Ethyope marcheth estward to the great wyldernesse westward to the londe of Nuby southward to the londe of Maritane and northward to the red se and than is marytane that lasteth fro the hylles of Ethiope unto lyby the high and the lowe that lasteth to the greate se of spayne.

Cotton ch. 29

Lamb-fruit and Barnacle Geese

Gog and Magog

NOwe have I saide and spoken of many on this side of the great kingdom of Chatay of Whom many ar obeysaunt to the greate chane. ≠ Nowe shall I say of som londes and countres and Iles that ar beyonde the londe of chatay. who so goth fro chatay to ynde the hyghe and the lowe he shal go thorough a kingdom that men call caldilhe that is a great londe/ there groweth a maner of frute as [h2ʳ] it were goordes. and whan it is rype men shere asonder and they fynde therin a best as it were of flesshe of bone and blode as it were a lytel lambe withoute wolle and men ete the best and the frute also and that is a great marveyle. Neverthelesse I sayde them that I helde that for no marveyle. For I sayde in my countre ar trees that bere frute that becom birdes fleynge and they ar gode to ete and that that falleth in water lyveth/ and that that fallethe on the erth dyethe and they had greate marvayle of this. In thys lond and many other aboute there ar trees that bere clowes and nutmygges and canel and many oter spyces and there ar vynes that beere so greate grapes that a stronge man shall have ynough to do to bere a cluster of the grapes. In that same londe ar the hylles of Caspe that men call uber. and amonge those hylles that ar there/ the Iewes of the x. kyndes enclosed that men call Gog and magog and they may nat come oute on no syde. There was enclosed xxii. kynges with their folke that dwelled before betwene the hylles of Syche and the kynge alysaunder chased theym theder amonge those hylles for he trowed to have enclosed theym there thoroughe workynge of men but he myght nat. but whan he sawe that he myght nat/ he prayed to god that he wolde fulfyll that he had begon/ and god herde his prayer and enclosed the hilles togeder so that the Iewes dwell there as they were locked in/ and there is hylles all aboute theym. but at one syde and there is see of gaspy. And some men myght aske. there is a see on one syde/ Why go they nat oute there. for therto answere I that all if it be called a see. It is no see/ but a stange standynge amonge hylles/ and it is the gretteste stange of all the worlde. And if [h2ᵛ] they went over the see they wote nat where for to aryve. for they can no speche but their owne. and ye shall understonde that the Iewes have no lawe eft their owne lawe in all the world. but they that dwell in these hylles/ and yet they pay trybute for their londe to the quene of armony. And somtyme it is so that som of the iewes go over the hylles but many men may nat passe there samen for the hilles ar so greate and so high. Nevertheles men say in that countre there by that in the tyme of antecryst they shal do moche harme to crysten men. And therfore all the Iewes that dwell in diverse partyes of the worlde lere for to speke Ebrewe. for they thatt the Iewes that dwell amonge the hylles beforesayde shall come oute of the hylles and they speke all ebrewe and nat elles. and than shall these Iewes speke ebrewe to them and lede theym into cristendom for to destroy cristen men. For these Iewes say they Wote by their prophesies that those Iewes that ar amonge those hylles of Caspy shall come oute/ and crysten men shalbe in their subieccion as they be under crysten men. and if ye woll wete howe they shall fynde the passage oute as I have understonde I shall tell you. In tyme of antecryst a fox shall make his den in the same place where kynge alysaundre dyd make the gates and he shall so in ther erthe and perse it thorough unto that he come among the Iewes. And whan they see this fox they shall have greate marvayle of hym for they sawe never such beste. for other bestes have they amonge them many. and they shall chase this fox and pursue hym unto that he be fled ageyne into his hole that he cam fro. and than shall they grave after as he wente unto they come to the gates that [h3ʳ] Alysaundre dyd make of greate stones well dight with symont. and they shal breke these gates and so shal they fynde the yssue. From this londe men shall go unto the londe of Bakary where ar many wycked men and fell. In that londe ar trees that bere woll as ist it were shepe of whych they

Hippopotami and Gryphons

make clothe. In this londe ar many Ipotaynes that dwell somtyme on londe/ somtyme on water and ar halfe man and half hors and they ete nat but men whan they may gete theym. In this londe ar many gryffons more than in another place. and som say they have the body before as an egle/ and behynde as a lyon. And they say soth. for they ar made so/ but the gryffon hathe a body gretter than viii. lyons and gretter and stalworthyer than an hundred egles. For certeynly he woll bere to his nest flyinge an horse and a man upon his backe or two oxen yocked samen as they go at ploughe for he hathe longe nayles on his fete and greate as it were hornes of oxen and of those they make cuppes there to drynk of and of his rybbes they make bowes to shote

Cotton ch. 30

The Empire of Prester John

FRo this londe of Bakary men go thorowe many iourneys to the londe of Prester Iohn that is a great emperoure of ynde and men call his londe the Ile of Pantoxore. ≠ This emperoure Prester Iohn holdeth greate londes and many and gode cytees/ and gode townes in his his† kyngdom many greate Iles and large. For this londe of ynde is all departed in Iles bicause of greate flodes that come oute of paradyse. and also in the see ar many greate Iles. The beste cyte that is in the **[h ii]** **[h3ᵛ]** Ile of Pentoxore is called Nyse for that is a noble cyte and ryche. Prester Iohn hath under hym many kynges. and many dyvers folke/ and his londe is gode and rych but nat so ryche as the londe of the great chane. for marchauntes com nat so moche theder as they do into the londe of the grete chan for it is so longe wey. And also they fynde in the Ile of Chatey† all that they have myster of/ as spicery clothes of golde and other rychesse. And all if they myght have better chepe in the lond of prester Iohn neverthelesse they lette for the longe wey and greate peryllis in the see. for there is many

The Lodestone Rocks

places in the see where ar greate roches of a stone that is called adamonde. the whiche of his owne kynde draweth to hym yron and for as moche that there shulde passe no ship that had nayles of yron. for it shulde drawe it to hym. therfore they dare nat wende into that countre with shippes for drede of adamandes. I went ones in that se and sawe as longe as it had bene a great yle of trees and stockes/ and braunches. growynge/ and the shypman sayde that those was of greate shyppes that were dwellynge there thoroughe vertue of the adamandes and of thynges that were in the shyppes were those trees sprongen and waxen.

¶ And suche roches are in many places in that see. and therfore dare no shypmen passe that wey. and another also they drede the longe wey. and therfore they wende too Chatay that is nere unto theym. and yet is it nat so nere that theym behoveth fro Venys or fro Geene be in see to warde Chatay xi. or xii. monethes.

The londe of Prester Iohn is longe/ and marchauntes passe theder thorough the londe of Persy and come unto [h4ʳ] a cyte that men call Ermes. for a Phylosopher that men called Ermes foundyd it/ and they passe an arme of the see and cometh to another cyte that men call Saboth and there fynde they all marchaundyses and popyniayes as greate plente as larkes in oure countre. In thys countre is lytell whete or barly. and therfore they ete ryse and mylke and chese and other frutes. This emperoure prester Iohn weddeth comonly the doughter of the greate chane. And the greate chan his doughter. In the lond of prester Iohn is many dyvers thynges and many precious stoones so greate and so large that they make of theym vessell platers and cuppes/ and many other thynges/ of whyche it were to longe to tel: but somwhat of his lawe and of his feyth shall I tell you. This emperoure prester Iohn is crysten and greate party of his londe. Also but they have nat all the artycles of oure feyth but they trowe wel in the fader and the son and the holy goost. and they are full devoute and true one to another. and they make no force of catell. and he hath under hym lxxii. provynces. and countrees and in eche one is a kynge/ and those kynges have other kynges under them. and in this londe are many marveyles. For in that londe is the gravelly see that is of sonde and of gravell and no drop of Water. and it ebbethe and floweth with right greate wawes/ as another see doth/ and it is never styll ne never in rest and no man may passe that londe beyonde it. And all if it so be that there be noo water in that see. yet men may fynde fysshe right gode and of other fasyon and shappe/ than is in any other sees. and also they are of full goode savoure/ [h4ᵛ] and swete and gode to ete. And at thre iournes froo that see ar greate hylles thorowe whyche cometh a greate flode that cometh fro paradyse and it is full of precious stones and no drop of water/ and it renneth with gret wawes into the gravelly see. And this flode thre dayes renneth so fast and stereth greate stones of the roches wyth hym that make moche noyse. and as sone they come into the gravelly see they ar nomore sene. and in those thre dayes whan

---

Of the Law and Faith of Prester John

The Gravelly Sea

it renneth thus noman dare come in it. but the other dayes men may go therin where they woll: and also beyonde that flode towarde the wyldernesse is a greate pleyne all sondy and gravelly amonge hylles/ and in that pleyne growe trees that at the rysinge of the son eche day begynne to growe/ and so growe they to mydday. and bere frutes but no man dar ete of that frute/ for it is a maner of yron/ and after mydday it turneth ageyne into the erthe. so that whan the sonne goth downe tt† is no thynge seene: And so doth it every day. and there is in that wyldernes many wylde men with hornes on their hedes/ and ryghte hydous/ and they speke nat but grunt as swyne. And in that countre ar many popyniayes that they calle in theyr langage pystak and they speke thorough ther owne kynde as apertly as a man. and those that speke well have longe tonges and large/ and on every fote fyve tose. there are som that hath but thre tose. and tho same speke noughte or very lytell

¶ This emperoure Prester Iohn whan he gothe to batayle he hath no baner borne before hym but he hath borne before hym iii. crosses of fyne golde and those are great [h5ʳ] and large and wel dight with precious stones and for to kepe eche a crosse is ordeyned a thousande men of armes and mo than an hundred thousande on fote in maner as men kepe a standard in bataile in other places and he hathe men withouten noumbre whan he goth to any batayle ageyne any other lord. And whan he hathe no batayle but rydeth with prevy company than doth he bere before hym but a cros of tre nat paynted and withoute golde and precyous stones and all playne in token that oure lord Iesu cryst suffred deth on a crosse of tre. And also he hathe borne before hym a plate of golde full of erthe in token that his lordship and nobley shall turne to nought and his flesshe shall turne to erthe. And there before hym also another vessell full of iewellys and golde and precyous stones in token of nobley and his myght. And he dwell comonly at the cyte of Suse/ and there is hys pryncipall palys that is so riche that marveyle is to tell. and above the princypal toure of the palys ar two pomelles of gold all rounde. and eche one of those hath two Carbuncles greate and large that shyne right clere on the nyght. And the pryncipal gates of this palys ar of precyous stones that men calle Sardyn. and the borders of the barres are of evory. and the wyndowes of the hall and chambers ar of crystal. And tables that they ete of som ar of emeraudes som ar of mastyk som of gold and pre-

Prester John's Palace

cious stones and the pyllers that bere the tables ar of such stones also and the greses on the whyche the emperoure goth to his see/ where he setteth at mete one is of mastyk and other of cystall†/ another of Iasby grene. another of dyasper. another of sardyn. another of Cormlyn. another of Sempton. And [h5ᵛ] that he setteth upon his fote is of crysolites and all these greses ar bordured with fyne golde and wel dight with greate perles and other precious stones/ and the sydes of his sege ar emeraudes bordured with gold and with precious stones. the pyllers in his chamber ar of fyne gold with many carbuncles and other such stones that gyve greate lyght on the nyght. and all if the charbuncles gyve great lyght. Nevertheles there brenneth eche nyght xii. great vessellis of crystall full of bame to gyve gode smel/ and to dryve awey wycked eyre. The forme of his bed is all of saphyre wel bounde with golde to make him to slepe wel and for to stroy lechery. for he woll nat lye by hys wyves but thryes in the yere after the sesons and all only for getynge of childre And he hath also a fayre palys at the cyte of Nyse where he dwelleth whan he wol but the eyre there is nat so wel tempered as it is at the cyte of Suse. and he hath eche day in his court mo than xxx. thousand men withoute comers and goers. but xxx. thousand there. And in the countre of the greate chane spende nat so moche as xii. thousand in our countre. he hath evermore vii. kynges in his court to serve hym. and echone of theym serveth a moneth. and with these kynges serve alwey. lxxii. dukes and ccc. erles/ and eche day they ete in his court xii. archebysshoppes and xx. bysshops The patryarke of saynt Thomas is as he were a pope. and archebysshops and bysshopes/ and abbottes all are kynges in that countre. And som of the lordes is mayster of the hall. som of the chamber. som stywarde. and somme marshal: and som other officers and therfore he his ful richely served. and his londe lastethe in brede foure monethes iourney/ and it is of length withoute mesure In this Ile of [h6ʳ] of† prester Iohn is greate plente of godes and moche riches and many precious stones In that londe was a riche man nat longe syth that men called there Catolonabes/ he was full riche and he had a fayre castell in an hyll and stronge and he had made a wall all aboute the hyll right strong and fayre within that he had a fayre gardeyne wherein were many trees beringe all maner of frutes that he might fynde/ and he dyd plant therin all maner of erbes of goode smell and that bare floures. and there Was

The Assassins' Paradise

many fayre welles/ and by them was made many fayre halles/ and chambers dight with gold and asure and he had made there divers storyes and bestes and birdes that songe and turned by engyne and orbage as they had be al quyk/ and he had in his gardeyne that he myght fynde to make a man solace/ and comfort. and he had also there in that gardeyne maydens wyth in the age of xv. yere the fayrest he myght fynde. and men chyldren of the same age. and they were cladde with clothes of golde/ and he sayde that tho same were aungellis and he had do made thre hylles fayre and gode all enclosed aboute with precious stones of Iaspy and crystall and well bounde with golde and perles/ and other maner of stones. and he had made a condyte under the erthe/ so that whan he wolde the walles ran somtyme with mylk. somtyme with wyne somtyme with hony. and this place is called Paradyse. ¶ And whanne any yonge bachelere of the countre knyght/ or Squyer cometh to hym for solace and disport. he ledeth hym into his Paradyse and shewe unto hym all these dyvers thynges/ and dyverse songes of byrdes and also of his damoselles/ and hys welles. and he dyd stryke dyvers instrumentes of musyke in an [h6ᵛ] hygh toure that myght be sene and sayde those were aungelles of god and that place was paradise that god hath graunted to those that beloved whan he sayde. ¶ Dabo vobis terram fluentem lac et mel [Leviticus 20:24]. That is to say I shal gyve you londe flowynge mylke and hony. And thanne thys riche man dyd these men drynke a maner of drynke of which they were dronken and he sayde to them if they wolde dye for his sake that whanne they were dede they shulde come into his paradyse. and they shulde be of the age of those maydens and shulde dwell alwey with them and he shulde put theym in a fayre paradyse where they shulde see god in his ioy and in his mageste/ and thanne they graunted to do all that he wolde and than he badde theym go and sle suche a lorde/ or a man of the countre that he was wroth with. and that they shulde have no drede of no man. and if they were slayne theym selfe for hys sake he shulde put theym in his paradyse whan they were dede. and so went these bachelers to sle greate lordes. of the countre. and were slayne theym self in hope to have that paradyse. and thus he venged of hys ennemyes thorough his desert. and whan ryche men of the countre perseyved this malice and cautele and the wyle of this Catolonabes they gadred theym togeder and assayled the Castell and slowe hym and destroyed all his godes and his fayre places and richesse that were in his Paradyse/ the place of the walles is there yet and som other thynges. but rychesse is nat there. and it is nat longe syth he was destroyed. ≠ A litell fro that place on the lyfte syde besyde the ryver of Physon is a greate marvayle. There is a vale betwene two hylles that foure myle is longe. som call it [i1ʳ] the valey Enchanted: som the valey of devylles. som the valey perylous and in that valey ar many tempestes and greate noyse and hydous every day and nyght. and somtyme as it were a noyse of Taburnes of nakers and of trompettes as it were at a greate fest. This valey is all full of devyllis and hath ben alwey and men say there that it is an entre to hell. In this valey is moche golde and sylver. wherfore many crysten men and other go theder for covetyse to have of that golde/ and sylver. but fewe of theym come oute ageyne for they ar as sone strangled of devylles. and in myddell of that vale upon a Roche is a vysage and the hede of a fende bodily right hidous and dredefull to se. and there is no thynge sene but the hede. to the shulders. but there is no man cristen in the worlde ne other so hardy that he ne shulde have greate drede for to behold it/ for he beholdeth eche man so sharply and so felly. and his iyen ar so styrynge and so sprenkelynge as fyre and he chaungeth so oft his countenaunce that no man dare come nere for all the worlde and oute of his mouth and his nose cometh greate plente of fyre of dyverse coloures. and somtyme is the fyre so stynkynge that no man may suffre it. but alwey a gode crysten man and that is stable in the feyth may go therin withoute harme if they shryve theym well and blysse them wyth the token of the crosse than shall the devyllis have no power of theym.

And ye shall understonde that whan my felowes and I were in that valey we had full greate thought if we shulde put oure bodyes in aventure to go thoroughe it/ and som of my felowes accorded therto .and som wolde nat accorde therto. and there was in oure company two freres [i i] [i1ᵛ] Mynours of lumbardy/ and they sayde if any of us wold go in they wolde go also. and whan they had sayde soo/ upon trust on theym we sayde that we wolde goo. and we dyd synge a messe and we were shryven and houseled and we went in xiiii. and whan we came oute we were but x. and we wyst nat Wheder oure felowes were lost there or they turned ageyne/ but we sawe nomore of theym

other of oure felawes that wold nat go with us in went aboute by another wey for to be before us and so they were and we went thorough the Valey/ and sawe there many marvelous thynges/ golde. sylver/ and precious stones and Iewellys greate plente on many sydes as us thoughte wheder it was as it semed I wote nat for I touched them nat. for the devylles ar so subtell and queynt that make many tymes a thynge to seme that it is nat for to desceyve men. and therfore I wolde touche no thynge for drede of ennemyes that I sawe in many lykenesses what of ded bodyes that I sawe lye in the valey/ but I dare nat say that they were nat all bodies but they semed bodies thorow makynge of devyllys. and we were oft casten downe to the erthe thorough wende and thonder and tempestes/ but god helped us alwey and so passed we thorowe that valey withoute peryll and harme thanked be god almyghty that us kept well. And beyonde that valey is a

<small>Giants and Dangerous Women</small>

gret Ile Where folke are as greate as geauntes of xxviii. fote or xxx. fote longe. and they have no clothynge but beestys skynnes that hange on theym/ and they ete no brede but flesshe rawe and drynke mylke and they have no houses and they ete gladlyer flessh of men than of other. and men sayd us that beyonde that yle is one yle where ar gretter geauntes [i2ʳ] as of xlv. or l. fote longe. and som say of l. cubytes longe but I sawe nat theym. and amonge those geauntes ar gret shepe as it were yonge oxen and they bere great Woll these shepe have I sene many tymes. Another yle is there occian in the see where ar many yll and fell women and they have precious stones in their iyen. and they have suche kynde that if they behold any man With wreth they sle theym of the beholdynge as the baselyk doth. another Ile is there of fayre folke and gode where the custume is such that the fyrste nyght that they ar wedded they take a certeyne man that is ordeyned therfore. and do hym ly by their wyves to have their maydenhede/ and they gyve hym greate reward for his travayle/ and those men ar called gadlibiriez. for men of that countre holde it a great thynge to make a woman no maydon and if it be so that the husbonde fynde hyr a maydon the nyght after. for peraventure he that lay by hir was dronken or for any other skyll the husbonde shall pleyne of hym to the lawe that he hath nat do his devoure/ and he shall grevuously be punysshed and chastysed/ but after the first night they kepe ther wyves well that they speke nat with those men and I asked what was the cause why they had that custom and they sayde somtyme men lay wyth their wyves first and none other. and their wyves had edders in their bodyes and stonged their husbonde on their yerde and their bodyes and so was many man slayne.

¶ And therfore hadde they that custom to lete other men have their maydenhede for drede of the dethe And thus they suffre theym to assay the passage or they put theym unto aventure.

[i2ᵛ] ¶ Another is there where women make moche sorowe whan their childre ar borne. and whan they ar dede they make greate ioy and cast theym in a greate fyre and brenne theym. and they that love well their husbondes whanne they ar dede they cast theym in a fyre to brenne also. for they say that fyre shall make theym clene of all fylthe and vyces and they shalbe cleene in another worlde. and the cause why they wepe and make sorowe whan their chyldren are borne. and that they make ioy at theyr deth. they say a chylde whan he is borne he cometh into this worlde for to traveyle and sorowe and hevynesse. and whanne they ar dede they go to paradyse where ryvers ar of mylke and hony. and there is lyfe and Ioy and plente of godes withoute travayle and sorowe. In this Ile they make theyr kynges by chesynge. and they chese hym nat for his rychesse ne his nobley/ but hym that is of gode condycyons and most rightwys and trewe/ that Iugethe eche man truly lytell and moche after their trespas. And the kynge may iuge no man to dethe wythoute counseyle of his barons and that all they assent. And if so be that the kynge do a greate trespasse as slee a man or suche other he shalbe dede. but he shalbe slayne. but they shall defende and forbede that no man be so hardy to make hym company ne to speke wyth hym ne gyve hym mete ne drynke and thus he shall dye. they spare no man that hath done trespas for love ne for lordshyp ne rychesse nor nobley that men do hym right after that he hathe done. And there is a nother Ile where is greate plente of folke. and they ete never flesshe of hares ne of hennes: ne of goose/ but yet there is many of theym/ but they ete gladly flesshe of all [i3ʳ] other bestes and they drynke mylke. In this countre they wedde their doughters and other of their kyn as theym lyketh. and if there be ten or twelve men in an house echon of their wyves shalbe comon to other. And a nyght shal one have one of the wyves and another nyghte another/ and if she have any chylde. she may gyve to which of them she woll. so that no man wote if it be his or nat. In this londe and many other places of ynde ar

Crocodiles and Other Strange Animals

many Cokadrilles that is a maner of a longe nedder and a nyghtis they dwelle on water/ and on dayes they dwell on londe and roches and they ete nat in wynter. This nedder slee men and eteth theym gretande and they have no tonge. In this countre and many other men cast sede of coton and sowe it eche yere and it groweth as it were smale trees that bere coton. In araby is many byrdes/ and som men calle Gyrsantis that is a full fayre best that is hygher than a greate courser or a stede/ but his necke is nere xx. cubites longe. and his croupe and his tayle is lyke to an herte/ and he may loke over an hyghe hous. and there is many Camylions that is a lytell best and he etethe/ and drynkethe never and he chaungeth oft hys coloure. for somtyme he is of one coloure and somtyme of another. and he maye chaunge hym into all colours that he woll but blacke and reede. There ar many wylde swyne of many colours/ and as greate as oxen. and they ar spotted as it were smale fawnes and there ar lyons all whyte. and there be other bestes as great as grete stedes that men call Lonhorans and som men call theym Tontes and their hede is blak/ and thre longe hornes in his fronte as cuttynge as a sharpe swerde. and he chaseth and woll sle the Olyfaunte. [i ii]

Cotton ch. 32

The Brahmins

[i3ᵛ] and there is many other maner of bestes of whom it were to longe to wryte. ≠ and there is another Ile gode and great and plenteuous where ar gode men and true and of gode lyfe after theyr feythe. and if all they be nat crysten. neverthelesse of kynde they ar full of gode vertues/ and they fle all vyces and all synne and malyce for they are nat envyous ne proude ne covetous ne lecherous ne glotenous/ and they do nat unto another man but that they wolde he dyd do theym/ and they fulfyll the x. commaundementes/ and they make no force of rychesse/ ne of havynge. and they swere nat but say nay/ and ye. for they say he that swereth he woll disceyve his neygboure. and som men call this the Ile of Bragamen and som call it the londe of feyth and thorough it renneth a greate ryver that men call Thebe. and generally all men in those Iles and other therby ar trewer and rightwyser than are in other countrees. In this Ile are no theves ne murderers ne comon women ne beggers. and for as moch they are so true and so gode that there is no tempest ne thunder ne warre ne hunger ne other tribulacions. and thus semeth well that god loveth theym well and is well payde of their trouth and their dedes/ and they trowe in god that made all thynge and hym worshyp they and they lyve so ordynatly in mete and drynke that they lyve ryghte longe and many of them dye withoute sykenesse that kynde fayleth theym for age. And kynge alysaunder somtyme sent his men to wynne that londe. and they sent hym letters that sayde thus. What behovethe a man to have all the worlde may nat suffyse thou shalt finde no thynge in us why thou shuldest warrey us for we have no ryches. [i4ʳ] ne tresoure. and all the godes and catell of oure countre ar comon. oure metes that we ete ar oure rychesse. And in sted of tresoure of golde and sylver we make oure tresoure peas and accord of love. and nought have we but a clothe upon oure bodyes. oure wyves are nat arrayed rychely to plesynge. for we holde it a greate foly a man to dyght his body to make it seme fayrer than god made it. we have be evermore in peas tyll nowe that thou wilt disherite us. We have a kinge amonge us nat for to law ne deme no man. for there is no trespassoure among us but all only to lere us to be obedyent to him and so may thou nought take fro us but oure gode peas. And whan alysaunder sawe this Letter. hym thoughte thus that he shulde do to moche harme if he troubled theym and sent to theym that they shulde kepe well their gode maners/ and have no drede of hym. Another Ile is there that is called Synople where also ar gode folke and true/ and full of gode feythe/ and they ar moch lyke in lyvygge† to men before sayde and they go all naked. and into that Ile cam kynge alysaunder. and whan he sawe their gode feythe and trouthe he sayde he shulde do theym noo harme and badde theym aske of hym rychesse and nought elles and they shulde have.

And they answered that they had ryches ynoughe whan they hadde mete and drynke to susteyne their bodyes and they sayde richesse of this worlde is nought worth but if it were so that he myght graunte theym that they shulde never dye that wolde they pray him. and alysaunder sayde that might he nat do for he was dedly and shuld dy as they shuld

[i4ᵛ] Than sayde they why art thou so proude and wold wynne all the worlde and have in thy subiecconn as it were a god and thou hast no terme of thy lyfe/ and thou wylte have all rychesse of the worlde the whyche shall forsake the/ or thou forsake it/ and thou shalt bere noo thynge with the. but it shall dwell to other but as thou was borne naked: so shalt thou be done in erthe. And alysaunder was gretly astonyed of this answere. and if it be so that they have nat the artycles of oure feyth. Nevertheles I trowe that god loveth theym well and their gode entencion and that he taketh their servyce to gre as he dyd of Iob that was a peyne the whyche he helde for his trewe servaunt/ and many other. I trowe well that god loveth Well all those that love hym and serve hym mekely and trewly and that despyse the vayne glory of the worlde as these men do and as Iob dyd. and therfore sayde oure lorde thoroughe the mouth of Isay† the prophete thus. Ponam eis multiplices leges meas [cf. Hosea 8:12]. That is to say I shall put to theym my lawes in many maners. and the gospell sayth thus. Alias oves habeo que non sunt ex hoc ovili [John 10:16]. That is to say. I have other shepe that ar nat of this folde/ and therto accordeth the avysion that saynt Peter sawe at Iaffe how the aungell cam fro heven and brought with hym of all maner of bestes and nedders and foules in all maner. and sayde to saynt peter Take and ete/ and saynt Peter answered. I ete never of bestes unclene/ and the aungel sayde to hym. Non dicas imunda† que deus mundavit [Acts 11:9]. That is to say Call thou nat those thynges unclene that god hath clensed. this was done in token that men shuld nat have many men in despite for ther divers lawes. for we wote never [i5ʳ] whom god loveth. and whom god hateth. And there is a nother Ile that men call Pytan. Men of thys lond tyll no londe for they ete nought. and they ar smale men but nat so smale as pegmanes. These men lyve with smell of wylde apples. And whan they go ferre oute of the countre they bere apples with theym. for as sone they lese the savoure of apples they dye/ they are nat full resonable/ but as it were bestes. And than is there another Ile where the folke ar all feders but the face and the pames of their handes. These men go as well above the see as on the londe and they ete flesshe and fysshe all rawe. ¶ In this Ile is a greate ryver that is two myle brode and halfe that men call Renemar. and beyonde that ryver is great wyldernesse as men that have be there say. In such wyldernesse as men say ar the trees of the son and the mone that spake to kynge alysander and tolde hym of his dethe and men say that folke that kepe these trees and ete of the frute of theym. they lyfe CCCC. or fyve hundred yere thorough vertue of the frute. and we wold gladly have go heder.²⁵ but I trowe that an hundred thou-

The Trees of the Sun and Moon

---

²⁵ Possibly "theder."

sande men of armes shulde nat passe the wyldernesse for greate plente of wyld bestes as dragons and edders that sle men whan they have any. In this londe is many Olyfauntes all white and blewe withoute noumbre and unycornes and lyons of many maners. Many other yles ar in the lond of Prester Iohn that were to longe to tell and moche rychesse and nobley of precyous stones in greate plente. I trowe that we have herde say whys† thy Emperoure is called Prester Iohn. but for those that wote nat I shall say. ¶ There was somtyme an Emperoure that was [i5ᵛ] a noble prynce and doughty/ and he hadde many crysten knyghtes with hym. and the emperoure thought he wolde se the maner of servyce in crysten churches/ and than was churches of cristendom in turky surry and tartary Ierusalem Palestyn araby harap and all the londes of egypt And this emperoure cam with a cristen knight into a churche of egypt and it was on a Saturday after wytsonday[26] whan the bysshop made orders and he behelde to the servyce and he asked of the knyght what folke those shulde be that stode before the bisshop/ and the knyght sayd they shulde be prestes. and he sayde he wolde nomore be called kynge ne emperoure but prest and he wolde have the name of hym that cam first oute of the prestes/ and he was called Iohn and so have all themperours sythen be called prestre Iohn. In that londe ar many crysten men of gode feyth and gode lawe/ and they have prestes to sing messe and they make the sacrament as men of grece doo but they say nat so many thynges as oure prestes do for they sey nat but that the apostles sayde as saynt Peter/ and saynt Thomas/ and other apostles whanne they sange messe and sayde Pater noster. And the wordes with the whyche goddis body is sacred. we have many addyconns of popes that have ben ordeyned of whyche men of those countrees knowe nat.

≠ ¶ Towarde the Est syde of the londe of prester Iohn is an Ile that men call Tabrobane/ that is right gode and fructuouse. and there is a greate kynge and a ryche and he is obedyent unto prester Iohn/ and that kynge is alwey made by chesynge. ¶ In this Ile ar two wynters/ [i6ʳ] and two somers:

Why the Emperor is called Prester John

Cotton ch. 33

---

[26] Described by Higgins (*Writing East*, 195) as a "pointlessly precise date," this may actually correspond to one of the prescribed days for ordinations in the Coptic church. See O. H. E. Burmester, *Ordination Rites of the Coptic Church* (Cairo: Société d'Archéologie Copte, 1986), 17–19.

and they shere corne twyes in the yere. And all tymes in the yere ar gardeyns florysshed. There dwell gode folke and resonable and many crysten folke amonge theym that ar full ryche. and the water betwene the londe of prestre Iohn and this Ile is nat full depe for men may see the grounde in many places. and there ar more Estwarde two other Iles. the one is called Orrell and the other Argete of whom all the londe is myne of golde and sylver. In those Iles may men see no sterres clere shinynge. but one sterre that is called Canapos And there may nat men se the mone but in the last quarter. In that Ile is a greate hyll of golde that pyssmyres kepe and they do the fyne golde from the other that is nat fyne golde/ and the pyssmyres ar as gret as houndes so that no man dare come there for drede of pyssmyres that shulde assayle theym so that men may nat werke in that golde ne gete therof but queyntyse/ and therfore whan it is right hote the pyssmyres hyde theym in the erthe from Onderne[27] to none of the day. And than men of the countre take camellys and dromaderyes and other bestes/ and goo theder and charge theym With golde and go awey fast or the pyssmyres come oute of the erthe. And other tymes whan it is nat so hote that the pissmyres hyde them nat they take meres that have foles. and they lay upon these Meres two vesselles as it were two smale barelis tome and the mouthe upwardes and dryve theym theder/ and holden their foles at home.

[i6ᵛ] And whan the pyssmyres sene theyse vesselles. for they have of kynde to leve no thyuge† to me†. They fylle these vesselles of golde. and whan men trowe that the vesselles ar full/ they take the foles and brynge theym as nere as they dare and they whyne and the meres here theym and as sone they come to ther foles. and so men take the gold so than for these pyssemyres woll suffre bestes to goo amonge theym but no men. Beyonde the Iles of the lond of Prester Iohn and his lordship of wyldernesse to goo right est men shall nat fynde but hylles great roches and other myrke londe where no man may see on day/ ne on nyght as men of the countre say. and this wyldernes and myrke londe lasteth to paradyse terrestre where Adam and eve were sette/ but they were there but a lytell whyle and that is towarde the est at begynnynge of the erthe/ but that is nat oure est that we call

The Gold-Digging Ants

The Earthly Paradise

---

[27] Possibly "Underne."

where the sonne rysethe in those countrees towarde paradyse. than it is mydnight in oure countre. for the roundnesse of the erthe for oure lord made the erthe all rounde in myddes of firmament. Of paradyse can I nat speke propirly. for I have nat be there. and that angoreth me. but that I have herde I shal say you. Men say that paradyse terrestre is the hyghest londe of the worlde/ and it is so high that it toucheth nere to the sercle of the mone/ for it is so highe that Noes flode myght nat come therto. the whyche covered all the erthe aboute.
¶ And this Paradyse terrestre is enclosed all aboute with a walle. and that wall is all covered with mosse as it semethe that men may se no stone ne no thynge ellis wherof it is. and the hyghest place of paradyse in the mydes of it [k1ʳ] is one wall that casteth oute the foure flodes that renne thorowe dyvers londes. The first flode is called physon or ganges: and that renneth thorough ynde in that ryver are many precious stones and moche lignum aloes/ and gravell of golde. Another is called Nylus or Gyron and that rennethe thorough Ethiope and egypt. The thirde is called Tygre and that renneth thorough Assary and Ermony the grete. And the forth is called Eufrates that rennethe thorough Ermony and Persy/ and men say that all the swete and fresshe water of the world take theyr springynge of theym. The first ryver is called Physon that is to say a gaderynge of many ryvers to geder and falle into that ryver. and som call it Canges† for a kynge that was in ynde that men called Tangeras for it renneth thorough hys lond And this ryvere is in som place clere in som place troble in som place hote in som place colde. The secounde ryvere is called Nylus or Gyron for it is ever troble. for gyron is to say troble. The third ryver is called Tygris. That is to say fast rennynge. for it renneth faster than any of the other. and so is a best that men call tygrys for he renneth fast. The forth ryver is called Eufrates/ that is to say well brennynge/ for there groweth many gode thynges upon the ryver/ and ye shall understonde that no man lyvynge may go unto that Paradyse. For by land he may nat go for wylde bestes which ar in the wyldernes and for hylles and roches where no man may passe. Ne by those ryvers may no man passe for they come with so greate course and so great wawes that no shyp may go/ ne sayle ageyne theym. Many greate lordes have asayed many tymes to go by those ryvers to Paradyse/ but they [k] [k1ᵛ] myght nat spede in their wey/ for som dyed for wery of rowynge som wex blynde/ and som deefe for noyse

of the waters. so no man may passe there but thorough special grace of god. And for I can tell you nomore of that place I shall say you of that I have sene ≠ in these Iles of the londe of prester Iohn and they ar under the erthe/ to us. and other Iles ar there Who so wolde pursue them for to environ the erthe who so had grace of god to holde the wey he myght come right too the same countrees that he were come of and come fro and so go aboute the erthe and for it were to longe tyme and also many perylles too pas/ fewe men assay to go so/ and yet might be done/ and therfore men came fro these Iles to other Iles coostynge of the lordshyp of Prester Iohn. And men come in the comynge to one Ile that men call Cassoy. and that countre is nere sexty iournes longe/ and more than. l. of brede that is the best londe that is in those countrees save chatay. and if marchauntes come theder as comonly as they do unto chatay. it shuld be better than chatay/ for it is so thyk of cytees and townes that whan a man gothe oute of a cyte he seth as sone another on eche syde/ there is greate plente of spyces and other godes.

¶ The kynge of this yle is full ryche and myghty/ and he holdeth his londe of the great chane/ for that is one of the xii. provynces that the greate chane hath under hym with oute his owne londe/ Fro thys Ile men goo to another kyngdom that men calle Ryboth. and that is also under the greate chane this is a gode countre and plenteuous of corne/ Wyne/ and other thynges. men of this londe have none houses. but they dwell in tentes made of tre.

[k2ʳ] And the pryncipall cyte is all blacke made of blake stones and whyte. And all the stretes are paved with suche stones/ and in that cyte is no man so hardy to spyll blode of man ne beest. for worshyp of a mawmet that is worshypped there. In that cyte dwelle the pope of their lawe that they call lobassy and he gyveth all dignytee and benefyses that fall to the mawmet. And men of relygyon and men that have churches in that countre ar obedyente to hym as men ar here to the pope. In this Ile they have a custume thoroughe all the countre that whan a mans fader is dede they woll do hym greate worship. they send after all his frendes religious prestes and other many. and they bere the body to an hyll with greate ioy and myrth and whan it is there the grettest prelate smyteth of his hede and layeth it upon a greate plate of golde or sylver/ and he gyveth it to his son/ and the son takethe it too his other frendes syngynge and saynge many orysons. and

than the prestys and the religyous cutte the flesshe of the
body in peces and say orysons. and the byrdes of the countre
come theder. For they knowe Well the custome. and they
flye above theym as they were Egles and other byrdes: that
ete flesshe. And the preestys cast the peces unto them And
they bere it awey a lytell from thens and than they ete it and
as prestes in oure countre synge for soules.

 Subvenite sancti dei[28] and so forth. So those prestes
there synge with highe voyce in their langage in this maner
of wyse. Se and beholde howe goode/ and gracyous a man
this was that the aungellys of god come for to fett hym and
bere hym into paradyse.

 And than thinketh the son of the samen man that he is
gretly [k2ᵛ] worshypped whan byrdes have eten his fader and
where ar most plente of byrdes there is most worshyp/ and
thanne cometh the son home with all his frendes/ and makethe them a great feest and the son maketh clene hys faders
hede and gyveth at drynke therof/ and the flesshe of the hede
he shereth and gyveth to his most specyall frendes. som a lytell and som a lytell for a deynte/ and in rememberaunce of
this holy man that the byrdes have eten. and of the scalpe of
the hede the son doth make a cup and therof drynketh he all
his lyfe in rememberaunce of his fader. And from thens to go
x. iournes thoroughe the londe of the greate chane is a full
gode Ile and a great kyngdom/ and the kynge is full myghty
for he hath eche yere CCC. hors charged with rys and other
tentes/ and he hath a noble and a rych lyfe after the maner
of the countre/ for he hath l. damsellis that serve hym eche
day at his mete and bed and do what he woll. and whan he
sitteth at the table they brynge hym mete/ and at eche tyme
v. meases togeder and they synge in the bryngynge a songe/
and they cut his mete and put it in his mouth/ and they have
Long Nails right longe nayles on their handes/ that is a gret nobley in
and that countre and therfore they late their nayles growe as
Small Feet longe as they may/ and som late growe soo longe that they
come aboute their handes and that is a greate nobley: and
gentry/ and the gentry of women is to have smale fete and
therfore as sone as they ar borne: they bynde their fete so
streyte that they may nat wex halfe as they shulde. And he
hath a full fayre paleys and riche where he dwelleth of the

---

[28] The responsory at the beginning of a funeral mass.

which the wall is ii. myle aboute and therin is many faire gardeyns. and all the pament of the hall and chambers is of golde and sylver. And in the myddes of one of theyse gardeynes [k3ʳ] is a lytell hyll wheron is a place made with toures and pynnacles all of golde/ and there woll he syt oft to take the ayre and disport for it is made for no thynge ellys. Fro this londe men may go thorough the londe of the greate chane and ye shall understonde that all these men and folke that have reason that I have spoken of have some artycles of oure feyth if all they be of dyvers lawes and dyvers trowynges they have som gode poyntes of oure trouth and they trowe in god of kynde as their prophesye sayth. Et metuent eum omnes fines terre [Psalm 66:4] That is to say/ and all endes of erth shall drede hym. And in another place. Omnes gentes servient ei [Psalm 72:11]. That is to say. Al folke shal serve hym/ but they can nat speke perfihgtly† but as ther kyndly wytte techeth theym nouther of the son nor of the holy gost can they speke but they can speke wel of the byble and speciall of Genesys and of the bokes of Moyses. And they say that those creatures that they worship ar no goddes/ but they worshyp theym for great vertue that is in theym whyche may nat be wythoute specyall grace of god. and of symulacres and ydols/ they sey that all men have symulacres and that sey they for us cristen men have Images of oure lady/ and other. but they wote nat that we worshyppe nat the ymages of stone ne of tre/ but the sayntes of whom they are made for as the letter techethe clerkes. howe they shall trowe so ymages and paynture techeth leude men/ they say also that the aungel of god speketh to theym in their ydols and do myracles. they sey sothe but it is an yll aungell that doth myracles to mayntene them in their ydolatry. There are many other countreys where I have nat ben nor sene. and therfore I can natte [k3ᵛ] speke propyrly of theym. Also in countrees where I have ben ar many marveyles that I spake nat of for it were to longe tale. and therfore holde you payde at this tyme that I have sayde. for I woll say nomore of marveylis that ar there. so that other men that go theder may fynde ynoughe to say that I have nat tolde. ¶ And I Iohn Maundvyle that went oute of my countre and passed the se the yere of oure lorde a M ccc. xxxii. and I have passed thorowe many londes and Iles and countrees/ and nowe am come to rest I have compyled this boke and do wryte it the yere of oure lorde M. ccc. lxvi. at xxxiii. yere after my departynge fro my countre. and for as

The
Visit to
the Pope

moch as many men trowe nat but that they se with theyr iyen or that they may conceyve in their kyndly wytte therfore I made my way to rome in my comynge homwarde to shewe my boke to the holy fader the pope and tell hym of the marveylis that I had sene in dyvers countrees so that he with his wise counsell wold examyne it wyth dyverse folke that ar at rome for there dwell men of al nacions of the worlde. and a lytell tyme after whan he/ and hys counseyle had examyned it all thorowe he sayde to me for certeyne that all was sothe. for he sayde he had a boke of laten that conteyned all that and moche more of the whych the Mapa mundi is made/ the whych boke I sawe. and therfor the holy fader the pope hath ratyfyed and confermed my boke in all poyntes. And I pray to all those that rede thys boke that they woll pray for me/ and I shall pray for them and all those that say for me a Pater noster and an Ave maria that god forgyve me my synnes. I make them parteners and graunt theym part of all my gode pylgrymages [k4ʳ] and other gode dedes which I ever dyd or shall do to my lyves ende and I pray to god of whom all grace comethe that he woll all the reders and herers that ar cristen men fulfyll of his grace/ and save them body and soule and brynge theym to his ioy that ever shall last he that is in the trynyte fader/ son/ and holy goost that lyvethe and regneth god withoute ende amen

¶ Here endeth the boke of Iohn Maundvyle.
knyght of wayes to Ierusalem and of marveylys
of ynde and of other countrees.
Emprented by Rychard Pynson.

APPENDIX I:

THE ENGLISH MANUSCRIPTS OF

THE BOOK OF JOHN MANDEVILLE[1]

DEFECTIVE VERSION

Group A:[2]
1. Corning, N.Y., Corning Museum of Glass MS 6
2. Cambridge, Magdalene College MS Pepys 1955
3. Cambridge, University Library MS Dd. i. 17
4. Oxford, Balliol College MS 239
5. Oxford, The Queen's College MS 383
6. Oxford, Bodleian Library MS Rawlinson D. 101
7. Oxford, Bodleian Library MS Douce 33
8. Cambridge, University Library MS Ff. v. 35

---

[1] This listing is adapted from M. C. Seymour's 1966 and 1993 catalogues in "English Manuscripts" and *Sir John Mandeville*, with reference to Bennett's catalogue in *Rediscovery* and Deluz's in *Livre*, as well as to my own investigation of the manuscripts. Seymour has located several texts not listed by Bennett or by Deluz, who uses Bennet as her major source for the English manuscripts.
    I list here 35 manuscripts of the Defective version. Higgins (*Writing East*, 22) says there are "c. 38," perhaps including my Related Texts, numbers 3, 4, and 5 in that accounting.

[2] Seymour's delineation of subgroups A-i, A-ii, and A-iii has undergone substantive changes between the 1966 classification ("English Manuscripts") and the 1993 (*Sir John Mandeville*, 42–46). In 1966, Ai, Aii, and Aiii corresponded to manuscripts 1–2, 3–7, and 8–9. The "Extracts" (Oxford, Bodleian Library MS Ashmole 751, listed here as Related Text no. 4) were listed separately but associated with a lost manuscript of the Aii subgroup. In the 1993 classification, Ai, Aii, and Aiii correspond to 1–2, 3–5, and 8–9. Numbers 6 and 7, as well as the Ashmole extracts, are now listed as unaffiliated A-texts, somewhat complicating Seymour's earlier assertion of a clear tripartite division of the A-texts. No explanation for these changes in classification has so far appeared. Cf. pp. xxxvi–xxxviii and n. 44.

Group B:
10. London, British Library MS Arundel 140
11. London, British Library MS Royal 17 B. xliii
12. London, British Library MS Harley 2386
13. London, British Library MS Harley 3954. [Illustrated: 100 colored drawings, with space left for 38 more. Seymour speculates that "Leaf 9 of the 8th quire (now lost) probably contained two full-page drawings" ("English Manuscripts," 188), which seems likely as the surrounding text is continuous. Seymour also notes that the text has been edited so that drawings appear at paragraph breaks.]
14. San Marino, Calif., Huntington Library MS HM 114

Independently derived:
15. London, British Library MS Royal 17 C. xxxviii. [Illustrated: 110 tinted drawings in the margins of the text, mainly at the base of the page.]

Group C:
16. Rugby School MS Bloxam 1008
17. London, British Library MS Additional 33758
18. Cambridge, Trinity College MS R. 4. 20. [Decorated: "on ff. 1, 89, 92, foliated borders and pictorial initials. ... The first depicts a knight 'Sir John Mandeville', and the second a walled town 'Thebes'. Gilded chapter initials throughout" (Seymour, "English Manuscripts," 190-91).]
19. Oxford, Bodleian Library MS Douce 109
20. Oxford, Bodleian Library MS Rawlinson B. 216
21. Oxford, Bodleian Library MS Rawlinson D. 100
22. Oxford, Bodleian Library MS Lat. misc. e 85 [Fragment—corresponding to Cotton chaps. 13-15]
23. Sneyd Manuscript [Missing since its sale at Sotheby's, October 1945][3]
24. Cambridge, Fitzwilliam Museum MS Bradfer-Lawrence Dep. BL 7

Group D:
25. Cambridge, University Library MS Gg. i. 34, part 3
26. Oxford, Bodleian Library MS Additional C. 285
27. Oxford, Bodleian Library MS Tanner 405

---

[3] Seymour 1966 lists this manuscript as "subgroup and whereabouts unknown," but the 1993 classification lists it as a C-text. It is unclear how, if the manuscript remains missing, it has been reclassified, but I here follow Seymour 1993, having no fuller information to offer.

28. Princeton, University Library MS Taylor 10[4]
29. Manchester, Chetham's Library MS 6711

Group E:
30. Edinburgh, National Library of Scotland MS Advocates 19. 1. 11
31. Dublin, Trinity College MS E. 5. 6
32. Oxford, Bodleian Library MS Rawlinson D. 652
33. Oxford, Bodleian Library MS Laud Misc. 699
34. London, British Library MS Sloane 2319
35. London, British Library MS Additional 37049[5] [Epitome. Illustrated: full-page, marginal, and interlinear tinted drawings. Edition: M. C. Seymour, "The English Epitome of *Mandeville's Travels,*" *Anglia* 84 (1966): 27–58.]

COTTON VERSION

36. London, British Library MS Cotton Titus C. xvi [Editions: A. W. Pollard, *The Travels of Sir John Mandeville* (London: Macmillan, 1900; New York: Dover, 1964); P. Hamelius, *Mandeville's Travels,* 2 vols., Early English Text Society os 153–54 (London, Kegan Paul, 1919); M. C. Seymour, *Mandeville's Travels* (Oxford: Clarendon Press, 1967); and others.]

EGERTON VERSION

37. London, British Library MS Egerton 1982 [Editions: G. Warner, *The Buke of John Maundeuill* (London: Roxburghe Club, 1889); M. Letts, *Mandeville's Travels,* Vol. 1. Hakluyt Society 2nd ser. 101 (London: Hakluyt Society, 1953); C. W. Moseley, *The Travels of Sir John Mandeville* (New York: Penguin, 1983), with additions from Cotton.]

BODLEY VERSION

38. Oxford, Bodleian Library MS Rawlinson D. 99 [Edition: M. Letts, *Mandeville's Travels,* Vol. 2, Hakluyt Society 2nd ser. 102 (London: Hakluyt Society, 1953).]
39. Oxford, Bodleian Library MS e Musaeo 116 [Edition: M. C. Seymour, *The Bodley Version of Mandeville's Travels* (London: Oxford University Press, 1963).]

---

[4] Listed by Seymour in 1966 as an E-text, "MS owned by Mr. B. Penrose" ("English Manuscripts," 171). In 1993 it has been silently reclassified as a D-text.

[5] I include the epitome among the manuscripts of the *Book* rather than as a related text because, while much abridged, it seems to me to be a form of the *Book* in a way that the extracts and poetic versions, which rather use the *Book* as a source, are not.

Related Texts [6]

1. Coventry, City Record Office MS. A "Metrical version" of 2, 947 lines, in couplets [Decorated: marginal scrollwork and gold initials. Edition: M. C. Seymour, *The Metrical Version of Mandeville's Travels* (London: Oxford University Press, 1973).]
2. Oxford, Bodleian Library MS e Musaeo 160. The "Stanzaic fragment," based on *The Book of John Mandeville* and Marco Polo's *Travels*. [Edition: M. C. Seymour, "Mandeville and Marco Polo: A Stanzaic Fragment," *Australian University Modern Language Association* 21 (1964): 39-52.]
3. Oxford, Bodleian Library MS Ashmole 751. The "Extracts," noted in Seymour ("English Manuscripts," 172) as "based on ... a lost manuscript of sub-group A (ii) of the Defective Version." [Edition: M. C. Seymour, "Secundum Iohannem Maundvyle," *English Studies in Africa* 4 (1961): 148-58.]
4. Oxford, Bodleian Library MS Digby 88 fol. 28. A recently discovered set of extracts—root text unknown. [Edition: P. J. Horner, "*Mandeville's Travels*: A New Manuscript Extract," *Manuscripta* 24 (1980): 171-75.]
5. Ripon, Library of Ripon Cathedral. Two discontinuous leaves in the book, *Petri Carpentarii ... Epistola*. The "Ripon fragment." [Edition: A. C. Cawley, "A Ripon Fragment of *Mandeville's Travels*," *English Studies* 38 (1957): 262-65.]

---

[6] Seymour 1993 lists numbers 1 and 2 as separate versions, number 3 as a manuscript of Group A, and numbers 4 and 5 as unaffiliated fragments, possibly associated with Group E.

APPENDIX II:
EARLY ENGLISH EDITIONS OF
THE BOOK OF JOHN MANDEVILLE[1]

While there is speculation that William Caxton may have planned an English edition of the *Book* as early as 1490, when he is said to have acquired the Egerton manuscript (British Library MS Egerton 1982), there is no evidence that such an edition ever came into being. Indeed, the Egerton text would wait for publication until 1889, when George Warner edited it for the Roxburghe Club (*Buke*).

Pynson's 1496 edition is now generally considered by scholars the first in English. Based on a manuscript of the Defective version, it became the basis for three editions by Wynkyn de Worde within the next fifteen years: a fact suggestive of a wide popular readership for the Defective version in the late fifteenth and early sixteenth centuries. Thomas East's 1568 modernization introduced conflation with another Defective text, but it was not until 1725 that the Defective version, traceable to Pynson's 1496 edition, was supplanted as the base text for English editions of the *Book*.

Pynson thus occupies an important position in the transmission and dissemination of the *Book* to a wide English readership. As M. C. Seymour remarks, "the earliest English version of *Mandeville's Travels* [Defective] has not been without honour in its own country. Much of the credit for this is due to its three earliest editors" ("Early English Editions," 207).[2]

---

[1] Major sources for this listing are Seymour, *Sir John Mandeville*, 50–51; Bennett, "Woodcut Illustrations"; and Moseley, "Availability of *Mandeville's Travels*." The description of the editions relies heavily upon Seymour's "Early English Editions" as well, which offers more thorough discussions of many of the earliest.

Several of the editions listed are available through University Microfilms, Ann Arbor, Michigan.

[2] He goes on to add, "and most of all to Thomas East," which may well be true, but for those of us interested in the *Book*'s earlier reception, the emphasis must lie elsewhere.

c. 1496   Richard Pynson.
           British Library G. 6713
           Bodleian Library Arch. G. d. 31 (1) [one leaf]

           A blackletter incunabular edition, apparently stemming from what Seymour classifies as the B-text of the Defective version. Overall, this edition preserves a greater number of readings attributable to its French antecedents than most extant Defective manuscripts. Not illustrated. No chapter headings.

1499   Wynkyn de Worde.
           Cambridge University Library Inc. 5. J. I. 2

           Uses Pynson's edition as copy-text, with minor corrections and linguistic modernizations. Introduces to English audiences 72 woodcut illustrations adapted from those of Anton Sorg's second Augsburg edition, 1481, which have since become synonymous with the *Book*.[3] Includes rubrics, chapter numbers, and a table of contents (present in the Insular version, but lost in transmission to the Defective version).

1503   Wynkyn de Worde.
           Bodleian Library A. e. 89
           Bodleian Library Douce frag. e. 8 [fragment]
           Stonyhurst College Library collection.

           A nearly exact, though reset, reprinting of the 1499 edition.

c. 1510   Wynkyn de Worde.
           Bodleian Library Arch. G. d. 31 (2) [two leaves]
           British Library Harley 5919, #16 [one leaf]

           Apparently another resetting of the 1499 edition.

1568   Thomas East.
           British Library 1045. h. 2

So far no thorough study of the extant editions has been undertaken, and while my research into the Defective texts has brought me into contact with many of the editions listed here, I have by no means seen them all. To provide a comprehensive guide would be a lengthy task, and far beyond the scope of the present work. Thus I offer only what I know, and hope that it will assist others in a more thorough study of the *Book*'s print transmission.

[3] Cf. Bennett, "Woodcut Illustrations," 60. Reproductions of Sorg's 121 woodcut illustrations are printed in Albert Schramm, *Der Bilderschmuck der Frühdrucke*, IV, "Die Drucke von Anton Sorg in Augsburg" (Leipzig, 1921), nos. 579–700.

Largely a reprinting of De Worde, slightly modernized and with some evidence of conflation with a C-text of the Defective version.[4] Bennett notes that the blocks used for East's woodcuts (adapted from De Worde's) are an incomplete set and show signs of wear, which may indicate that they were used for other editions between de Worde 1510 and East 1568 ("Woodcut Illustrations," 66).

East's edition provides the basis for all those following, up to the 1725 Cotton edition.

1582/3   Thomas East.
Bodleian Library Douce MM 489
Folger Shakespeare Library collection

A reprint of the 1568 edition, in different type and with seventeen recut pictures.

1612   Thomas Snodham.
Library of Congress collection

A reprint of East 1582/3, with two blocks recut reversed, and four from East 1568.

1618   Thomas Snodham [often erroneously associated with Thomas Stansby].
British Library G. 6715

1625   Thomas Snodham.
Folger Shakespeare Library collection [the Britwell Court copy]
Huntington Library collection

Reprints the same blocks as 1612, except for twelve recut and five from East 1568.

1632   William Stansby.
British Library G. 6714[5]
Yale University Library Ecd 322 gk

---

[4] Cf. Seymour, "Early English Manuscripts," 206–7, for a more detailed discussion of the evidence for conflation.

[5] Moseley ("Availability," 129 n. 25) dates G. 6714 ca. 1660, adding that conflicting notes appended to the text claim that it was printed by East, and that it was printed c. 1680, not by East.

Includes 72 new woodcuts of "the traditional subjects" (Bennett, "Woodcut Illustrations," 67).

1640   Richard Bishop.
Folger Shakespeare Library collection
Huntington Library collection

Uses Stansby's new blocks as far as sig. L, mingling new with old thereafter.

1650   Richard Bishop ["for E. Dod and N. Ekins"].
John Rylands Library collection

1657   Richard Bishop ["By R. B. and are to sold [sic] by A. Crooke"].
British Library G. 6716

1670   "For Andrew Crooke."
British Library 10055 a. 6

1677   "For R. Scott, T. Basset, J. Wright and R. Chiswell."
"For B. Tooke" [apprentice to A. Crooke's brother, J. Crooke].
British Library C. 32. d. 42
Huntington Library collection

1684   "For R. Scott, T. Basset, J. Wright and R. Chiswell."
British Library G. 6717
British Library 1045 h. 30

Apparently a reprint of East 1658.

1696   "For Rich. Chiswell, B. Walford, Mat. Wotton, and Geo. Conyers."
British Library 6718

In quarto.[6] Includes 70 woodcuts, recut but closely modelled on those of Bishop 1640.

---

[6] Almost all known early editions of the *Book* are in what Moseley calls "the cheap octavo format" ("Availability," 129).

1704[7]	"For Rich. Chiswell, B. Walford, Mat. Wotton, and Geo. Conyers."
	In quarto.
1705	Richard Chiswell. British Library 1077 g. 35 (2)
1722[8]	A. Wilde [for G. Conyers, T. Norris, and A. Bettesworth]. British Library 10056 c. 22
	With its "132 numbered pages, followed by a table of 109 chapters" and "sixty-nine pictures, still in the Sorg tradition," this is "the last to appear in the tradition of Wynkyn de Worde's text and Anton Sorg's illustrations" (Bennett, "Woodcut Illustrations," 68-69).
1725	"Printed for J. Woodman and D. Lyon and C. Davis."
	A new edition, taken from the Cotton text (BL MS Cotton Titus C. xvi). Not illustrated.

---

[7] Bennett ("Woodcut Illustrations," 68) notes a reference in B. Quaritch's 1887 *General Catalogue* (784, 2852) to an undated duodecimo editon, which he assigns a date of "ca. 1700," but I have been able to unearth no further information about this possible intervening edition.

[8] Bennett notes an undated edition (ca. 1710), in quarto, which she says is British Library 10056 ("Woodcut Illustrations," 68). The British Library has nothing at that shelfmark, but does hold a copy of the Wilde 1722 edition, for which Bennett gives no holding information, at shelfmark 10056 c. 22.

Letts (*Sir John Mandeville*, 179) references a chapbook version, British Library 10055a which he dates as "c. 1720" and describes as "an honest, although an abridged, edition, based on East, not hack-work like the others." He claims to have a copy dated 1704.

GLOSSARY OF PROPER NAMES

I have had recourse, in glossing the proper names of the text, to both George Warner's and C. W. Moseley's Egerton editions and to M. C. Seymour's Cotton edition, as well as to a broad array of atlases and geographical databases.[1] Other useful sources for locating the places in the *Book* have been the *Times Atlas of World Exploration* (1991), Deschamps' *Dictionnaire de géographie ancienne et moderne* (1870), Kenneth Nebenzahl's *Maps of the Holy Land* (1986), Scullard's *Atlas of the Classical World* (1959), the Rand-McNally *Bible Atlas* (1962), Christiane Deluz's Appendices III and IV to *Livre* (including maps), and the online cartographic resources from the University of Texas, Stanford University, and Yale University. In an effort to minimize the effect of changing borders and nomenclatures in the modern East, I have attempted to locate places for the reader in historical terms where possible, with reference to unchanging features and place-names of long standing.

Personal names have been cross-checked with a variety of biblical concordances and encyclopediae.

Abachare, Abcaz, Abeacaz (72, 73): Abkhazia, region in northwest Georgia on the Black Sea

Abdenago (14): Abednego, one of the three young companions of Daniel thrown into the fiery furnace by King Nebuchadnezzar

Abdon (31): probably the prophet Obadiah

Abel (16, 36): Abel, son of Adam

Abior, hyll of (73): Mount Elbruz, in the Caucasus Mountains between the Black and Caspian Seas

---

[1] Warner's copious notes to his Egerton edition (*Buke*) are an invaluable and often overlooked resource for location of places and interpretation of difficult nomenclatures. I am much indebted to them here.

Glossary of Proper Names 105

Abraham, Abram (16, 17, 18, 29, 31, 36, 42, 44): Abraham the Patriarch
Acheldemak (28): Aceldama, the Field of Blood, bought with the wages of Judas's sin
Acon, Dacres (13, 14, 39): Acre (formerly Ptolemais), port city north of Haifa. See also Tholomayda.
Adam (1, 5, 16, 17, 55, 88): Adam
Adryan (23): Hadrian; Roman Emperor (117–138 A.D.)
Affe, Iaffe (13, 34, 37, 39, 86): the city of Jaffa (aka Joppa, later Tel Aviv-Yafo), an important port of entry for pilgrims to Jerusalem. See also Iops.
Affryke (12, 64): Africa
Affynpayn (4): the city of Philippopolis (later Plovdiv), on the Maritsa River in Bulgaria
Agar (44): Hagar, the Egyptian handmaiden who became the mother of Ishmael by Abraham
Alape, Alappe, Anaple, Harap (14, 15, 21, 87): the city of Aleppo, in northern Syria
Alban, ryver (38): the Abana River, in Lebanon
Albany (60): alternate name for the province of Manzi, in southern China. See also Mancy. The application of the name *Albany* to this region appears to be original to the *Book*.
Aldema (29): the city of Admah, on the Red Sea
Alkaron (19, 40–43): the Koran. See also Harme, Massap.
Alle (6): King Coel of Britain
Allesey, Allesy (3): the region of Silesia, in the Oder River valley
Almayne, Almaygne, Almaigne (3, 7, 39): Germany
Alysander, Alysaunder, Alysaundre: 1. Alexander the Great (8, 49, 51, 72, 74, 75, 85, 86); 2. the Egyptian city of Alexandria, of which Athanasius was Bishop (46); 3. the city of Alexandria Margiane (later Merv/Mary) in southern Turkestan (later Turkmeniya) (49); 4. the city of Derbend, on the west coast of the Caspian Sea, mythically associated with Alexander the Great (72). See also Berbent.
Ameas (32): the city of Amiens, in northern France
Amonites (44): the Ammonites, an ancient Semitic people who lived east of the Jordan River
Amos (38): the prophet Amos
Amosony, Amozonde, Amozome (3, 48, 49): Amazonia, believed to be near Scythia
Amours, Castell of (12): Deudamour (Dieu d'Amour), Frankish name for the Castle of Saint Hilarion in northern Cyprus
Anania (14): Hananiah, original name of Shadrach. See Sydrach.
Anaple. See Alape.
Andrewe, saynt (32): Saint Andrew the Apostle, brother of Simon Peter

Anna (31): Hannah, mother of the prophet Samuel
Anne (6, 27): Ananias, the High Priest at Jerusalem
Anne, An saynt (7, 25, 26): Saint Anne, mother of the Virgin Mary
Antyoche (38): the city of Antioch (later Antakya) on the Syrian coast
Antyoche the better (38): the city of Antiochia Pisidiae (later Yalvac) in Asia Minor
Araby, Arab (2, 4, 15, 21, 29, 34, 43, 44, 45, 50, 84, 87): Arabia
Arabyns (16): the Arabs
Ararach (47): Mount Ararat, in Eastern Turkey. See also Thano.
Arboth (17): Caryatharba (Place of the Patriarchs). See also Caryatharba.
Archades, playn of (38): the plain of Archades, near Damascus
Archellek (14): the Syrian Desert (Et-tîh)
Archetryclyne (33): ἀεχιτεικλίνιος: the governor of the feast [John 2:8]
Archiporta papaton (53): reported title of the prelate of Polumbum (Quilon) on the Malabar coast of India. Probably from the Nestorian title *archiprotopapas*, mentioned in Prester John's Letter to the Greek Emperor Manuel, which may have been the *Book*'s source here.
Argete (88): Pliny's Argyre, a mythical island in the Great Sea Ocean
Armony, Ermony. See Ermony.
Aron (24): Aaron
Artoyse (38): the city of Artah, near Greater Antioch (Antiochia Pisidiae)
Artyron (47): the city of Erzerum, in eastern Turkey
Aryens (36): the Arian heretical sect of Christianity, characterized especially by the belief that the Son is not of the same substance as the Father. Possibly meant here simply as *Armenians*.
Arystotyll (8): Aristotle
Ascopardes (16): an Arab tribe, possibly the Sudanese
Askalon, Ascalon (14, 20): the city of Askalon, in south Palestine
Assy, Assary: 1. Asia Minor (21, 64, 89); 2. Asia: also *Assy the deep* (71)
Assy the Lesse (4, 9): Asia Minor
Athanas, saynt (46): Saint Athanasius; Bishop of Alexandria, c. 325–373. Contrary to the *Book*'s report, Athanasius did return to his bishopric in his lifetime.
Athos, mount: 1. Mount Athanasi, on the Greek isle of Lemnos (7); 2. Mount Athos, on the Acte peninsula in northeast Greece (8)
Austen, saynt (35): Saint Augustine; Bishop of Hippo, 396–430 A.D.
Azaria (14): Azariah, original name of Abednago. See Abdenago.

Babylone, Babylony, Babilon: 1. Cairo (14, 32, 37, 45, 69). See also Kayre; 2. Babylon (14)
Bacirida (72): the city of Bokhara, in southern Turkestan (later Uzbekistan)
Bakary (75, 76): probably Bactria (later Afghanistan), but possibly the city

of Bokhara, in southern Turkestan (later Uzbekistan)
Balthasar (19): one of the Magi
Barbara, saynt (14): Saint Barbara
Baudewyn (30): Baldwin I; King of Jerusalem, 1100–1118, and brother of Godfrey of Bouillon
Bedoyns, Bedoynes (15, 16): the Bedouins
Belet (24): Bethel (Moriah), northwest of Jerusalem, where stood the ark of God. *See also* Moriach.
Beleth (14): the city of Bilbeis, north of Cairo, possibly conflated in the text with the town of Ba'albek east of Beirut, on the site of the ancient city of Heliopolis. *See also* Manbek.
Belgrave (3): the city of Belgrade in Yugoslavia
Belyan, mount (65): probably a conflation of the Baldjuna Desert, east of Lake Baikal (considered the northern boundary of Cathay), and the Altai Mountains (sometimes called the Belgian Mountains)
Belyon, ryver (13): the ancient river Belus (now the Nahr N'amein) near Acre. North of the River Abellin, with which Moseley identifies the Belyon.
Beniamyn: 1. Benjamin, the youngest son of Jacob (20); 2. the Portion of Benjamin, where the tribe of Benjamin dwelt (31)
Berbent (72): the city of Derbend, on the west coast of the Caspian Sea. From Persian *dar-band*: narrow passage. *See also* Alysander, Port de Fear.
Bernarde, saynte (12): Saint Bernard
Bersabe (16, 34): the city of Beersheba, west of the Dead Sea. Not named for Bathsheba, it means in Arabic *Well of the Oath*.
Beruth, Beruch (12, 37): Beirut
Besayda, Bsayda (32, 33): the town of Bethsaida, northeast of the Sea of Galilee
Bessamorn (4): Byzantium (later Constantinople, Istanbul). *See also* Constantynople.
Bethany (7): the ancient country of Bithynia in Asia Minor, bordering on the Black Sea
Bethleem, Betheleem, Bethelem (18, 19, 20, 27, 48, 71): Bethlehem. *See also* Effrata.
Botron (30): the city of Bosra, south of Damascus. *See also* Cofraa.
Bouche of Constantynople, the (7): The Mouth of Constantynople (The (Hellespont). *See also* Brache of Saynte George, Hellespount.
Brache of Saynt George, Brace of Saynt George (7, 38): The Arm of Saint George (The Hellespont). *See also* Bouche of Constantynople, Hellespount.
Bragamen (84): the Brahmins
Bretaygne, greate (6): Great Britain

Bryke (74): Phrygia, in central Asia Minor
Bugers (3): the Bulgarians (Bulgars)
Bulgary (3): Bulgaria
Burgoyne (37): Burgundy, in eastern France
Byble (32, 35, 42, 92): the Bible

Cadom (62): the great court of the Mongols, near Beijing
Calabre (13): the region of Calabria, in southern Italy
Calamy (54): probably the city of Mailapur (later Madras), in southeast India, but possibly the city of Calama in Gedrosia, west of the Indus River
Calaphes (15): probably not a place name. "He holdethe Calaphes" apparently means "he holds the title of Caliph," as the sentence continues "... that is to say amonge theym Roys [king]." The term *Caliph* in fact means *heir* rather than *king*.
Calastre (7): the Greek isle of Thera (Santorin)
Calcas (7): the Greek isle of Carki
Caldee, Calde (3, 44, 45, 48, 49, 73, 74): Chaldea, region of southwest Asia on the Persian Gulf and the Euphrates River
Caldilhe (74): Warner suggests that *Caldilhe* is a form of *Kao-li* (Marco Polo's *Cauly*: Korea). Its location vis-à-vis the Caspian region is problematic, but no more compelling identification offers itself.
Calofe (16): Caleb, an Israelite scout
Calonach (57): apparently the *Zampa* of Odoric of Pordenone: the southern part of South Vietnam. The derivation of the name *Calonach* is unclear.
Calvary, mount (6, 21): Mount Calvary (Golgotha), outside ancient Jerusalem, where Christ was crucified
Cam, Cham (64): Ham, son of Noah. The *Book* refutes the legend that the title *Chan* [Mongolian *khan*: lord] stems from Ham, deriving it instead from Changuys [Genghis], the first Khan.
Camalach (68): Beijing. From Mongolian *kaan-baligh*: city of the Great Khan.
Cambre (38): the city of Edessa (later Homs) in Syria
Cana (51, 52): the district of Thána, along the Bombay coast of India
Canane (12): the ancient region of Canaan, roughly corresponding to later Palestine. *See also* Chan.
Canapos (88): the star Canopus
Cane. *See* Chan.
Canges. *See* Ganges.
Canopat, Canopate (14, 15): Egypt. *See also* Egypt, Mersyne.
Canryssy, Tanziro (47, 72): the city of Tabriz in northwest Persia, between the Caspian Sea and the Lake of Urmia
Capadoce (38, 74): the ancient district of Cappadocia in eastern Asia Minor
Capharnaym (32): the ancient city of Capernaum, on the Sea of Galilee

Cardabago (48): the city of Isfahán, in Persia. Probably from the Persian *chau bagh*: royal gardens. See also Saphan.
Carme, hyll (13): Mount Carmel, the dwelling place of Elijah, near Haifa
Carmes, ordre of (13): the Order of Carmelite Friars
Carnaa (48): unclear; Warner notes that " 'Carnaa' or 'Cornaa' is in Odoric Comerum; but the latter is only one of the many various readings of the Latin MSS (Comum, Conium, Karum, etc.). Col. Yule identifies it with the Camara of Barbaro and the Kinara of modern maps, marking the site of the great city of Persepolis" (*Buke*, 201n).
Carpate (7): the Greek isle of Carpathos (later Scarpanto)
Carras (30): the town of Kerak, just east of the Dead Sea, seems here to be conflated with Le Krak des Chevaliers, the Crusader castle Mont Royal in Syria. See also Reale mount, Sermoys.
Cartage (12): the ancient city-state of Carthage, on the north coast of Africa. Fortified by Baldwin I in 1115. See also Didonsart.
Caryatharba (17): the Place of the Patriarchs. From *kirjath arba*: city of the four, because of the tradition that four of the biblical patriarchs are buried there. See also Arboth.
Caspe, Caspy, hylles of (74, 75): the Caucasus Mountains near the Caspian Sea. See also Uber.
Caspy, Gaspy, see of (72, 75): the Caspian Sea
Cassage, Chasak (19, 48): the city of Kashan in Persia, south of the Caspian Sea
Cassay (60): the city of Hangchow on the East China Sea. From *kingszé*: capital.
Cassoy (90): the province of Shansi, in northern China
Catolonabes (79, 80): Hasan ibn Sabbāh, founder of the Hashishi'yun (Assassins). Warner (*Buke*, 216n) offers a thorough discussion of the various branches of this sect.
Caym (16, 36): Cain, the son of Adam
Cayphas: 1. Caiaphas, the High Priest (7, 13, 28, 39); 2. the city of Haifa. The name does not derive from *Caiaphas* (13, 39).
Ceromosan, ryver (61): the Huang-ho (Yellow) River in northern China. From Mongolian *karamuren*: black river.
Certege (7): the Greek isle of Ortygia (Delos)
Cesare, Cesary (14): Caesarea, seaport south of Haifa
Cesary Phylyp (39): the ancient city of Caesarea Philippi, in northern Palestine
Cham. See Cam.
Chan, Chane, Cane: 1. Khan, title of Mongol rulers (39, 56, 58, 60-62, 64-66, 68, 69, 72-74, 76, 77, 79, 90-92); 2. Canaan (33). See also Canane.
Chananee, woman of (33): the woman of Canaan, wife of Simon Chananeus (Simon the Canaanite)

Changuys (64): Genghis Khan (c. 1162-1227); Great Khan of the Mongols

Charlemayne (23): Charlemagne (Charles I); Frankish king, 768-814, and Emperor of the West, 800-814. The fiction of Charlemagne's expedition to the Holy Land was in wide circulation from the eleventh century. The story of his acquisition of the foreskin of Christ originates in the twelfth century.

Charles, kynge (23): Charles the Bald; king of France, 840-877, and Holy Roman Emperor, 875-877

Chasak. *See* Cassage.

Chatay, Chatey (56, 58, 61, 62, 64, 66, 71, 72, 74, 76, 77, 90): Cathay (later China)

Chibens, Chybense (61): the city of Nanking in eastern China, on the Yangtze River

Chmay, castell of (38): the castle of Emmaus (later Imwas) between Jaffa and Jerusalem. *See also* Emaux.

Chyppron (3): the city of Sopron in Hungary

Cofraa (48): *Cofraa* is probably an adaptation of *Bosra*. Jobab, "Cofraas son," was the son of Zerah of Bosra. *See also* Botron.

Colles (11): the Greek isle of Rhodes, often called Colos in the Middle Ages by a back formation from *colossus*. *See also* Roodes.

Colocenses (11): the city of Colossae, in Phrygia. Conflated on 8^r with Colos (Rhodes).

Comame, Comange, Comayn, Cosmane (3, 8, 71, 72): Cumania. Refers to the land or people of the Cumans, a Turanian tribe from the north of the Caspian and Black Seas who later spread into Hungary.

Constance (6): Constantine I; Roman Emperor, 306-337

Constantynople, Constantynoble (4, 6-8, 11, 21, 38, 45, 46): Constantinople. *See also* Bessamorn.

Cophos (10): the Greek isle of Cos. *See also* Lango.

Cordynz (73): the Kurds

Corodan, prynce (44): used here as the prince's name; probably an error for the Prince of Khorasan. *See also* Corosaym.

Corosaym: 1. Kharesm [from the Persian *kharizm*: lowland] the lowland between the Aral and Caspian Seas. The major city of the region was Urghendj (71); 2. the city of Chorozin, in Galilee (32, 33)

Crist, Criste, Cryst, Cryste. *See* Iesu cryst.

Cycyle (13): Sicily

Cypre (4, 11-13, 37, 50): Cyprus

Cythoco Chane (66): Ogadai; Great Khan of the Mongols, 1229-1241. Ogadai was the third, not the eldest, son of Genghis Khan

Dacres. *See* Acon, Tholomayda.

Damas, Damasse (13, 15, 17, 36, 38, 39): the city of Damascus, in southwest Syria
Damazyne (21): Armenia. See also Armony, Ermony. The derivation of Damazyne is unclear.
Dameth (15): Hamath (later Hama) in western Syria
Darke (37): the Crusader castle of Archas (later Arqa), near Tripoli
Daunby, river of (3): the Danube River
David, Davyd (15, 16, 20, 24, 27, 29, 35): King David of Jerusalem
Dayr, Castell (14): the Crusader castle of Darum, south of Gaza
Deane (10): Diana, a goddess of Cyprus in the Mediterranean pantheon
Dedde See, Ded see, Dedde se (29–31): the Dead Sea
Didonsart (12): Carthage. See also Cartage.
Dodym (58): possibly the Andaman Islands, in the Bay of Bengal
Donke (38): apparently Tekoa, the town just south of Bethlehem where Amos was born
Dotaym, vale of (31): the vale of Dothan, near Mount Gilboa
Duras (37): the port city of Dyrrhachium (later Durazzo) on the Albanian coast of the Adriatic Sea
Dydo (12): Dido
Dydon (12): Sidon (Saida), the birthplace of Dido. Because of the omission of some text, the edition here says Sidon is Beirut, rather than that Sidon is at some distance from Beirut. See also Sydon.
Dysmael. See Ismael.
Dysmas (4, 11): Dismas, the good thief crucified alongside Christ

Ebrewe (5, 8, 75): the Hebrew language
Ebron: 1. the vale of Hebron, in southern Palestine (16–18, 20, 31). See also Teres, vale of; 2. the Hebrew language (19). See also Ebrewe.
Echel, ryvere (71): the Volga River. From Turkish *idil*: river.
Effrata (18): ancient name of Bethlehem. See also Bethleem.
Effraym, hyll of (31): Mount Ephraim
Egypt, Egipt, Egypte (2, 4, 14, 15, 19, 21, 31, 43, 87, 89): Egypt. See also Mersyne, Canopat.
Ekale de Tyrreyes (13): The Scale (Ladder) of Tyre, later known as Ras en Nakurah. Refers to both the steep headland between Acre and Tyre, and the road that climbs it.
Elyas (12, 13): the prophet Elijah the Tishbite
Elyne, Elyn, saynt (6, 7, 21, 26): Saint Helena, mother of Constantine and finder of the True Cross
Elysabethe (28): Saint Elizabeth, mother of John the Baptist
Emaux (28, 39): the town of Emmaus (later Imwas), between Jaffa and Jerusalem. See also Chmay.
Eneas (12): the Trojan Aeneas

Englonde, Englond (2, 3, 6, 45): England
Englysshe (7, 19, 35, 55): the English language
Ephesym (9): Ephesus, city near the Aegean coast of Asia Minor
Ermen, mount (32): Mount Hermon, inland between Tyre and Damascus
Ermes: 1. the city of Ormuz, on the Strait of Ormuz in southern Iran, at the outlet of the Persian Gulf (77). See also Hermes; 2. the wise man, Hermes Trismegistus (who was not, in fact, the founder of the city of Ormuz) (77). See also Ermogynes.
Ermogynes (8): the wise man, Hermes Trismegistus. See also Ermes.
Ermony, Armony (2, 46, 47, 72–75, 89): Armenia. "Little Armenia" was in southern Asia Minor, in Cilicia. See also Damazyne.
Ernax, vale of (38): the town of Ormanx in Asia Minor
Ethyope, Ethyops, Ethiope (3, 21, 49, 74, 89): Ethiopia
Euphrate, Eufraten, Eufrates, flom/flode (45, 74, 89): the Euphrates River
Eurace (64): a tribe of Tartary, corresponding to Hayton's *Cunat*
Europe (64): Europe
Eustache, saynt (38): Saint Eustace
Eve (16, 17, 55, 88): Eve

Famagost (11, 12, 37): the city of Famagusta, in Cyprus
Fassar, ryver (38): the biblical river Pharpar, flowing from Mount Hermon past Damascus. See also Ferne.
Faxton (7): the Greek isle of Naxos
Ferne (38): possibly the city of Ilgun, in Asia Minor
Ferne, ryver (38): the biblical river Pharphar. See also Fassar.
Flagine (39): unclear; perhaps a port town between Acre and Haifa
Flaunders (39): Flanders
Floraghe, castell (38): Castle Florach, on the south coast of Asia Minor
Fnnes (45): Phoenicia. See also Phenys.
Fraunce (6, 30, 37, 39): France
Frenche, French (30, 43): the French language

Gabaon (31): probably the town of Gibeon, in the Portion of Benjamin, just north of Jerusalem
Gabryell (33, 41, 43, 44): the Archangel Gabriel
Gaffolos (57): possibly Parlák, in Sumatra, or a garbled reference to Caffo, on the Crimean peninsula. The *Book* appears to use as its source here a passage from Vincent of Beauvais about the Caspian region. It is unclear why the story is relocated to the Far East.
Galgalagh, Galgalath (19): offered as an alternative name for one of the Magi
Galyle (30, 32, 33, 36): the region of Galilee, north of Jerusalem
Galyle, see of (34): the Sea of Galilee (Lake of Gennesaret), east of Nazareth

Ganges, Canges, flode (89): the Ganges River. *See also* Physon.
Garryson (31): Mount Gerazim, north of Jerusalem
Gaspy, see of. *See* Caspy.
Gayus Cesar (20): Julius Caesar (100–44 B.C.)
Gaza, Gasa (14): Gaza (formerly Philistia), south of Jaffa. *See also* Phylistyen.
Geeble (38): the city of Gebal (later Jeble) in Syria
Geene, Geen (32, 37, 45, 51, 61, 77): the city of Genoa, Italy
Gelboe, mount (30): Mount Gilboa in northern Palestine, west of the Jordan River
Genesys (92): the biblical book of Genesis
Geneth (74): the ancient country and Roman province of Paphlagonia in northern Asia Minor, bordering on the Black Sea
George: 1. the ancient and medieval kingdom of Georgia, south of the Caucasus Mountains and bordering on the Black Sea (73); 2. Georgia: with Abkhazia, one of the lesser kingdoms within the kingdom of Georgia (73)
George, saynt (29, 36, 38): Saint George the Cappadocian, patron saint of England
Georgyns (29, 36): followers of St. George the Cappadocian, patron saint of England
Gog and Magog (74): the Gog and Magog of Ezekial 38–39, conflated here with the Jews of the ten lost tribes of Israel
Gomor (29): the city of Gomorrah in ancient Palestine
Gononon, saynt (12): Sozomen, fifth century bishop of Potamia
Graften (39): possibly a corruption of *Dorestena*, the ancient name for the province of Silistria in eastern Europe
Great, Grete se (45, 73): the Black Sea, thought to be an arm of the Great Sea Ocean. *See also* Maure, Port de Pounce, Occean.
Grece. *See* Gresses.
Grece, Ile of (13): the Greek island of Crete
Grecon (39): the city of Krakow
Gregory, saynt (35): Gregory I; Pope, 590–604
Gregours (36): the Greeks
Grekes (36): the Greeks
Grekes see (72): the Sea of Greece
Gresses, Grece (3–5, 7–9, 19, 36–38, 73, 87): Greece
Grewe (5, 8): the Greek language
Gryff (37): the Greek isle of Corfu
Gyron (89): the Nile River. *See also* Nylus; Nyke, flode.

Hamfon (73): the district of Hamschen, near the Black Sea
Harap. *See* Alape.

Harme (19, 40): Arabic *horme*: holy; an alternative name for the Koran. See also Alkaron, Massap.
Hay (30): the town of Ai, just north of Jerusalem
Hellespount (7): the Hellespont (Dardanelles), strait in northwest Turkey. See also Bouche of Constantynople, Brache of Saynt George.
Hely (31, 34): the prophet Eli
Helyam (23): Aelia (Jerusalem). See also Ierusalem, Iebus, Salomee.
Helyseus (31): the prophet Elisha
Helyseus Damaske (36): Abraham's steward, Eliezer the Damascene
Hercules (52): the demigod Hercules
Hermes, yle of (51): probably the city of Ormuz, although the island of Ormuz is quite nearby. See also Ermes.
Herode, Heraude, kynge (14, 26): King Herod the Great. See also Herode Ascolonyte.
Herode Agrippa (26): Herod Agrippa
Herode Antipa (26): Herod Antipas
Herode Ascolonyte (26): King Herod the Great. See also Herode, kynge.
Holy Crosse, Hyll of (4, 11): the Mountain of the Holy Cross
Holy Sepulchre, Churche of the (23): the Church of the Holy Sepulchre, in Jerusalem
Hospitelers, Hospytalers (11, 22): the religious military order of Knights Hospitallers, established in Jerusalem in the twelfth century
Hungery, Hungry (3): Hungary
Hyllary (35): Saint Hilary of Poitiers
Hyllaryon (12): Saint Hilarion

Iacob, Iocob (16, 20, 24, 31, 32): Jacob the Patriarch
Iacobynes (35): the Jacobites (Monophysites), followers of the sixth-century Syrian monk Jacob Baradaeus
Iaffe. See Affe.
Iames, Iame, saynt: 1. Saint James the Apostle, son of Zebedee (13, 26, 27, 34, 35, 54); 2. St. James the Bishop of Jerusalem (25)
Iana (56): the Indonesian island of Java
Iapheth, Iaphet: 1. Japhet, son of Noah (13, 64); 2. The city of Jaffa, said to have been founded by Japheth (14)
Iasper (19): Jaspar, one of the Magi
Idones, Idumea (30, 48): the ancient country of Idumaea, south of Judea and the Dead Sea
Iebus (20): early name for Jerusalem. See also Ierusalem, Helyam, Salomee.
Ierom, saynt (19): Saint Jerome
Ierusalem, Iebusalem (1, 3, 4, 7, 12-17, 20, 21, 23-25, 28-33, 36-39, 87, 93): Jerusalem. See also Iebus, Helyam, Salomee.
Ieryco, Ierico (29, 34): the city of Jericho, northwest of the Dead Sea

Glossary of Proper Names 115

Iesu cryst, Iesu criste, Iesu crist, Iesu cryste, Ihesu cryst (1, 2, 4–9, 20, 23–25, 27–29, 33, 34, 41–43, 54, 78): Jesus Christ
Iewes (1, 4–7, 14, 17, 18, 21–25, 27–29, 31–33, 41, 42, 47, 74, 75): the Jews
Inde, Indee, Ynde, Ynd: 1. India. The medieval conception of *Inde* does not, however, correspond well with the modern boundaries of India. The *Book* associates *Inde* variously with northern, eastern, and western Asia, and even with east Africa. On the well-known confusion of India with East Africa, stemming from late antiquity, cf. A. Kazhdan and A. Cutler, "India," *Oxford Dictionary of Byzantium*, 3 vols. (New York: Oxford University Press (1991), 2: 992–93 (3, 4, 21, 45, 49–51, 59, 72, 74, 76, 83, 89, 93); 2. Judea (probably an error for "Iude") (20, 29)
Indyns (36): the Indian followers of Saint Thomas
Ioachim (26): Saint Joachim
Iob, Iobab: 1. Job the Patriarch (30, 86); 2. Iobab, King of Idumea (48)
Iohn (baptyst), saynt (25, 26, 28, 31, 32): Saint John the Baptist
Iohn Crysostom, saynt (7, 27): Saint John Chrysostom
Iohn Maundevyle, Iohn Maundvyle (2, 92, 93): John Mandeville
Iohn, Ion, saynt (9, 13, 22, 27, 34, 35): Saint John the Evangelist
Iohn the bysshop, saynt (31, 32): Saint John, Bishop of Jerusalem
Iohn the xxii, pope (9): John the XXII; Pope, 1316–1334
Ionas (12): Jonah, the widow's son raised from the dead by Elijah
Ionays (9): the Genoese
Iops (13): the city of Joppa (Jaffa). *See also* Affe.
Iordan, Iordane, Iardon, flom (29, 30, 34, 39): the River Jordan, in northeast Palestine
Iosaphat, Iasaphat, vale of (22, 27, 28, 34): the vale of Jehosaphat, between Jerusalem and the Mount of Olives
Ioseph: 1. Joseph, eleventh son of Jacob (14, 31); 2. Joseph the Patriarch (20); 3. Joseph, husband of the Virgin Mary (33)
Ioseph of Aramathy (21): Joseph of Arimathea
Iosue (16, 30): Joshua, the successor of Moses
Iosyas (36): unclear; the reference is to Isaac, son of Abraham. *See also* Isaac.
Ioy, mount (28, 31, 38): Mount Joy (Montjoie, Neby Samwil), just northwest of Jerusalem
Ipocras (10): the Greek physician Hippocrates
Irlande (3): Ireland
Isaac (29, 31): Isaac, son of Abraham. *See also* Iosyas.
Isakan (65): from Mongolian *yasa khan*: the code of the Khan
Isay (86): the prophet Hosea
Ismael, Dysmael (30, 44): Ishmael, son of Abraham
Israel: 1. the land or generations of Israel (16, 24, 30, 31); 2. Jacob, second

son of Isaac, whose name is changed to Israel [Genesis 32:28 and 35:10] (24)

Iudas (28): Judas Iscariot

Iulian, Iulius (23, 31): Julian the Apostate; Roman Emperor, 361-363

Iustinian (4): Justinian I (483-565); Byzantine Emperor, 527-565

Karmen (73): used here as a name for the Kurds. Probably a reference to one of the Persian cities they inhabit: Kerman or Kermanshah.

Katheryn, saynte (15, 27): Saint Catherine of Alexandria (a.k.a. Saint Catherine of the Wheel). The Mount of Saint Catherine is one of the peaks of Sinai, to which her body was miraculously transported after she was beheaded in Alexandria.

Kayre (14): Cairo. See also Babylone.

Kenet, saynt (22): unclear; the canons are associated with Saint Augustine in most other texts of the *Book*, as well as in the probable source, Jacques de Vitry

Lamaton (37): unclear; given as a port city on Cyprus, but no convincing identification offers itself

Lambardy. See Lumbardy.

Lamory (55): part of the Indonesian island of Sumatra

Lango (10): probably the Greek isle of Cos. Although the text refers to Cophos (Cos) and Lango as separate islands, the story of Hippocrates' daughter is associated with Cos, and *Lango* is as yet unidentifiable as a place name. See also Cophos.

Larcheslevyn (44): a Saracen religious leader. The Cotton text reads "the archiflamyn or the flamyn, as oure archbisschopp or bisschop."

Laten, Latyn (5, 8, 19, 20, 35, 93): the Latin language

Latorym (60): the port city of Canton (Guang-zhou) in southeast China

Lay, ryver (38): probably the Lake of Nicaea (later Iznik Lake) in northwest Turkey

Lectowe (39): medieval Lithuania, extending from the Baltic to the Black Sea

Lempne (7): the Greek isle of Lemnos

Lobassy (90): the Dalai Lama. The term apparently stems from Odoric: "Lo Abassi, id est Papa in lingua sua. . . ."

Locuth (38): the port city of Laodicea (later Latakia) in northwest Syria

Lombardy. See Lumbardy.

Lombe, Polomes (52): the city of Quilon (Polumbum), on the Malabar coast of India. See also Polombe, hyll.

Loth (17, 29, 44): Lot

Luke, saynt (7): Saint Luke the Evangelist

Lumbardy, Lambardy, Lombardy (3, 13, 37, 38, 45, 61, 81): the region of

Glossary of Proper Names 117

Lombardy in northern Italy. The Lombardy mile is generally used as the standard mile for the *Book*, although distances are by no means accurate.

Lybany, Lybane, Lyban mount (30, 34, 38): the Libanus (Lebanon) mountains

Lyby (3, 74): Libya

Lyson, hyll (74): Mount Lyson, in northern Iraq

Mabaron (54): the coastal region of Coromandel, in southeast India on the Bay of Bengal

Machabe (38): Judas Maccabaeus

Machomete (19, 40, 42–44): Mohammed

Macydone, Macidone, Macydony (8, 50): Macedonia, on the Balkan peninsula

Makaryn (31): the Jewish fortress of Machaerus, on the Dead Sea

Mallebriuz (38): the vales of Malabrunia, in Asia Minor

Mambre, vale of (16, 30): the vale of Mamre (later Ramel el Khalil) north of Hebron. *See also* Marbre.

Manbek, castell (39): the Crusader castle at Ba'albek. *See also* Beleth.

Mancy (59, 60, 61, 63): the province of Manzi, in southern China. *See also* Albany.

Marbre, mount (17): the Mount of Mamre. *See also* Mambre.

Marca (9): the city of Myra, in Asia Minor, on the Lycian coast

Maritane, Marytane (74): Mauretania

Maroch (45): Morocco

Marroke, ryver (3): the Maritsa River, in Bulgaria

Mary (1, 8, 33, 40, 41): the virgin Mary

Mary Cleofe (22): Mary Cleophas

Mary Magdalen, Mary Magdeleyne (22): Mary Magdalen

Massap, Mesap (19, 40): Arabic *mashaf*: book; an alternative name for the Koran. *See also* Alkaron, Harme.

Maure (72): the Black Sea, *mare maurum* (then thought to be an arm of the Great Sea Ocean). *See also* Great Se, Port de Pounce, Occean.

Mediteran, see (45): the Mediterranean Sea.

Medoynes (46): the Medes, inhabitants of Media

Megon (73): the Moghan steppe, west of the Caspian Sea

Melchior (19): Melchior, one of the Magi

Melchysedech (25): Melchizedek, priest and king of Salem, west of the Jordan River [Genesis 14:18]

Meldane (30): from Arabic *maidan*: open space or market, which may be taken here as a specific place name. Other texts refer to the term meaning fair or market in "Sarmoyz" or "Sarazinois": the Arabic language

Melke (57): possibly Malacca, on the west coast of Malaysia

Menchi (64): a tribe of Tartary, corresponding to Hayton's *Monghi*
Menk (61): the city of Ningpo in eastern China
Mersyne (14): Egypt, from Arabic *Misr*. See also Egypt, Canopat.
Mesap. See Massap.
Messopotany, Messopotayne (21, 45, 74): Mesopotamia (later Iraq)
Minona (7): the Greek isle of Paros
Moabites (44): an ancient Semitic people, related to the Hebrews
Modyn, mount (38): Mount Modin (later Mount Latron) near Jerusalem
Molo (7): the Greek isle of Melos
Moriach (24): Moriah (later Bethel), where stood the ark of God. See also Belet.
Mormant, alpes of (38): possibly the Phrygian Black Hills
Moryache (38): the city of Marash in south central Turkey
Mosel (74): the city of Mosul, east of the Sindjar mountains in northern Iraq
Moyses (15, 24, 42, 92): Moses
Moyses, mount (15, 34): the Mount of Moses (Mount Sinai)
Mydy, Myddy (45, 72, 73): the kingdom of Media, part of the Persian Empire in southwest Asia
Myghell, saynt (2): Saint Michael
Mymon, Fosse of (13): the Fosse of Memnon near the Belus River, reportedly named for a monument to Memnon that stood nearby
Myroche, port (37, 38): the city of Mavrovo, near Valona (Vlonë) on the Albanian coast of the Strait of Otranto
Mysael (14): Meschach, one of the young princes thrown into the fiery furnace by King Nebuchadnezzar

Naaman (30): Naaman of Aram, cured of his leprosy by Elisha [2 Kings 5]
Nabugodonozor (14): King Nebuchadnezzar
Narde. See Pyncy.
Natumeran (58): the Nicobar Islands, in the Indian Ocean
Naym, Namy (32, 34): the city of Naym (Nain), in Galilee
Nazareth, Nazarethe (30, 33): the city of Nazareth, in Galilee
Neople (31): Neapolis (later Nablus), the ancient city of Shechem, north of Jerusalem in Samaria. See also Sychem.
Nessabor (72): the city of Nishapúr, in northeast Persia
Nestorynes (36): the Nestorian heretical sect of Christianity, characterized especially by the belief that the divine and human persons of Christ remained separate in the incarnation
Newburgh (3): the city of Wieselburg (Moszon, Hungary) on the Leytha, northeast of Odenburg (Sopron) and so clearly not on the way thence to Belgrade. Newburgh corresponds with Albert of Aix's *praesidium Meseburch* and William of Tyre's *Meeszburg*. Seymour glosses this as

"Odenburg, now Wieselburg, in Hungary" but the two are separate cities.
Noe (5, 13, 29, 47, 64, 89): Noah
Norwey (3): Norway
Nuby (74): the region of Nubia in northeast Africa, south of Egypt
Nubyens (36): the Nubians
Nycholas, saynt (9, 19): Saint Nicholas
Nycosy (11): the city of Nicosia, in Cyprus
Nyflond, Nyflande (3, 39): Livonia, central European region bordering the Baltic Sea
Nyke (38): the ancient Byzantine city of Nicaea in northwest Turkey, later Iznik
Nyke, flode (45): the Nile River. See also Gyron, Nylus.
Nylus (89): the Nile River. See also Gyron, Nyke.
Nyse (76, 79): the city of Nisa/Neyseh in southern Persia

Occean, Occian, see: 1. the Great Sea Ocean, believed to surround the three known continents (45, 51, 59); 2. The Black Sea (once believed to be an arm of the Great Sea Ocean) (71). See also Maure, Great Se, Port de Pounce.
Olymphus (8): Mount Olympus, in northeast Greece
Orda (39): the city of Serai, on the Volga. From Mongolian *ordu*: camp or court (whence the term *horde*). John of Plano Carpini, probably the *Book*'s source here, visited Batu Khan's ordu at Serai on his way to meet Kuyuk Khan. See also Sarachys.
Orrell (88): Pliny's Chryse, a mythical island in the Great Sea Ocean

Palestyne, Palastyne, Palestyn (19, 20, 45, 87): Palestine
Pannony (3): the Roman province of Pannonia, in southwest Europe
Pantoxore, Pentoxore, Ile of (76): Pentoxoire, Prester John's mythical kingdom. Associated with India/Abyssinia. See also Inde.
Paradyse Terrestre (45, 53, 68, 76, 77, 88, 89): Eden, the earthly paradise
Parys, Paryse (6, 7, 23, 60): the city of Paris, France
Paten. See Salamasse.
Pateran (9): Patera, in Asia Minor, the birthplace of Saint Nicholas
Paul, Poule, saynt (11, 36, 42): Saint Paul the Apostle
Pellerinz, castell. See Pylleryns.
Percy, Persy, Perse (2, 4, 21, 45, 48, 69, 72, 77, 89): Persia. See also Poy.
Persans (46): the Persians
Peter, Petyr, saynt (6, 27, 28, 32, 34, 35, 86, 87): Saint Peter the Apostle
Pharao, Desart of (30): the desert of Pharan (Arabia Deserta), the northern part of the Arabian peninsula
Phenne (38): the city of Philomelium, in the ancient country of Pisidia, in southern Asia Minor

Phenys (30): Phoenicia. *See also* Fnnes.
Philistiens (16): the Philistines
Phylistyen (14): the city of Philistia (later Gaza). *See also* Gaza.
Physon, ryver: 1. the Oxus River, between the Aral Sea and the Hindu Kush (72, 81); 2. the Ganges River (89). *See also* Ganges, Canges.
Polombe, hyll (53): Mount Polumbum, named here as the site of the Fountain of Youth. *See also* Lombe.
Polomes. *See* Lombe.
Port de Fear, Port de Feare (72): Alexander's Iron Gate (*port du fer*); the pass of Derbend, between the Caspian Sea and the Caucasus Mountains. *See also* Berbent.
Port de Pounce (45): Pontus Euxinus, the Black Sea. Here the name is applied to Trebizond, a port city on the Black Sea. *See also* Maure, Great Se, Occean.
Poule, saynt. *See* Paul.
Poy (73): Persia. *See also* Percy.
Poyalme (3): Poland
Preter Iohn, Prester Iohn, Prestyr Iohn, Prestre Iohn (36, 69, 76–79, 87, 88, 90): Prester John, legendary emperor of India/Abyssinia. No source has yet been located for the *Book*'s derivation of the title.
Pruysse, Pruys, Pruyse (3, 39, 40, 66, 71, 72): Prussia
Pulverall (38): the port of Bafra, on the south coast of the Black Sea near Sinope
Pycardy (32): Picardy, in northern France
Pylates, Pylate (7, 26): Pontius Pilate
Pylleryns, Pellerinz, Castel of (14, 39): Château Pelerin, the fortress of the Knights Templar at Athlît, south of Haifa, held against the Saracens from 1218 to 1291, when it fell just before the fall of Acre
Pyncy, Narde (8): the land of the Petschenegs (Pincenarii), early inhabitants of the area along the lower Danube in Bulgaria. The complete name *Pyncynarde* has been split here into *Pyncy* and *Narde*. *See also* Pynteras.
Pynteras (3): the Petschenegs (Pincenarii), early inhabitants of the area along the lower Danube in Bulgaria, their land. *See also* Pyncy.
Pytan: 1. the ancient country of Bithynia in northwest Asia Minor (74); 2. Pytan; an unclear reference, possibly a back formation from the Trispithami, a people mentioned in one of the book's sources for this section (86). (Cf. Warner, *Buke*, 219n.)

Quadryge (44): Khadija, wife of Mohammed
Quesicion (74): the ancient country of Lydia, in western Asia Minor

Rachell (20): Rachel, wife of Jacob

Glossary of Proper Names 121

Raco (39): Batu; grandson of Genghis Khan and Khan of Kypchak (the Golden Horde), 1242–1255. For his court, see Orda, Sarachys.
Rama Beniamin (31): the city of Ramah in the Portion of Benjamin, just north of Jerusalem
Ramatha, Sophym (30, 38): the city of Ramatha (often called Rama) in the Portion of Ephraim, north of Jerusalem
Ramos, Rames (37–39): the town of Ramleh, southeast of Jaffa
Raphane (37): Jacques de Vitry's *Raphaneam*, identified by editors of the *Book* variously as *Rafinêh* or *Rafaniyeh*, although it has never been clearly located. From context, it should be northeast of Tripoli.
Reale mount (30): the pilgrim castle of Mont Royal, in Syria. *See also* Carras, Sermoys.
Rebecca (16): wife of Isaac (whose name has been omitted from the text at page 16)
Redde See, Red Se (16, 24, 38): the Red Sea
Renemar, ryver (86): in most texts some form of Buemare. Warner notes that "The *Ep. Alex.* speaks also ... of the 'amnis Buemar' [cf. Fr. text] in the furthest forests of India" (*Buke*, 219n). The river's reported width of two and a half miles is almost certainly a confusion of that source, which speaks of Alexander's vast camp—two and a half leagues across—on the banks of the river.
Rochayz (74): the city of Roha (ancient Edessa, Urfa), on the Euphrates River
Romayn, Romayne (4, 38, 61): Romany, in Asia Minor
Romayn See (38): the Roman Sea
Rome (9, 20, 23, 24, 46, 93): Rome
Roodes, Rodes (10, 11, 37): the Greek isle of Rhodes, base of the Knights Hospitallers from 1306 to 1523. *See also* Colles.
Rosse, Rossye, Russy, Rosy (3, 39, 66, 71, 72): Russia
Roys Ile (15): used here as a synonym for *Caliph*. Probably a corruption arising from the French, with *Roi* as synonym for *Caliph*, and *Il* beginning a new sentence the rest of which is lost in the "Egypt Gap."
Ryboth (90): Tibet. The "pryncipall cyte" is probably Lhasa.
Rychay (38): usually glossed as *Heraclea*, although Heraclea is neither a river, nor very near Greater Antioch

Saba (49): This probably refers to Persian Saba, of which the magus Balthasar was said to be king. It has been conflated here with Ethiopian Saba, in Meroe, perhaps owing to the the tradition, grounded in Psalms 68:31 and 72:10, that one of the Magi was from Ethiopia
Sabaoth (30): the town of Shobek, fifty miles southeast of the Dead Sea
Sabatory ryver (37): possibly a spring near Arqa
Saboth (77): the port city of Cambay, in western India

Sabyssatoll (47): probably Mount Sabissa Collasassius, near Erzerum in northwest Turkey

Saffre (13): the town of Shefa 'Amr, east of Haifa, often identified as the birthplace of Saints John and James. Sometimes conflated in the text with the city of Seffûrich, near Nazareth

Salamasse, Paten (56): unclear; Warner notes that Salamasse and Paten are "the Thalamasyn and Panten (al. Paten) of Od[oric] ... but what place is meant must be left to conjecture. Col. Yule supposes it to be upon the coast of Borneo, and suggests Banjermasin" (*Buke*, 201n).

Salomee (20): the early Canaanite name of Jerusalem. See also Ierusalem, Iebus, Helyam.

Salon, Salamon (15, 16, 20, 22, 25, 27, 28): King Solomon of Israel

Samary (31): Samaria, district of ancient Palestine between Galilee and Judea. Also its capital city, Samaria (Sebastia, Sebaste). See also Sebast.

Samarytane, Samaritane, Samaritan, Samarytan (31, 32): Samaritan

Samson (14): Samson

Samuel (28, 31): the prophet Samuel

Saphan (72): the city of Isfahán, in Persia. See also Cardabago.

Saphen (12): the city of Saphon. Conflated at page 12 with Sodom.

Sara (16): Sara, wife of Abraham the Patriarch

Sarachys (72): the city of Serai [from *serai*: palace] in Cumania, onetime capital of Kypchak (the Golden Horde). Identified with the city of Tsarev, on the Akhtûba branch of the Volga. See also Orda.

Saraphy (19): offered as an alternative name for one of the Magi

Sarasyns, Sarrasyns, Sarasynes (11, 12, 17-19, 21-23, 28, 30, 32, 34, 40-44, 47, 48, 60, 68, 73): Saracens

Sarchis (52): the city of Baroch, in western India north of Surat

Sardemarke, Sardena (13, 36): the town of Saidenaya, north of Damascus

Sarduz (68): the Great Khan's summer court at Kaipingfu. From *shangtu* (*xanadu*): upper court.

Sarept (12): the town of Sûrafend, southeast of Jaffa. Conflated at page 12 with Sodom.

Sarmasse (72): unclear; listed as one of the principal cities of western Persia, but no convincing identification offers itself

Sarra (44): possibly the city of Shiraz, in southwestern Persia

Sarrasyns. See Sarasyns

Sathalay (11): either Adalia (later Antalya), port city on the south coast of Asia Minor, or Eski Adalia, the site of ancient Side

Saturne (51): the planet Saturn

Saure (74): the ancient district of Isauria, near Pisidia, in Asia Minor

Saures (73): Shapur II; Emperor of Persia, c. 309-379

Saveoure, saynt (12): Saint Savior

Savoy (3): the region of Slavonia, in eastern Croatia

Saynt Albone (2): Saint Albans, the town in England whence the narrator hails
Scotlonde (3): Scotland
Sebast (31, 32): the city of Sebastiyeh, in Samaria
Segor (29): the city of Zoar, on the Dead Sea
Sem (64): Shem, son of Noah
Semeth (64): a tribe of Tartary, corresponding to either Hayton's *Tebeth* or *Sonich*
Sercy (71): the ancient maritime country of Tarshish, referred to in the Bible but not clearly located
Sermoys: 1. the language of the Saracens (30). *See also* Meldane; 2. alternative name for the pilgrim castle of Mount Royal in Syria (30). *See also* Carras, Reale Mount.
Seth (5, 17): Seth, son of Adam
Sicar, Sycar (31): Sychar, another name for the city of Shechem. *See also* Sychem.
Sobeth (64): a tribe of Tartary, corresponding to either Hayton's *Tebeth* or *Sonich*
Sodom (12, 29): the city of Sodom in ancient Palestine
Solome (29): the city of Zeboiim, on the Dead Sea
Solopenco (48): legendary king of Amazonia, before the female takeover. Variously *Scolopitus* or *Colopheus*.
Somober (56): part of the Indonesian island of Sumatra
Sophy, saynt (4, 8): Saint Sophia
Sophym. *See* Ramatha.
Sormagnant (72): the city of Samarkand, east of Bokhara in Turkestan
Spayne, se of (45, 74): the Spanish Sea
Spernere, castell of (46): the fabled Castle of the Sparrowhawk
Stephyn, Stephen, saynt (22, 27): Saint Stephen
Sterny (4): the city of Sofia, in Bulgaria
Strages (8): the town of Stagira, on the Macedonian peninsula of Chalcidice, birthplace of Aristotle
Sure, Sur (12, 37): Sûr (Tyre), port of entry for Syria. *See also* Tyre.
Surry, Surrey, Syry (2, 4, 12, 13, 14, 15, 20, 21, 30, 34, 36, 38, 45, 87): Syria
Surryens (36): the Syrians
Suse (78, 79): the city of Susa (Shushan in the Old Testament), ancient capital of the Persian province of Susiana. The winter residence of Persian kings, here identified as Prester John's capital city.
Swere (48): possibly the ancient kingdom of Susiana (Elam), at the head of the Persian Gulf
Sybola (31): the town of Shiloh on Mount Ephraim, east of Jaffa
Syche, Sychy (45, 48, 74): the ancient kingdom of Scythia, including parts of Europe and Asia north of the Black Sea and east of the Aral Sea

Sychem, Sicar (31): the ancient city of Shechem (Neapolis, later Nablus) north of Jerusalem in Samaria. See also Neople.
Sydon (12): the city of Sidon (Saida), south of Beirut; an important Phoenician port and the birthplace of Dido
Sydrach (14): Shadrach, one of the young princes thrown into the fiery furnace by King Nebuchadnezzar
Sylvester, saynt (31): Saint Sylvester
Symar, hyll (74): the Sindjar mountains, in northern Iraq
Symeon, saynt (25): Simeon, a holy Jew present at the Purification
Synay, mount(e) (14, 15, 27, 37, 44, 45): Mount Sinai; several peaks of Sinai are referred to in the text. At sig. c7^r "synay" is used in error for Mt. Zion.
Synople (85): unclear; the Egerton text gives two iles here: Oxidrace and Gynoscriphe. Warner notes that the "Oxidracae were a great tribe of the Panjáb, on the banks of the Hydaspes, who vigorously opposed the advance of Alexander" (Buke, 218n). This may give some sense of location, though it does not explain the use of Synople in this context.
Synople, castell of (38): the port city of Sinope/Sinop, on the Black Sea in northern Turkey
Syon, mount (27, 28): Mount Zion, in eastern Jerusalem. See also Synay, mount.
Syry. See Surry.

Tabrobane (87): Greek name for the island of Ceylon (later Sri Lanka) in the Indian Ocean
Takyna (41): fabled enchanter/evil spirit, seducer of maidens
Tagneras (89): offered here as a king in India
Tanghot (64): a tribe of Tartary, corresponding to Hayton's Tangot
Tanziro. See Canryssy.
Tartary: 1. Tartary (2, 39, 45, 64, 66, 71, 87); 2. the Tartars, a tribe of Tartary (Hayton's Tatars) (64)
Tartarynes, Tartaryns (62, 66, 70): the Mongols. The word is also used in the text as a common noun to mean silk.
Tecle, saynt (31): probably Saint Thecla the virgin, follower of Paul, but Warner suggests this may be a different person, a pilgrim from Maurienne (cf. Warner, Buke, 188n)
Templers (25): the religious military order of the the Knights Templar, established in Jerusalem in the twelfth century
Teres, vale of (16): the vale of Tears (Hebron). See also Ebron.
Tesbyria (7): the isle of Lesbos, off the coast of Asia Minor
Thabor, mount (33, 34): Mount Tabor, in northern Palestine
Thano (47): another name for Mount Ararat. Possibly from the Persian kuh-i-nuh: mountain of Noah. See also Ararach.

Thebe, ryver (84): probably the Hydaspes River (later the Jhelum River), on the Indian subcontinent
Theosody (31): Theodosius I; Roman Emperor, 379-395
Thirry. See Tyre.
Tholomayda (13): Ptolemais (later Acre), port city north of Mount Carmel. See also Acon.
Thomar (48): the city of Carmana (later Kerman), in Persia
Thomas, saynt (27, 54, 79, 87): Saint Thomas the Apostle (Doubting Thomas)
Topazonde. See Trapazonde.
Tortouse, Tourtouse (38, 39): the port town of Tartous, north of Beirut
Tracota (58): the name has been identified with Dragoian in Sumatra, Trinkat in the Nicobar Islands, and Tringano on the Malay peninsula. The story, however, refers to Vincent of Beauvais' account of the Ethiopian Troglodytes. The similarity of names may account for the relocation
Tracy, Trachy (3, 8): Thrace
Trapazonde, Topazonde (45, 46, 47): Trebizond (later Trabzon). Port city in northeast Turkey, on the Black Sea.
Troyse, Troy, Troys (7, 23): the city of Troy, on the coast of Asia Minor
Trypelle (39): the port city of Tripoli, north of Beirut
Turcople (8): used here as a place name, probably arising from the Turcopoli, a tribe of mixed Turkish and Greek descent
Turkes (9, 11, 46, 47): the Turks
Turkeston, Turkescon (72): the central Asian region of Turkestan, between Iran and Siberia
Turky (2, 9, 21, 38, 72, 73, 87): Turkey
Turmagute (49): Terra Marginen (Turkmeniya), east of the Caspian Sea
Tyborne (34): the city of Tiberias, on the Sea of Galilee
Tygre, Tygris, flode/flom (45, 74, 89): the Tigris River
Tyre, Thirry (12, 13, 37): Tyre (Sûr), port of entry for Syria. See also Sure.
Tytus (23, 24): Titus; Roman Emperor, 79-81, son of Vespasian

Uber (74): the Caucasus Mountains, probably from *ubera aquilonis*: the breasts of the north wind. See also Caspe, hylles of.
Urrey, Ury (16, 25): Uriah

Valayre (64): a tribe of Tartary, corresponding to Hayton's *Ialair*
Valon (37): Valona (Vlonë), port city on the Strait of Otranto, between the Adriatic and Ionian Seas
Vaspasiane (23): Vespasian; Roman Emperor, 69-79
Venys (13, 37, 38, 44, 45, 51, 61, 77): the city of Venice, Italy

Wales (3): Wales

Ynde, Ynd, Inde. *See* Inde.

Ysan (48): probably the name *Esau*. The text here says that Jobab was king of Idumea, "and after king of Ysan," rather than "after King Esau."

Zachary (25): the prophet Zechariah, son of Barachius, stoned for rebuking the people

BIBLIOGRAPHY

Manuscripts and early editions referred to in the text are listed in the Appendices.

Ambrose. "De Fide." *Patrologiae Cursus Completus. Series Latinae.* xvi: 527-693.
Aristotle. *Nicomachean Ethics.* Trans. Martin Ostwald. New York: Bobbs-Merrill, 1962.
Atiya, Aziz. *The Crusade in the Later Middle Ages.* London: Methuen, 1938.
Augustine. "Sermo 46." *Patrologiae Cursus Completus. Series Latina.* xl: 1325-26.
Bedier, Joseph. *La Traditione Manuscrite du Lai de L'Ombre.* Paris, 1929.
Bennett, Josephine Waters. "Chaucer and *Mandeville's Travels.*" *Modern Language Notes* 68 (1953): 531-34.
———. *The Rediscovery of Sir John Mandeville.* Modern Language Association monograph ser. 19. New York: Modern Language Association, 1954.
———. "The Woodcut Illustrations in the English Editions of *Mandeville's Travels.*" *Papers of the Bibliographic Society of America* 47 (1953): 59-69.
Bovenschen, Albert. "Untersuchungen über Johann von Mandeville und die Quellen seiner Reisebeschreibung." *Zeitschrift der Gesellschaft für Erdkunde zu Berlin* 23 (1888): 177-306.
Bramont, Jules, ed. *The Travels of Sir John Mandeville and the Journal of Friar Odoric.* London: J. M. Dent, 1928.
Brown, Carleton. "Note on the Dependence of *Cleanness* on *The Book of Mandeville.*" *Publications of the Modern Language Association* 19 (1904): 149-53.
Brunetto Latini. *Li Livres dou Tresor.* Ed. Francis J. Carmody. University of California Publications in Modern Philology 22. Berkeley, Calif.: University of California Press, 1948.
Bruns, Gerald R. "The Originality of Texts in a Manuscript Culture." *Comparative Literature* 32 (1980): 113-29.

Burmester, Oswald Hugh Ewart. *Ordination Rites of the Coptic Church.* Cairo: Société d' Archéoligie Copte, 1986.
Campbell, Mary B. *The Witness and the Other World: Exotic European Travel Writing, 400–1600.* New York: Cornell University Press, 1991.
Cappelli, Adriano. *The Elements of Abbreviation in Medieval Latin Paleography.* Trans. David Heimann and Richard Kay. Lawrence, Kan.: University of Kansas Libraries, 1982.
Cawley, A. C. "A Ripon Fragment of *Mandeville's Travels.*" *English Studies* 38 (1957): 262–65.
Cerquiglini, Bernard. *In Praise of the Variant: A Critical History of Philology.* Trans. Betsy Wing. Baltimore: Johns Hopkins University Press, 1999.
Cicero. "On Duties." *Brutus. On the Nature of the Gods. On Divination. On Duties.* Trans. Hubert M. Poteat. Chicago: Chicago University Press, 1950. 463–610.
de Poerck, Guy. "La traditione manuscrite des *Voyages* de Jean de Mandeville." *Romanica Gandensia* 4 (1955): 125–58.
Deluz, Christiane. *Le livre de Jehan de Mandeville: Une "géographie" au XIVe siècle.* Louvain-la-Neuve: Institut d'Etudes Médiévales de l'Université Catholique de Louvain, 1988.
Ganser, W. G. *Die niederländische Version der Reisebeschreibung Johnns von Mandeville: Untersuchungen zur handschriftlichen Überlieferung.* Amsterdamer Publikationen zur Sprache und Literatur 63. Amsterdam: Rodopi, 1985.
Hamelius, Paul, ed. *Mandeville's Travels, Translated from the French of Jean d'Outremeuse.* 2 vols. Early English Text Society os 153–54. London: Kegan Paul, 1919.
———. "The Travels of Sir John Mandeville." *Quarterly Review* 227 (1917): 331–52.
Hanna, Ralph, III. "Mandeville." *Middle English Prose: A Critical Guide to Major Authors and Genres.* Ed. A. S. G. Edwards. New Brunswick, N.J.: Rutgers University Press, 1984. 121–32.
Hayton the Armenian. *La Flor des estoires de la terre d'Orient.* Ed. Charles Kohler et al. In *Recueil des Historiens des Croisades. Documents arméniens.* Vol. 2. Paris: Imprimerie Nationale, 1906. xxiii–cxlii, 111–363. Rpt. Farnborough, England: Gregg Press, 1967.
Higgins, Iain. *Writing East: The "Travels" of Sir John Mandeville.* Philadelphia: University of Pennsylvania Press, 1997.
Holub, Robert C. *Reception Theory: A Critical Introduction.* London: Methuen, 1984.
Horner, P. J. "*Mandeville's Travels*: A New Manuscript Extract." *Manuscripta* 24 (1980): 171–75.
Howard, Donald R. "The World of *Mandeville's Travels.*" *Yearbook of English Studies* 1 (1971): 1–17.

———. *Writers and Pilgrims.* Berkeley, Calif.: University of California Press, 1980.
Jacques de Vitry. *Historia Orientalis. Libri duo. Quorum prior orientalis, sive hierosolymitanae: alter, occidentalis historiae nomine inscribitur.* Ed. Francis Moschus. Douai, 1597. 1-258.
John of Plano Carpini. *History of the Mongols. Mission to Asia.* Ed. Christopher Dawson. Medieval Academy Reprints for Teaching 8. Toronto: University of Toronto Press, 1980. 1-76.
———. *The Voyage of Johannes de Plano Carpini. The Travels of Sir John Mandeville.* Ed. A. W. Pollard. London: MacMillan, 1923. 213-60.
Jusserand, J. J. *English Wayfaring Life in the Middle Ages.* 1890. Trans. Lucy T. Smith. New York: Putnam, 1930.
Kazhdan, A. and A. Cutler. "India." *Oxford Dictionary of Byzantium.* 3 vols. New York: Oxford University Press, 1991. 2: 992-93.
Kimble, George. *Geography in the Middle Ages.* London: Methuen, 1938.
Kohanski, Tamarah. "Picturing the East: The Harley 3954 Illustrations to *The Book of John Mandeville.*" *Allegorica*, forthcoming.
Lejeune, Rita. "Jean de Mandeville et les Liégois." *Mélanges de linguistique romane et de philologie médiévale offerts à Maurice Delbouille.* Vol. 2. Gembloux: J. Duculot, 1964. 409-37.
Letts, Malcolm, ed. *Mandeville's Travels: Texts and Translations.* 2 vols. Hakluyt Society 2nd ser. 101-2. London: Hakluyt Society, 1953.
———. *Sir John Mandeville: The Man and His Book.* London: Batchworth Press, 1949.
Lyall, R. J. "Materials: The Paper Revolution." *Book Production and Publishing in Britain: 1375-1475.* Ed. Derek Pearsall and Jeremy Griffiths. Cambridge: Cambridge University Press, 1989. 11-29.
May, David. "Dating the English Translation of *Mandeville's Travels*: The Papal Interpolation." *Notes and Queries* ns 34 (1987): 175-78.
———. "*Mandeville's Travels*, Chaucer, and the House of Fame." *Notes and Queries* ns 34 (1987): 178-82.
McGann, Jerome J., ed. *Textual Criticism and Literary Interpretation.* Chicago: Chicago University Press, 1985.
Montegut, Emile. "Sir John Maundeville." *Heures de Lecture d'un Critique.* Paris: Librairie Hachette, 1891. 235-337.
Moseley, C. W. R. D. "The Availability of *Mandeville's Travels* in England." *The Library* 5th ser. 30 (1975): 125-33.
———. "Chaucer, Sir John Mandeville, and the Alliterative Revival: A Hypothesis Concerning Relationships." *Modern Philology* 72 (1974): 182-84.
———. "Sir John Mandeville's Visit to the Pope." *Neophilologus* 54 (1970): 77-80.
———, ed. *The Travels of Sir John Mandeville.* New York: Penguin, 1983.

Newton, Arthur P., ed. *Travel and Travellers in the Middle Ages*. London: Kegan Paul, 1926.
Nicholson, E. B. "John of Burgundy, alias 'Sir John Mandeville'." *Academy* 25 (12 April 1884): 261.
Nicholson, E. B. and Henry Yule. "Mandeville, Jehan de." *Encyclopedia Brittanica*. 9th ed. 1883.
———. "Mandeville, Jehan de." *Encyclopedia Brittanica*. 11th ed. 1911.
Odoric of Pordenone. *The Eastern Parts of the World Described. Cathay and the Way Thither*. Vol. 2. Ed. Henry Yule. London: Hakluyt Society, 1914.
———. *The Journal of Friar Odoric*. *The Travels of Sir John Mandeville*. Ed. A. W. Pollard. London: MacMillan, 1923. 326-62.
Patrologiae Cursus Completus. Series Latina. Ed. J. P. Migne. 221 vols. Paris, 1844-64.
Pollard, A. W., ed. *The Travels of Sir John Mandeville*. London: MacMillan, 1923. New York: Dover, 1964.
Polo, Marco. *The Travels*. Transl. Ronald Latham. Harmondsworth: Penguin, 1958.
Pseudo-Ambrose. "Hymnus ad Sextam." *Patrologiae Cursus Completus. Series Latinae*. xvii: 1178-79.
Purdon, Liam. "Sodom and Gomorrah: The Use of *Mandeville's Travels* in *Cleanness*." *Journal of the Rocky Mountain Medieval and Renaissance Association* 9 (1988): 63-69.
Ridder, Klaus. *Jean de Mandeville's "Reisen": Studien zur Überlieferungsgeschichte der deutschen Übersetzung des Otto von Diemeringen*. Munchener Texte und Untersuchungen zur deutschen Literatur des Mittelalters 99. Munich: Artemis, 1991.
Ruddy, David W. "Scribes, Printers, and Vernacular Authority: A Study in the Late-Medieval and Early-Modern Reception of Mandeville's Travels." Ph.D. Diss., University of Michigan, 1995.
Ryding, William. *Structure in Medieval Narrative*. The Hague: Mouton, 1971.
Said, Edward. *Orientalism*. New York: Vintage, 1979.
Schepens, Luc. "Au sujet de deux manuscrits de Jean de Mandeville." *Scriptorium* 16 (1962): 377-78.
Seymour, M. C., ed. *The Bodley Version of Mandeville's Travels*. Early English Text Society os 253. London: Oxford University Press, 1963.
———. "The Early English Editions of *Mandeville's Travels*." *The Library* 5th ser. 19 (1964): 202-7.
———. "The English Epitome of *Mandeville's Travels*." *Anglia* 84 (1966): 27-58.
———. "The English Manuscripts of *Mandeville's Travels*." *Edinburgh Bibliographic Society Transactions* 4 (1966): 169-210.

——. "Mandeville and Marco Polo: A Stanzaic Fragment." *Australian University Modern Language Association* 21 (1964): 39-52.

——, ed. *Mandeville's Travels.* Oxford: Clarendon Press, 1967.

——, ed. *The Metrical Version of Mandeville's Travels.* Early English Text Society os 269. London: Oxford University Press, 1973.

——. "The Origin of the Egerton Version of *Mandeville's Travels.*" *Medium Aevum* 30 (1961): 159-69.

——. "The Scribal Tradition of *Mandeville's Travels.*" *Scriptorium* 18 (1964): 34-48.

——. "Secundum Iohannem Maundvyle." *English Studies in Africa* 6 (1961): 148-58.

——. *Sir John Mandeville.* Authors of the Middle Ages 1. Aldershot, Hants: Variorum, 1993.

Singer, D. W. "Note." *The Library* 3rd ser. 9 (1918): 275-76.

Sisam, Kenneth. *Fourteenth Century Verse and Prose.* Oxford: Clarendon Press, 1975.

Steiner, Arpad. "The Date of Composition of *Mandeville's Travels.*" *Speculum* 9 (1934): 144-47.

Thomas, J. D. "The Date of *Mandeville's Travels.*" *Modern Language Notes* 72 (1957): 165-69.

The Travels of Sir John Mandeville: Facsimile of Pynson's Edition of 1496. Exeter Medieval English Texts and Studies. Exeter: University of Exeter Press, 1980.

Vincent of Beauvais. *Speculum historiale.* Douai, 1624. Rpt. in *Speculum quadruplex sive Speculum maius: naturale/doctrinale/morale/ historiale,* pt. 4. Graz: Akademische Druck- und Verlagsanstalt, 1964-65.

Vogels, Johann. "Handschriftliche Untersuchungen über die englische Version Mandevilles." *Jahresbericht über das Realgymnasium zu Crefeld.* Crefeld: Gustav Kuhler, 1891.

Warner, George F., ed. *The Buke of John Maundeuill.* London: Roxburghe Club, 1889.

——. "Sir John Mandeville." *Dictionary of National Biography from the Earliest Times to the Present.* 1922-23. 12: 908-914.

William of Boldensele. "Des Edelherrn Wilhelm von Boldensele Reise nach dem gelobten Lande." Ed. C. L. Grotefend. *Zeitschrift des historischen Vereins für Niedersachsen* 1852. Hannover, 1855. 209-86.

William of Rubruck. "The Journal of Friar William de Rubruquis." *The Travels of Sir John Mandeville.* Ed. A. W. Pollard. London: MacMillan, 1923. 261-325.

William of Tripoli. *Tractatus de statu Saracenorum.* Ed. Hans Prutz. *Kulturgeschichte der Kreuzzüge.* Berlin, 1883. Hildesheim: Georg Olms, 1964. 573-98.

Yule, Henry, ed. *Cathay and the Way Thither, Being a Collection of Medieval*

Notices of China. 4 vols. Hakluyt Society 2nd ser. 33, 37-38, 41. London: Hakluyt Society, 1913-16.

Zacher, Christian K. *Curiosity and Pilgrimage: The Literature of Discovery in Fourteenth-Century England*. Baltimore: Johns Hopkins University Press, 1976.